PENGUIN BOOKS

ZERO TOLERANCE

Peter C. Emberley received his Ph.D. at the London School of Economics in 1983 and is currently Professor of Political Science at Carleton University in Ottawa. He is also the Director of the University's new College of the Humanities, which offers a core curriculum in the liberal arts to gifted undergraduates. He is the author of *Values Education and Technology* and co-author of *Bankrupt Education: The Decline of Liberal Education in Canada.*

ZERO TOLERANCE

Hot Button Politics in Canada's Universities

Peter C. Emberley

Penguin Books

PENGUIN BOOKS
Published by the Penguin Group
Penguin Books Canada Ltd, 10 Alcorn Avenue, Toronto,
Ontario, Canada M4V 3B2
Penguin Books Ltd, 27 Wrights Lane, London W8 5TZ, England
Penguin Books USA Inc., 375 Hudson Street, New York,
New York 10014, U.S.A.
Penguin Books Australia Ltd, Ringwood, Victoria, Australia
Penguin Books (NZ) Ltd, 182–190 Wairau Road, Auckland 10,
New Zealand

Penguin Books Ltd, Registered Offices: Harmondsworth,
Middlesex, England

Published in Penguin Books, 1996
1 3 5 7 9 10 8 6 4 2

Canadian Cataloguing in Publication Data

Emberley, Peter C. (Peter Christopher), 1956–
Zero tolerance: hot button politics in Canada's universities

ISBN 0-14-025347-5

1. Universities and colleges – Canada. 2. Education, Higher –
Canada. I. Title.

LA417.5.E52 1996   378.71   C95-930898-9

Copyright acknowledgments appear on page 306.

For Cheryl

hot button

hot button *noun*
Slang.
  1. A psychological propensity for immediate or pre-
     dictable response or reaction, as to a political
     issue or marketing tactic: *an issue that presses vo-
     ters' hot buttons.*
  2. Something that is of great interest or is known to
     elicit immediate or predictable response or reac-
     tion: *a new product that is a hot button among
     young consumers.*
—**hot´-but´ton** (hŏt´ bŭt´n) *adjective*

The American Heritage Dictionary of the
English Language, 3rd edition

No one ought to meddle with the universities, who does not know them well and love them well.

Matthew Arnold

Acknowledgments

One's judgments and overall perspective so often originate in the contingencies and happenstance of personal experience. In the late 1970s I decided to pursue my postgraduate training in Britain, to the incredulity of my American-trained advisors at the University of Toronto. British postgraduate study is seen as a rather whimsical affair. I found that to be true, but in time I came to understand it differently.

The London School of Economics is a somewhat dilapidated, even ramshackle, establishment in central London, cast between the clean efficiencies of London's banking street, Southampton Row, the tourist trade of Aldwych Street and the overwrought energy of Fleet Street, the home of Britain's newspaper empire. The school itself is spread across a clutter of buildings and houses going off in every direction, each comprised of endless dark nooks and crannies, blind hallways and staircases that lead nowhere. In brief the LSE, as it is fondly known, is a rabbit warren. Various notorious old creaking paternosters shunt students from floor to floor within these buildings and in the process terrify most of them nearly to death. Although the LSE does not have, like University College London, an embalmed Jeremy Bentham at its entrance, the ghosts of Beatrice and Sidney

Webb, H.G. Wells and Harold Laski roam freely. In brief, the LSE is very unlike the brash and polished campuses found in the suburbs or on the periphery of many a city in North America.

At the LSE, and this realization was reinforced by my sustained acquaintance with the university cultures of Oxford and Cambridge, I learned that the *modus operandi* of British postsecondary education was less professional training than a kind of mellowing. As doctoral students we were never really *taught* anything, though we brushed up against some marvellously witty conversation and some ponderous scholarship. Lectures were hit-and-miss, and idiosyncracy flourished. Nonetheless, it was expected that in time we would develop a richly yellowed patina and that we would age as old casks of madeira do. As the joke went, echoing Stephen Leacock's observation about British universities, we were there to be smoked at—not trained, not accredited, not even supervised by any meaning of the word. We were merely smoked at. And it did seem that most of the faculty there had only a passing interest in us, since most were aloof and, at best, ironic, a situation vastly contrasting with the professional crispness many of us had experienced in North American universities. In any event, for a number of years I was smoked at by Michael Oakeshott, Elie Kedourie, Kenneth Minogue, Maurice Cranston and Wolfgang von Leyden, though the effects of their gnomic utterances would not reveal themselves until much later. Disenchanted, I fled for a time to Chicago for professional training and I am forever grateful for the kind patronage of Joseph Cropsey there.

Time brings retrospective reassessment. Years later I came to understand that education is not a magic potion that immediately transforms one upon being imbibed. Nor is it the silver bullet that will solve all our human problems. Rather, it is something ineffable and not always recognized at the moment for what it is. Michael Oakeshott, the school's greatest scholar and teacher, once said that university education is not a beginning and not an end, but a middle. Its ways, then, are poorly grasped by those who think in terms of learner-centred or outcomes-based models, for what these approaches overlook is the only process that really counts—the mysterious interaction of the needs of students and the scholarly culture. The London School of Economics gave me the opportunity to learn the true meaning of liberal education.

More recently and directly, many conversations, debates, interviews and experimental talks or lectures have contributed to this book taking its present form. I am particularly grateful for the friendship of Barry Cooper and Timothy Fuller. These two wonderful individuals have spent much time schooling me in the appropriate idiom to express the university experience. I am also grateful to Stuart Adam, Dean of Arts, Carleton University, who gave me the opportunity to create a College of the Humanities with a core curriculum degree program at that university. Its development demanded a continuous attention to the issues that form the core of this book.

I found very useful the comments made by conference participants—particularly Hamid Dabashi (Columbia University), Eva Brann (St. John's College) and Harvey Schulmann (Concordia University)—at the inaugural meeting of the Association of Core Texts and Curriculum. I am in debt to the many people who provided me with accounts of the state of their universities—particularly George Feaver, James Keeley, Robert Jackson, Frederic Vaughan, Zdravko Planinc, David Warrick, Mark Zacher, John Wood, Hamish Telford, Jim Moore, Rainer Knopff, Tom Flanagan, Lynda Erickson, Jonathan Vance and Kim Campbell. Michel Gaulin gave unstintingly of his time and expertise. Don Savage patiently endured many questions. I vastly appreciate the methodic and tireless work of my research assistants Simon Kow, Leanne Wright, Keith Haysom and Tabitha Kollar. I owe a special word of thanks to my colleague Philippe Azzie for his research assistance. I am grateful for research funds from the Dean of Graduate Studies and the Dean of Social Sciences at Carleton University, as well as the Donner Canadian Foundation. I would like to acknowledge the staff at the Association of Universities and Colleges of Canada, the Ontario Confederation of University Faculty Associations, the Canadian Association of University Teachers, the Social Sciences and Humanities Research Council, the Ontario Council on University Affairs, the Council of Ontario Universities, the Canadian Students' Federation, the Association of Atlantic Universities, the Council of Ministers of Education, the Centre for Philanthropy and many universities across the country for generously and expeditiously supplying me with their reports or policy statements. None of these individuals or agencies are responsible for the ideas or the errors that will be found in this book.

I appreciate the support and enthusiasm of Jackie Kaiser, my sponsoring editor at Penguin Books Canada Limited, who initiated the process and was a fellow-traveller during every stage of writing this book. I am grateful to my editor, Kathryn Dean, for her care as a reader, her lively commentary and the sense of balance she helped me bring to the text.

My greatest debt is to my wife, Cheryl, for her infinite patience, humour, indulgence and insight.

Peter C. Emberley
Ottawa, Ontario
December 1995

Contents

Chapter 1

Wilting Ivy?

*Because half a dozen grasshoppers under a fern make the field
ring with their importunate chink...do not imagine that those
who make the noise are the only inhabitants of the field.*

Edmund Burke

School taxes, user fees, capital punishment, immigration,
Quebec separation, the future of health care, clear-cut log-
ging—these are the big-ticket political issues that coax
Canadians, if not out on the street, at least into writing letters to
the editor, irately phoning their elected politicians and signing
petitions. To many Canadians these are matters which are either
of immediate concern or on which it is not hard to whip up a little strong-minded moral objection, especially in a day when entitlements are starting to be eroded.

But meanwhile, behind the facade of ivied gothic spires and
tweeds-and-pipe-tobacco professors, a far darker battle is being
played out, as one of Canada's most venerable institutions—the
university—is under siege. As various impassioned sectarians
contend to control the future of Canada's universities, the institution itself is on the verge of financial, spiritual and political
collapse. Unlike the big-ticket political issues, little more than
an occasional murmur of protest has been heard until recently
about this crisis. The academic world, with its high levels of
abstraction and apparent remoteness from the immediacy of the
political fray in which social issues are debated, has seemed not
particularly pertinent to the well-being of Canadians.

1

To be sure, the gradual erosion of the university is less visible, its effects less immediate and its overall consequence hardly understood. Occasionally, events (even of great magnitude) percolate up, alarm bells ring, and pundits clamour doom and gloom. However, these episodes are seen by the general public less as something symptomatic than as the sporadic upsets with which all institutions are typically beset.

Yet today some of the most important stakes of our times are being played out in our universities. And all of us will be influenced by the way the chips are played and the outcomes won. The university is both the barometer and the initiator of historical change, and no one can deny that great historical changes are afoot. Empires have fallen, old ethnic nationalisms are being revisited, economies have globalized, previously marginalized peoples are being recognized and new technologies are proliferating. Where does the university stand amidst all this change? For thirty years, the outer face of the university has been placid, and the Canadian public has innocently assumed that all was therefore well. Only now are warning bells ringing.

In the United States, the wake-up call came much earlier. For fifteen years the American public has been alert to the clashes occurring on college campuses: the denunciations of the European inheritance, the ascendancy of race and gender as potent social forces, the wars over freedom of speech and political correctness and the shift from "sage on a stage" lecturing to teaching through new interactive technologies. *The New York Review of Books, Harper's, The National Review, The American Spectator* and *The Atlantic Monthly*, even television and radio stations from the northwest to the deep south, covered the university debate so extensively that many Americans are now familiar with the names of its chief protagonists—Allan Bloom, E.D. Hirsch, Dinesh D'Souza, Roger Kimball, Gerald Graff and Stanley Fish, to name a few—and the philosophical traditions that lie behind them. Books like *The Closing of the American Mind* and *Cultural Literacy* actually became national bestsellers! Some, like Dinesh D'Souza (author of *Illiberal Education*) and

Stanley Fish (author of *There's No Such Thing as Free Speech...
And It's a Good Thing Too*), have made the university debate a
travelling roadshow. Most importantly, the American public
appreciates that what is at stake has massive implications for
society generally.

In Canada, until recently, hardly any national debate on these
issues has transpired. Little fulminations by the *Globe and Mail*'s
columnists—Michael Valpy, Bronwyn Drainie, Robert Fulford
and Lesley Krueger—and an occasional episode on *Studio Two*,
W5 or *Face Off* have been mere tempests in a teacup. When the
presidents of Yale or Berkeley pronounce on the economy,
crime, racial tension or the fortunes of the GOP, America listens. When the president of Canada's most prestigious university, the University of Toronto, condemns government zeal in
"restructuring" postsecondary education and warns of the
"betrayal of an entire generation of Canadians," his pronouncements fall on deaf ears.

We should be paying far greater attention. If for no other reason, the scale of our university enterprise should make us rethink
our indifference. Canada commits more to postsecondary education than any other OECD country, to the tune of 2.6 percent
of its gross domestic product (the others are around 1.5 percent).
Our ninety degree-granting institutions receive $9.8 billion in
subsidies annually, of which $2.6 billion make up federal grants
to the provinces. In the last decade alone, a 30 percent increase
in university enrolment has translated into the fact that 900,000
students, or 20 percent of Canadians between 18 and 25, are
today registered in Canada's colleges and universities. In 1992,
120,000 bachelor's and first professional degrees, 18,000 master's
degrees and 3,100 doctorates were awarded. To date, $8 billion
of student loans have been made to over two million students. A
total of 61,845 full- and part-time faculty and 25,000 sessional
appointments provide the teaching and research of Canada's universities. Twenty-six percent of all Canadian research and development is done by universities. In Ontario alone, universities
contribute as much as $6.2 billion to the economy.[1]

In the last six years, however, our indifference has been shattered. Canadians are starting to wake up to troubling newspaper headlines: "Universities get more bad news," "Government *—Jehral* hangs sword over colleges," "Universities strangled by 'PC' politicians," "Walkman University: Sony, Inc. buys a vote at McGill." The editorial introduction to the second annual *Maclean's* university survey sums up the new awareness succinctly: "The post-secondary educational system is in a crisis far more profound than millions of Canadians realize. It is, indeed, a system under severe siege."[2]

And amidst tremors that are making themselves felt from the University of British Columbia in Vancouver to Memorial University in St. John's, Newfoundland, our spin-doctors have identified the early warning of the "crisis" in Canada's universities.

Two dark and sobering events in particular stand out vividly in the public's mind:

- In 1989, Marc Lépine, an engineering student at the École Polytechnique of Montreal, armed himself with a semiautomatic rifle, entered a classroom, separated out men from women and slaughtered fourteen women. Investigators later found a hit-list of prominent Canadian women and a suicide note stating that feminists had ruined his life. In the wake of this event, interpreted by many feminists as further indication of the pervasive sexism in society, university associations, supported by government ministries, commissioned a survival guide for women in academe (*Lifting a Ton of Feathers*) and pledged to wage war on discrimination and harassment. "The Montreal massacre," the editorial in the Canadian Association of University Teachers' bulletin read, "is only the visible expression of a complex hostility and systemic bias against women."[3]

- On August 24, 1992, Concordia engineering professor Valery Fabrikant shot and killed four of his colleagues, allegedly because he was denied tenure and out of frustration with what he had perceived as irregularities in research funding and

4

scholarly recognition in the department of which he was a member. One important investigation of the incident concluded that the "production-driven research culture" (the "publish or perish" mentality) governing accountability in universities was in part to blame for the incident.[4] A report on the Fabrikant murders blamed the hit-and-miss management and absence of line-authority in Concordia's university administration for having failed to take action against Fabrikant's history of abusive behaviour long before the events of August 24.[5]

On a less horrific scale, but for some observers every bit as symptomatic of the internal collapse of the university, consider the following incidents:

- In 1989, Philippe Rushton published a study showing that women had less intelligence than men, and that Asians outranked whites and blacks. Ontario premier David Peterson called for Rushton's immediate dismissal on the grounds that the study was "morally offensive to the way that Ontario thinks."[6] The controversy continues over whether Rushton's tenure should be revoked.

- In 1990, anthropology instructor Jeanne Cannizzo's Royal Ontario Museum exhibit "Into the Heart of Africa"—a display of Canadian soldiers and missionaries in nineteenth century Africa meant to show Victorian biases and prejudices—was panned by black groups, and Cannizzo was subject to verbal attacks, as well as physical threats in her classes and at home, that ultimately led to her permanent departure from the University of Toronto.

- In 1993, Queen's student newspaper *Surface* featured a story entitled "What If the Queen Were Born a Brown Bread," suggesting that to be white was to be "bland, pudgy and limp." When a student of colour protested, he was denounced in the

5

newspaper as a "chocolate-covered almond"—brown outside, white inside. Subsequent issues of *Surface* included a poem denouncing Jesus Christ as a "flaming faggot," a collage of photographs of known campus figures superimposed on pictures of bodies cut out from gay pornographic magazines and a poem proposing that killing white people is forgivable in the context of a racist society. A Queen's professor defended the racist and salacious materials pointing to differences of power in society: "When you've been part of the excluded and subordinated, you may use things as a rhetorical device to make a dominant group understand what they're doing."[7]

- In 1993, University of New Brunswick mathematics professor Matin Yaqzan wrote in the campus newspaper that "any woman who enters a man's bedroom at night should consider it an invitation for sexual intercourse" and that the date-rape of a "promiscuous" girl was more an "inconvenience" than a "moral outrage," significantly less serious than the violation of a virgin. Yaqzan was suspended, subsequently reinstated, and then chose to take early retirement. What followed was a countrywide campaign against date-rape and an impassioned debate on the nature of academic freedom.

- In 1990, Alberta chemistry professor Gordon Freeman wrote an article for the *Canadian Journal of Physics*, arguing that working women are responsible for many family and social problems, among them increased student cheating, drug abuse, embezzlement and corrupt business practices, and even the massacre of women students at l'École Polytechnique.[8] The National Research Council was asked to recall the journal and to reprint it without the offending article.

- In 1995, pursuant to a $236,000 investigation, University of British Columbia's political science department was denied the right to admit further graduate students amidst allegations of systemic racism and sexism among its faculty. Similar allegations of harassment or discrimination have been raised in political science departments at the University of Victoria and the University of Manitoba. In the former, the department was obliged to search for a new chairperson from outside the university to take the department beyond its "chilly climate." Two women faculty left the department at the University of Manitoba and university investigations continue.

- At the University of Guelph a 1994 policy banned whites from a section of the lounge of the Clarence Munford student centre. The area was to be considered a "safe space" refuge for nonwhites only. When charged with supporting reverse racism, advisors to the university harassment office stated that racism couldn't be reversed against a group holding power and privilege. "There is a fundamental difference between what is at play when a group that holds power chooses to exclude another less powerful group and when a marginalized group chooses to gather in solidarity and support."[9] "The future," Jack Granatstein, distinguished historian at York University, said in a convocation address referring to incidents of this sort, "is exceedingly bleak. We are moving into the Dark Ages again, where knowledge is not something that is going to be subjected to the tests of truth, but to the tests of race, ideology and gender. I find it terrifying."[10]

- In 1994, the Washington-based Office of Research Integrity found that Dr. Roger Poisson, a Université de Montréal cancer specialist, had falsified records of patients in an international breast-cancer study. Governments were immediately pressured to initiate procedures for more accountability and review of research practices in universities, and the Social Sciences and Humanities Research Council, tying its $1-billion grant budget to universities' willingness to produce ethics policies, warned, "We have a stick. We have funding."[11]

- In 1994, University of Toronto professor Herbert Richardson was released from his teaching position for neglect of his classroom responsibilities, because of his involvement in the $2-million business enterprise of Mellen Press and Mellen University based in the Turks and Caicos Islands. The cry arose for abolition of tenure, a platform upon which two Canadian premiers, Ralph Klein and Mike Harris, came to office in 1993 and 1995 (nothing more than a "job guarantee," as Harris put it, echoing general public sentiment, "whether you're pulling your weight or not"). Many mused equally about academic sabbaticals. Were they anything more than paid vacations?

- In 1994 and 1995, governments in Alberta, Manitoba, Ontario and New Brunswick announced major cuts (up to $400 million in each province) in funding grants to universities and closure of professional programs. In anticipation of the financial squeeze, schools of business at Queen's University, University of Manitoba and Athabasca University began to run their programs on the basis of full-cost recovery. Other programs are poised to follow suit.

- Dissatisfied with the theoretical approach of traditional business schools, Manitoba's Palliser Furniture opened its own "university" program in 1993, delivering MBA-quality curricula to meet Manitoba's "real" needs. In Nova Scotia, meanwhile, permission was given in 1994 to some faculty to apply "shock treatment" to postsecondary education by opening a no-frills university that would operate without public funds in an abandoned school.[12]

The warning bells continue to toll. Faculty (who for years had enjoyed small classes, generous research grants and modest assessments of their productivity) and support staff (who for years have sheltered and carried the burden of university administration) are being asked to do more with far, far less. Their grumbling is becoming louder every day.

I do hope the author intends to deal with the abuse of students & staff coercing graduate students in particular into doing their student academic requirements — i.e. thesis/research on the area in which the staff member is working or publishing — this practice is almost normal & has been for at least 30 years [when I attended graduate school & observed such shameful practices first hand]

- At Mount Allison University, despite their recurring top ranking by *Maclean's*, faculty and staff associations have initiated two strikes and a vote of nonconfidence in the president who balanced the budget and eliminated the university's debt, but did so in a highly adversarial manner.

- Accusing academics of "driving our universities into the dust," the Nova Scotia government is undertaking a sweeping rationalization of its university system. In 1995, when the Chair of the Nova Scotia Council on Higher Education warned of amalgamations, closures and quotas, and stated that "no programs, policies or practices are sacrosanct," she was denounced as a "bully."[13] At the University of British Columbia the faculty association called in a forensic auditor to reveal waste. At Carleton University, amidst rancorous debate, faculty petitioned and overthrew the university administration's "open-admission" policy.

Cracks are appearing all over the academic landscape. Votes of nonconfidence in university presidents are spreading. Boards of governors are wrestling with university senates in efforts to expand their jurisdiction over academic matters. Testy relations have formed between universities and provincial governments. As one senior government officer stated in response to a survey of the perception of universities among provincial government officials: "Our approach is just to starve the buggers to death and hope they'll react as we'd like."[14]

The general mood is discouraging. Many students admit that they are beside themselves with the spiralling sticker price of their education and with concerns about their futures. Parents are confused and angry. Overextended governments are gleeful to have finally spotted a cash cow that can be milked to finance the $420 billion national debt. Interest groups are flexing their muscles and staking out their political ground. Professors are burning out, many eager to take early retirement incentive packages. Support staff are stretched to the limit and increasingly are taking stress-leave. Boards of governors are divided by sectarian battles. Senior university officials, rather than exhibiting moral and intellectual leadership and making tough decisions, are walking on eggshells and in the process of playing the game of offending no one often alienating those they represent. Financial officers are desperately trying to keep the balance sheets from showing too much red ink. Professional university associations are scrambling to protect the privileges of an aging professorate—perceived by many to be a gerontocracy shielded by academic freedom and tenure.

One constituency after another is attempting to seize the high ground by claiming to hold the monopoly on the language of "excellence," "quality," "performance" and "common sense," concepts that have become, in Uwe Poerksen's terms, "plastic words"—words that can be used to mean anything.[15] While university departments, unskilled in marketing their wares, frantically search for ways to protect themselves, sectarians from both the left and the right are homing in like birds of prey gyring around a fallen and terrified quarry. Some of these sectarians, authorized by government commission to regulate and micromanage the university for equity, accountability and efficiency are now, like privateers, ransacking the institution. As if all this were not enough, drastically reduced budgets have led to deferred maintenance of aging facilities, obsolete laboratory equipment, severe cutbacks in library acquisition and the visible impact of growing squalor on university campuses. In a desperate pitch to raise themselves above the general bedlam and jockeying for power across Canada, Queen's University, McGill University and the University of Toronto compete to bill themselves as the "Harvard of the North."

Meanwhile, maverick scholars like John Ralston Saul, Neil Bissoondath, Robert Reich, Michael Ignatieff and Francis Fukuyama, and academic outsiders like Allan Bloom, Conor Cruise O'Brien and Camille Paglia are engaging our social and cultural world in a way that most academic research does not. And when governments and corporations look for innovative research, for thought that challenges the status quo, they look not to the universities but to independent think tanks like the Fraser Institute, C.D. Howe Institute or the Institute of Advanced Research, in Canada; the Woodrow Wilson Center and the Brookings Institution or Heritage Foundation in the United States. As a provocative editorial read in last year's *Economist*: "Today, knowledge is too important to be left to academics."[16]

"*C'est une révolte?*" Louis XVI asked when he heard of the storming of the Bastille. "*Non, Sire,*" the Duc de la Rochefoucauld-Liancourt retorted, "*c'est une révolution.*" Can we today doubt, in light of the tumult in Canada's universities, that we are in the midst of anything less than a revolution—one that will forever change these institutions?

But what is the true nature of this revolution? A succession of incidents added up, however great, does not in itself translate into a substantive crisis. Yet they become a "crisis," and random occurrences develop into "systemic problems" when one simple, but potent, ingredient is added: *turf wars*. We must, I believe, entertain the possibility that the plainly evident collapse of the university is not merely the cumulative total of a series of incidents but the consequence of a plethora of invented crises and the intense politicization of education. For if we examine these incidents carefully and impartially, we find that what we are witnessing is less an expression of detached reflection on the idea of the university than a fierce jockeying for power and control. Contenders of both the left and the right are struggling to be the university's new gatekeeper. The fractious debate in this country about the fate of the university is not being conducted by those who know and love the university well, as Matthew Arnold would have had it, but by competitors who are pursuing their own political agendas because they see their fortunes tied to who controls the university. Their rhetoric alone reveals their true intentions.

These contenders—who reside both within and outside the university—have observed the events of the last six years, have "theorized" them (as they like to put it) and found underlying "causes," "symptoms" and "deep structures." And from them now emanates a single cry: "Clean up your house, or we will do it for you."[17] The loudest voices have been the corporate right and the cultural left, the one committed to applying free-market principles to all facets of university life, the other agitating to denounce all remaining forms of intellectual and social authority. But many others have joined the clamour for putting the house in order, unwittingly reinforcing the antics of the right and left. To hear these whistle blowers, one would almost believe that Canada's universities have become utterly irrelevant and the primary source of all our social and personal problems. Yet in truth, Canada's universities do not play a marginal role, nor until recently has dissatisfaction been great. Indeed, a 1993 survey of 140,000 university graduates revealed that 84.3 percent were satisfied or very satisfied with the quality of their education.[18] Such satisfaction notwithstanding, the new revolutionaries express the keenest desire to have the universities believe they have a "perception problem" and to have the universities turned on their heads.

Quick fixes and silver-bullet "restructuring" plans abound. To "clean house" means letting the molly-maids of industry and politically polarized interest groups loose on the university—with their brushes and mops of "transparency," "program rationalization," "accountability," "measurable outcomes," "learner responsive delivery," "employer guarantees," "dating contracts," "discipline codes," "inclusive curricula," "value-for-money audits," and "total quality management."

Business, governments, university professional associations and lobby organizations, multicultural and feminist groups, policy wonks who pretend to speak for a disaffected public—each presumes it has diagnosed the ills of the university and each is quick to offer a cure: institute user fees, abolish tenure, design modularized curricula, demand greater productivity from academics, convert library holdings to CD-ROM, change delivery systems, enshrine lifelong learning, use electronic broadcasting to create virtual classrooms, enforce education equity legislation, institute discipline codes, contract out university services, design more partnerships and cooperative ventures with the private sector, monitor outcomes, create self-directed learning structures. Charges of waste and inefficiency, elitism and privilege, irrelevance and antiquarianism, come from both left and right—and, curiously, political camps within and outside the institution often converge on the same issues in their rejection of the traditional university. Each believes that it has grasped the first principle that will restore the university to order. Much heat but little light and understanding is generated by these contenders for the public's approval as successive hot buttons are pressed.

As one looks at the hot-button politics gripping Canada's universities, it becomes apparent that the schemes and mechanisms are one and all seductively simplistic plans guaranteed to mobilize special-interest groups and to seize the imagination of the general public so that it believes an enormous con-game is being played with its tax-dollars and its children. Nearly all are fantastical dreams of "reinventing" or "re-engineering" the university, often evoked with the powerful rhetoric that the impending twenty-first century signals a major millennial change and no one must miss the parade.

Unfortunately, it seems that however simplistic these shortcuts to paradise are, the constituencies at which they are aimed, including the general public, are invariably seduced by the proposals. Social engineering—for that is what is replacing genuine education—is so much easier to understand and to rally behind than the elusive processes of higher learning. As one listens to the complaints and agendas, one is struck by their intolerance for the imperfections, uncertainty, freedom, leisure, withdrawal and authority of university culture. There is little appreciation that the search for those elusive riches—understanding, good judgment, happiness, freedom and truth—cannot and must not permit of a final solution. The university is an institution with the bedrock of over seven centuries of maturation and refinement. Its core is sustained by enduring traditions stemming from the Near and Far East, classical Greece and Rome, mediaeval

Christianity, the Enlightenment and, in the nineteenth century, from evocative writings on liberal education by Matthew Arnold and John Newman. The university is an institution formed to cultivate intellectual and spiritual passion, discerning moral judgment, imagination and the methodic discipline associated with scientific research. In its capacity to question prevailing social practices and to stimulate intellectual knowing and moral doing that transcend the immediate practicalities of the world, the university serves society by offering it a higher idea of itself and endowing it with decency and grace.

All this now stands at risk. With the demand that the university acquire a new and crisp efficiency, and be transparent to the economic and social priorities of society, the opportunity for having one haven in which intellectuals and scholars can distance themselves from prejudice and bargaining is vanishing. The new clean-up would perhaps be at home in the business or military enterprise or in government bureaucracy, but its intolerance for the university's natural (and healthy) ambiguity and free play has the capacity to destroy that institution's fundamental character. The scholarly culture thrives on an unending series of rejoinders of "Yes, but…" to every answer offered to any question. If this adventure is closed down, Canadians risk regressing to a self-image as "hewers of wood and drawers of water." We will no longer be equal participants in the ongoing renewal of world culture.

The intolerance shown the university today manifests itself in a vast number of syndromes: crisis mongering, high confidence in the ability to manage and control by technological, legalistic and bureaucratic means, zeal to overturn historical tradition, self-righteous moralizing and impatience with ambiguity and inconsistency. Few of the institution's current critics really understand the mystique of the university classroom, fewer yet appreciate the moral and intellectual contexts within which knowledge advances. We are increasingly seeing this intolerance translate into formulaic solutions and unprincipled expedience. The tragedy is that the discussion is being conducted like a zero-sum game: raise tuition fees or abolish tenure, cut funding or close universities, invoke reverse discrimination or establish an equity review monitor, establish inclusive curricula or withdraw faculty autonomy, provide distance education or overpack classes with students, undervalue teaching or shift all research to centres of excellence alone. There is little balance in what may be the most important debate of the century.

Let me illustrate with a concrete case. In 1993 the Ontario NDP government, harking back to the Reaganite language of the war on drugs, distributed to colleges and universities a "Framework Regarding Prevention of Harassment and Discrimination in Ontario Universities," which advocated a policy of "zero-tolerance for harassment and discrimination at Ontario universities."[19] The policy was not aimed at explicit acts of injustice alone. Among other mischiefs it ordered ended were the very elusive and undefined phenomena of "negative environments" and "poisonous atmospheres." The policy, with its vague and elusive language of sensed environments and systemic victimization, and its easy abandonment of the presumption of innocence and the accepted rules of evidence, was seen by many as a departure from due process. Reaction was swift and predictable. In opposition, professors banded together and formed societies under the banner of "academic freedom" and at Trent University even composed a charter enshrining the "right to offend." Numerous multicultural and women's groups mobilized, denounced the "backlash" particularly of "white males preserving their entrenched privileges" and called for more radical deconstruction of pervasive systemic forms of sexism and racism. University administrators, true to their primary objective, saw in this a golden opportunity to expand the already swollen budgets and bureaucracies of their equity offices.

The debate, filled with incriminations and denunciations, unholy pacts and alliances of convenience, was characteristic of the trouble into which Canada's universities have fallen. Everything was wrong here. Many academics worried that its expansive language would cause a proliferation of ill-founded, vexatious complaints. But the opposing appeals to "academic freedom" were equally abstract and formulaic. A dispassionate observer could hardly resist the conclusion of how self-serving it was that some of the professorate was seeking to entrench its privileges—especially with the scare tactics it employed in comparing the situation to Nazi Germany and the Salem witch hunts. Appeals to "empowerment" and "deconstruction" were equally rigid—intolerant of the distinctive and necessarily ambiguous processes of the scholarly culture. University equity bureaucracies swelled, diverting even more resources from the university's chief purposes of teaching and research. While faculty and academic administrators groused amongst themselves about the nature and limits of "academic freedom," special-interest groups were not hesitating to give away the whole shop.

This zero-tolerance policy was only one of innumerable interventions into, and agitations within, the culture of the university. But it is a striking illustration of the widespread desire to "re-engineer the university for the twenty-first century" and of the way that slogans and abstract formulae can mobilize diverse social constituencies, government, interest groups, faculty, students and administrators to act overzealously and recklessly. Zero tolerance invokes the sense of distrust of the idea of the university shifting priority from the free intellectual and spiritual adventures in human possibility comprising a genuine education, to limitless social engineering. As one of the last institutions inherited from the Middle Ages that has not been demystified and "rationalized," or recast to form a seamless web with contemporary demands for efficiency and mastery of all mysteries and contingencies, it appears that now finally the university, too, will have its doors thrown open wide to the glare of public scrutiny.

One blue ribbon committee after another asserts that the university's rituals and apprenticeships are quaint at best, oppressive at worst. "What universities are learning," as Xerox Canada's chairman said, "is that they aren't sacred ground." Canada's university system, as the media likes to state it, has a "perception problem." "The bottom line," Janet Halliwell, Nova Scotia's chairwoman of the Council on Higher Education has said, "is, if universities want to retain their position…they are going to have to change. Society has a lot more in the way of expectations and those expectations can be filled elsewhere."[20] But "bottom-line" thinking means intolerance for those leisurely and ambiguous but creative encounters and conversations that offer an opportunity for a brief transcendence and interlude from the rush and certainties of the business world or society in general. "Zero tolerance" is one appropriate metaphor for today's threat to our universities.

The decisive question for the Canadian public as it faces the real possibility of the university's collapse is whether these diagnosticians are identifying the true ailments. Coleridge once commented that we will not understand the real uses of an institution until we have destroyed it. Have we reached the point where the university, as an idea and institution, as the embodiment of the scholarly culture, is being irretrievably dismantled?

There are nearly always contexts to specific turbulences. It cannot be doubted that Canada is today at a watershed in its history. No better indication of this is the breakdown of the Meech Lake and Charlottetown accords and the confusions sown during the 1995 Quebec referendum. The lesson from these political agitations should be that the old-style politics of formula (and the "one-best-way") has reached its zenith. After all, in the gradual accomplishments since Meech Lake and Charlottetown, we should have learned that the proper acts of conciliation towards Quebec, aboriginals and visible minorities could more successfully be done administratively, through principled compromise and practical common sense. But we have not learned this lesson, and so formulaic sloganeering continues. The misreckonings, as well as the fortunes, of society and the university mirror and reinforce one another. We will not pass through our current woes until we recognize the mischief created by ideological posturing.

The current disorientation is not only the result of Canada's difficult politics and uncertain expectations. It is also a reflection of our world and our peculiar times. We are in a period of great transition, as the ways of the old world are passing and the shape of the world to come is seen but through a glass darkly. The character of all periods of transition is one of confusion and anxiety, as traditional political, moral and spiritual symbols collapse, as new ways are explored and old ways rediscovered and as cultures and beliefs mingle and form new syntheses. Our reaction to these changes has to be balanced. Nostalgia makes one impotent, while boosterism makes one superficial. As we discuss the future of the university, we must do so realizing that much of the doctrine and dogma of our past can no longer guide us, having exacted so heavy a toll from the earth we inhabit and having led us to cut ourselves off from the rich spiritual encounters still enjoyed, for example, by our aboriginal people. We must realize that if we do not acknowledge the losses and deprivals accompanying our global fate—the rise of technological civilization—and the evident and widespread alienation of our inner being from the momentum of the external world, we are shortchanging Canada's future generations.

In the following chapters as I examine the issues agitating Canada's campuses—tenure, political correctness, university funding, postmodernism, research, technological upgrading, curriculum reform, bureaucratic growth, the mood of Generation X, an irascible public—I will track the growing disaffection with the university as an institution that harbours privileges and forms of leisure, passions and ambiguities, of which our society is increasingly suspicious. My foil for bringing this disaffection to account is a specific image of the university—as a place of incubation where the most profound human needs and longings are released, formed and matured by exposure and initiation into a tapestry of scholarship—a culture that is *in* but not *of* the social world. It is an image based on the practices and experiences arising out of the sacred trust that develops between the genuine teacher and a student and out of the stewardship each participates in as they go through the process of understanding and renewing the world of culture.

This image may not be everyone's idea of the university—and more discouragingly not everyone's experience of higher learning—but I suggest that it is the image that makes most sense of what occurs in the classrooms, libraries and laboratories of our campuses. I believe that the portrait I depict of university education is truest to the experience of the millions of graduates who since 1789 have been admitted to convocation at Canada's universities. It should be acceptable to those who see the university as preserving the inheritance of our civilizational achievements, but also to those who see its purpose as initiating new directions. I have drawn the image from three writers: Northrop Frye, F.R. Leavis and Michael Oakeshott. Of necessity, in writing a book of this sort, one recalls and converses with Matthew Arnold and Cardinal John Newman, the great architects of the modern idea of a liberal education. But otherwise, the idea of the university I portray arises from my own experiences teaching, learning, writing and serving various administrative functions at four universities. To give as ample and concrete an account as possible, I have drawn my materials from incidents reported and discussed in the media, from conferences and academic bulletins, from university memoranda and journal articles, as well as from interviews with administrators, faculty and students across the country.

Zero Tolerance is intended as a book that does not bury Canada's universities, but praises them. How could one do otherwise when every fall one looks into the faces of nervous, excited young men and women, cracks open the first page of Homer's *Odyssey* and reads its magisterial first lines, anticipating the wonder and curiosity with which students will join in an adventure that has gone on for millennia, a spiritual journey whose goal is understanding of the self and of the worlds that surround us. That same adventure goes on in every science and engineering laboratory, at every library table, in every tutorial and in every common room. But the opportunity for future students to embark on this odyssey is at risk of coming to an end.

We are at a fork in the road, perhaps at a point of no return, and the decisions we make in the next decade will be of epochal significance. The moment of choice always involves both danger and opportunity. Will we choose well and judge soundly, or will we put the achievements represented by Canada's universities in direst jeopardy? Some believe that despite our acute problems, we live in the best of all possible worlds; others take the perspective that the future will take care of itself. I subscribe neither to the idea that all the follies I am about to describe are self-correcting nor to the overwrought language of "crisis." But I do believe that now is the time for unified opposition to the creeping politicization and internal collapse of Canada's universities. As a first step, the threat must be recognized.

Chapter 2

The Needs of Students and the Scholarly Culture

*[We] sail a boundless and bottomless sea; there is neither
harbour for shelter nor floor for anchorage, neither
starting-place nor appointed destination. The enterprise
is to keep afloat on an even keel; the sea is both friend and
enemy; and the seamanship consists in using the resources
of a traditional manner of behaviour in order to make a
friend of every hostile occasion.*

Michael Oakeshott

Every fall one hundred thousand new students arrive at
Canada's universities. They are curious and intellectually
hungry; they have known or are hoping to know love; they fear
or revere or are indifferent to their gods; many have seen or
heard about death; individually, they are tasting of that absolute
freedom which is given to human beings to enjoy; they have all
suffered some injustice at the hands of the stronger; they have
encountered mercy and charity and forgiveness; they have nearly
all appreciated in one form or another the essential mystery of
being. Their longings are beautiful, inchoate, passionate and
sometimes dark.

I refer to this vast range of longings and predicaments for two
reasons. The first reason is that increasingly the universities are
being required to see themselves as "engines of economic
growth," as "training centres," as the "cutting edge" of research
and development. University presidents in droves are capitulating
to this vision of the university, their own imagination and judgment harnessed to the soulless activity of devising performance
indicators and "quality management" tools. Academic administrators, who are in principle responsible for the efficient use of
resources in furthering the aims of the institution, are actually

21

ensnared in bureaucracies in which they have become functionaries of an exponential growth of budgets and regulations. In great part, they offer no vision beyond keeping an even keel, often hiding their own passions under the mask of "neutrality." Academics themselves are capitulating to the new agendas, claiming that students tell them they want only practical information to acquire jobs. "They want the facts," says a speaker at a meeting of the Canadian Society for Teaching in Higher Education, "They don't want to do the thinking."[1] And students themselves are parroting what society has told them to expect—"skills," "jobs," "competitive advantage," "productivity" and "relevance"—however much this may go against their strongest instincts.

In quieter moments, students wonder why their emptiness remains. Today's young students, like those of the previous generation, are attracted to the idea of extremes and still read books by Herman Hesse, Ayn Rand and William Golding, dreaming of absolute freedom or absolute hell. If the idiom in which these dreams and nightmares are expressed seems different to many of us (the music of Fine Young Cannibals, New Order or The Tragically Hip), the underlying drama of longings and predicaments is still the same. In opposition to the reduction of the scholarly culture urged upon us by those who would see education solely as vocational training, we must remind ourselves over and over again that students long for much more from their heavy investment and trust than skills and jobs. One student, Heather Bishop, recognized the miscue that was given her when she entered university and was encouraged to think of the university as a business corporation and of herself in terms of "learner satisfaction." "It's not until we've been in school for a couple of years," she candidly confessed later, "that we realize that just getting a degree and getting out fast isn't going to get us what we think we want."[2]

There is another reason for a far-reaching audit of students' needs. It is fashionable today in talking about teaching methods and curriculum, not to say the *purpose* of the university, to recognize that students come to the university with all kinds of "baggage," and that it is the university's business to deal with it. Such recognition has translated at nearly all universities into a vast and expanding network of student counsellors, race coordinators, harassment officers, equity officials, human rights charters, disability centres, retreats, caucuses and committees, personal mentors, special advisors, and workshops on re-engineering teaching and research, whose task it is to offer therapy (usually stimulating "empowerment" and focusing on "wellness" or "authenticity") to help heal the "wounded" and "scarred." The university's purpose, it is said, is fulfilled in being at the vanguard of the helping professions, supplying the knowledge base and the consolation to effect social change.

I am not discounting the importance of these vocations, nor the role the university should play in them. The erosion of the family, the general loosening of social morals and the concomitant rise of crime, the virtual disappearance of traditional healing institutions, the loss of public rituals of purification of grief or fear, the narrow focus of modern medicine—all these create a vacuum that some agency has to fill if we are to arrest the growing tide of personal and social disorder. Moreover, there is a long-standing and reasonably respectable opinion that the university is a laboratory for political and social reform and that this reform starts with a change in consciousness, or the kind of therapy that restores and stimulates a new gestalt. Whether one subscribes precisely to this opinion or not, other traditional viewpoints support the expectation that the university concern itself with the "whole person," the complete flourishing of those persons who form a community there, and the use of education as the means to realize the idea of a just society. It is the great error of the modern university to have devoted the preponderant part of its resources to fostering cognitive knowledge and skills and to have abandoned serious attention to the life of the spirit. The modern university has bought heavily into the simplistic and reductionist opinion that everything beyond the "cognitive" (read, quantifiable and capable of being operationalized) is merely the "affective realm." In one fell swoop, the life of imagination, the forms of poetic creativity, the soul-leading quality of genuine conversation, the "aha"-experience of understanding, the *pathos* of true friendship, the development of civic virtues and the exploration of meaning are all pushed under the rug as if they were embarrassing little oddities. Against this image of the student as a machine capable of being made clever with knowledge and skills, nearly any effort to expand the repertoire of the university is to be applauded.

Nonetheless, it is unfortunate that those who want the university to respond to the "whole person" and to the sediments of baggage do not do so with a deeper recognition that these young men and women, troubled with the anomie of their times and with the personal horrors that modern life has brought to visibility, also arrive with needs more enduring and potent than those arising from the contingencies of their personal and social lives. Their sense of drift and meaninglessness, their apparent inability to see the importance of meaningful personal and social relations, and the gulf between their interior lives and public institutions, while real, obscures other vibrant needs. For, lying dormant in their consciousness are layers of historical culture and legend, primordial fears and hopes, incipient conceptions of justice and charity, the awesome power of concentrated intelligence, anticipations of wholeness, entanglements with a vast array of destinies, and potential for madness, divine or otherwise. Furthermore, the opportunity to brush up against these forms is not the exclusive prerogative of students in arts and humanities. When psychology students use the word "mind," and biology students the word "life," and both raise fundamental questions about order and finitude, they are metaphorically evoking the same mysteries and orders of perfection of which the arts and humanities student has had some experience. What is given in the process of education, as Northrop Frye says, "is both mysterious and substantial, infinitely beyond us and yet inside us, something we can never reach and yet something that is essentially what we are."[3] The pathologization of these needs, and their management by the

24

network of university counsellors as if the university were a social welfare agency, disturbs not only the sacred stewardship between teacher and student, but risks converting education into social engineering.

If we do not undertake to address the perennial and elementary questions concerning humanity, we transform the university into a social welfare agency or a cynical supplier of tools to equip students in their climb up the pecking order of economic, social and political power. But this image of society as a war zone of contending parties is the very image against which the genuine spirit of the university stands. Knowledge and power are related, but anyone acquainted with the deeper processes of understanding and crafting meaning realizes that such processes would not be possible unless transcendence in principle were possible. The economic and material infrastructure of the university, around which power circulates, is not without significance, but it pales in relation to the intellectual and spiritual order that gives the scholarly community substance and purpose. The oldest injunction that defines the form of the university—"Know Yourself"—is an invitation to explore things in the heavens and on earth, the limits and possibilities of human thought and action, and the rich manifold of cultures that humans have created. Most importantly, however, it is a proposition that the one thing most needful for human happiness is an unceasing inquiry into the nature of the self that inquires.

The distinctive form that these student needs have taken in the Western world will be understood only if we explore a few elements of the history of the university. The university as an institution was founded in Europe in the thirteenth century. But the ideas at its core—the uninhibited pursuit of truth, the aspiration to cultivate independent-mindedness, the promotion of intellectual and spiritual order, the enhancement of moral vision through the humanizing force of the world of culture— have their origins much earlier in the fertile intersection of traditions in the Mediterranean region. At the centre of the university lie historical traces of the cultures of Mesopotamia,

Babylon and Egypt, then Judaea, Syria and Iran, and later Ionian natural philosophy and the Platonic Academy.[4] The essence of the university is more, however, than layers of historical sediment. From these cultures, the university also inherited distinctive symbols stemming from the perennial human need to interpret experiences. For example, one of the primary human experiences is a sense of oblivion or boundlessness. Symbols such as "evil," "death" and "freedom" are attempts to articulate this experience and assist us in establishing meaning in our personal lives, in society and in history. Other primary experiences such as the sacred, the tension between imperfection and perfection, and reconciliation were also symbolized in a distinct manner by these Mediterranean cultures, and Western civilization inherited these in the form of "god" or "wholeness," "love" or "justice," and "friendship" or "happiness." When the university, as an institution, was founded in the Middle Ages, these historical legacies and symbols were synthesized to create a tapestry of myriad invitations to rich explorations and encounters. The university has evolved since its mediaeval origins, absorbing traces of the transformations defining European history—the Renaissance, the birth of modern science, the Enlightenment and Romanticism. It also acquired a new range of symbols defining human endeavour, such as "history," "progress," "emancipation" and "alienation." The origins and development of the university have defined the human needs to which the university caters.

There are two dimensions to the university's beginnings that explain how students' needs are understood: the institutional and the symbolic. Although the symbols structuring those needs arose much earlier than the creation of the university as an institution, it is necessary to look at the later development first because it defined how those symbols would be appropriated.

Like other modern institutions such as the law court, the political state and the family, the university is the product of conflicts of the Middle Ages—between emperor and pope, city and monastery, clergy and layperson, faith and reason—and through them all, the theologies of Augustine and Aquinas. The university as an institution developed in the first place because the political unit known as the Holy Roman Empire saw that its survival depended on an equal conferral of power on political rule (*regnum*), the ecclesiastical teaching of salvation (*sacerdotium*) and study (*studium*). The precise historical origin of the universities was in the early thirteenth century when the major European universities—Bologna, Naples, Toulouse, Paris, Oxford and Cambridge—were established as guilds or corporations devoted to study and as places where masters and scholars could come together. The common concern was usually animated by a theological design, even when the explicit discipline of inquiry was medicine, law or letters. Many of the universities were supported directly by the papacy. Like the priesthood, its members were also granted a wide range of privileges, protections, immunities and exemptions, seen as beneficial to maintaining the distinctness and singlemindedness of the scholarly enterprise. The conferral of equal power on study is one of the most important legacies of the Middle Ages. That legacy is evident in the vast authority we still invest in the university, and many of today's debates about the scope of study have their source in mediaeval debates—for example, whether the curriculum should consist of specialized scholarship or the all-rounded education of the *trivium* (grammar, rhetoric and logic) and *quadrivium* (arithmetic, geometry, astronomy and music).

The understanding of *studium*, and thus of the university as an institution, was not undisputed or unchanging. One understanding that would continue to persevere into the nineteenth century when Cardinal John Newman made it the cornerstone of his account of liberal education, was the identity of the university with the Church. *Universitas* is a mediaeval designation that refers generally to a corporate enterprise with an identified common purpose. An *ecclesia*, or community of faithful tied together by common belief in orthodoxy, was a type of *universitas*. Generally, a *universitas* referred to an association that pursued some enduring interest (whether salvation, profit, military conquest or study) and it was ruled accordingly. As a guild, it was created by an act of authority endowing it with specific powers and franchises—a fact reflected in today's university charters. By the late thirteenth century, the term *universitas* came to refer especially and exclusively to a higher place of study—the university.

But the *universitas* was not the only form of association in mediaeval Europe, nor did its design alone define the emerging universities. An equally important mediaeval association was the *civitas*, one bound by rules, rather than common undertakings, by civic decencies rather than moral precepts. *Civitate* are associations whose members acknowledge the authority of civil laws specifying the conditions for undertaking a diverse range of actions.[5] One could say that instead of advancing from a common predicament or specifiable interest, *civitate* encourage merely the continuous exploration of the conditions of association. The idea of the university as a *civitas* also came to prevail at some European universities in the late Middle Ages. Michael Oakeshott, attentive to the theological nuance behind the emergence of *civitas*, suggests that the difference between *universitas* and *civitas* is best understood as a distinction between modes of understanding that continue to compete as options for our current debates about the university.

In a *universitas*, he writes, lingers the God of Thomist theology:

> [One is] a partner with others in a common enterprise and as a sharer in a common stock of resources and a common stock of talents with which to exploit it. The enterprise may be described in various terms: the search for Truth, the pursuit of the Common Good; "making nature yield what it has never yielded," etc. It is a cooperative undertaking and therefore in terms of managerial decisions about performances; and there is a notional "one best way" of conducting it. In this self-identification *outcomes are preferred to adventures and satisfactions to wants....* The deity corresponding to this disposition is

the Proprietor of an estate of vast resources ("Nature")
who, although he may be suspected of being somewhat
niggardly, is nevertheless (like the managers of the enterprise) a "providence," *not the author of rules of conduct but
the source of substantial benefits.*

The *civitas*, on the other hand, is distinctly Augustinian:

And since men are apt to make gods whose characters
reflect what they believe to be their own, the deity corresponding to this self-understanding is an Augustinian god
of majestic imagination who, when he might have devised
an untroublesome universe, had the nerve to create one
composed of *self-employed adventures of unpredictable
fancy,* to announce to them some *rules of conduct, and
thus to acquire convives capable of "answering back" in civil
tones with whom to pass eternity in conversation.*[6]

To the extent that these two modes of understanding still
define the character of today's university, neither the Thomist
nor the Augustinian mode prevails over the other. Indeed, one
could say that the modern university is comprised of the healthy
and often creative tension between *universitas* and *civitas*,
between certain outcomes as one goal and adventures as
another. This tension is clearly evident in the historical emergence of the university in the shape it has come down to us.

Universities began to proliferate and evolve significantly in the
latter part of the thirteenth century under various influences, one
of the most important being the formation of houses of study by
Franciscan and Dominican mendicants. The political meaning
of these houses is more complex than the oft-asserted claim and
criticism that there exists an identity between the Church and
the traditional idea of the university. In the context of the idea
of the Holy Roman Empire, these houses decentred papal power
and conferred upon the cities in which they were situated a political relevance vastly beyond their status as administrative units

under the authority of emperor and pope. Secondly, especially under Franciscan influence, the focus of theological reflection in these schools was no longer the ecclesiastical authority of the Church, with all of its hierarchies and privileges, as the embodiment of the mystical body of Christ. Rather, the focus was on the daily suffering and sacrifice of spiritually and socially destitute men and women and on an image of Christ with whom the worldly poor could identify. It is quite wrong, then, as the reconstructive history of some feminists would have it, to identify the origin of the university exclusively with the monastery and with the hierarchical and patriarchal order that prevailed there. The rise of the Franciscan and Dominican houses was a potent political alternative to the consolidation of power that had occurred during the monastic reforms at Cluny in 910. And this shift in power had the additional effect of creating an opening in the idea of *studium*, and thus of the university, for the greater influence of the idea of *civitas*.

Behind this pragmatic history of the university lies also an intellectual and spiritual culture that was institutionalized and given a precise symbolic definition in the Middle Ages. The idea of the scholarly culture identified two great primals in Western civilization: Athens and Rome, or even better, Socrates and Christ. Both figures became our symbols for expressing the natural human desire for perfection and the belief that the first cause of human striving is a desire for the good that is eternal. From the figure of Socrates emanates a set of symbols defining intellectual vision, or what Aristotle so magisterially identifies in the first line of the *Metaphysics* as our primary impulse: "All humans, by nature, desire to know." Socrates' legacy is evident in our continuing equations of goodness with reason, order with harmony and unity, and truth with statements of proof—all manifestations of how reason can become a living presence in society. And in our personal lives, our continuing endorsement of the Socratic accent on conversation (Yes, but…) as the vehicle of understanding (aha!) has decisively moulded our intercourse with others, especially our expectations concerning the purposes of friendship and citizenship. Our conception of the university as one of the chief means of cultivating citizens—by linking the life of reason and political order, and conceiving of the state as the individual soul writ large—is part of the Socratic heritage that the Platonic Academy transmitted. Our belief that the sense of justice derives from the common bond enjoyed by friends comes from the same root.

From the second primal and from the figure of Christ emerges a different imperative: the desire to do good in the world as a reflection of divine perfection. Christ's parables are paradigms of right action, affirming our capacity for compassion, forbearance, humility, charity, love and, above all, faith in the simple goodness and mystery of existence. The parables serve as way-markers in a spiritual pilgrimage, the purpose of which is to seek reconciliation with the divine and with other human beings. The injunction to live a moral life, within the rhythms of the spiritual pilgrimage and within a community of believers, is a recognition of the individual's free power to make the world better. It is an injunction to use our gifts to serve and to improve, as externalization of our interior struggles to heal ourselves. The symbol of Christ endures whenever individuals affirm in strict conscience their duty to do what is right, or exhibit redemptive hope in free actions and new beginnings, or demonstrate faith in the binding power of love with which human life can be graced, or dwell on the link between the richness of their interior lives and the capacity to do good in the world. But the moral imperative to do good in the world comes at the same time with an admonishment against letting our moral accomplishments become objects of pride. Christ's life is intended to be understood as a warning against virtue become irascible because it believes falsely that humankind's weakness and dependence on grace can be overcome. Such presumption, which gives rise to sinful fantasies and projects of self-deliverance and self-redemption, is a betrayal of the patience, forbearance and mercy also exhibited by Christ. And from that legacy flows the Western world's continuing recognition of the need for tolerance and of the capacity for forgiveness even in the face of evil.

However remote the lives of Socrates and Christ may appear from the daily enterprise of teaching and learning in university classrooms, the symbols of their lives still constitute the major forms of students' intellectual and spiritual searches. And the tension between them is, in great part, the source of the alternative positions put forward whenever reforms and restatements of the university's essential mission are undertaken. Indeed, even where we today affirm, in apparent opposition to Socrates and Christ, the primacy of individual freedom, the equality of all persons, the displacement of faith by secular learning, the progress of history and the preference for liberal democracy, these are but restatements of what we have inherited from that legacy.

These symbols come down to us through the distinctly mediaeval cross-fertilization of Near and Far Eastern, Judaic and Hellenic ideas, and became associated with the thirteenth-century doctrines of scholastic philosophers. However, it would be reducing severely the richness and suggestive quality of these symbols to believe they are narrowly "Western" or "Christian-Platonic." One might say, instead, that these two primals contain a vast range of meaning, and that vital threads present at the origins of the "West" are always available to be unearthed and used for their restorative possibilities. If we see "Socrates" and "Christ" in this way, it would not be inappropriate to suggest that these two symbols form a significant key to understanding our world culture. To speak of "our" culture is to see identities within world culture, convergences of need and expectation, or a universality of adventures and predicaments. Indeed, one of the great virtues of the present re-cognition of the achievements of other civilizations, and the creative efforts to recover ancient wisdom, is the discovery of the enormous impact Near Eastern and Far Eastern thought had on defining the legacy of Socrates and Christ. These discoveries are now serving, amidst great tumult and fertile creativity, to renew symbols like "intellectual knowing" and "moral doing" that have become partially dogmatic and sterile in Western life. Our growing reacquaintance, for example, with the cosmological visions and life-affirming rituals of our aboriginal peoples, with the Hindu understanding of the sacramental nature of everyday existence, with moral authenticity in Islam and the oral tradition amongst native peoples, is not a repudiation of the figures of Socrates and Christ, but a renewal of the deepest meaning of the symbols we have inherited from them.

The multifaceted quality of these symbols is evident in the way they were employed in the centuries following the twelfth and thirteenth century. The Renaissance of the late thirteenth century, represented by figures such as John of Trent, John of Salisbury and Joachim de Fiore, directed scholarly attention away from the idea of eternity and of "the mystical body of Christ" that transcends and unifies the political hierarchies of the world, to the idea of the worldly personality and to the work that could be done to transform the world by overcoming its social divisions. The symbol of Christ became the image of a more worldly Christ, who served the poor and suffering—a figure such as St. Francis. In the sixteenth century, the symbol of Socrates meant the pursuit of scientific knowledge for the purpose of "the relief of man's estate," to use Francis Bacon's expression. The eternal, dismissed as an "imaginary republic," and whose pursuit, it came to be believed, had distracted humans from effectually ordering the world, was replaced with an ideal of social wholeness that could be employed to achieve heaven on earth.

The turn to a project of using knowledge to perfect the world significantly changed many classical and mediaeval priorities. Where the Greek mathematician Archimedes was said to have been so mortified that his theoretical inquiries had led him to a practical invention that he destroyed the plans, the founders of modern science, René Descartes and Francis Bacon, conceived of the natural world as something to be experimented upon and mastered for mundane gain. Under the aegis of modern science, the search for knowledge became a project to order the world on a grid and subject it to precise measurement and correction, preferably under laboratory conditions. The very idea of "experiment," as opposed to theoretical detachment and reflection, suggests the new interplay of power and knowledge. It is also the source of what is meant by "technology"—the mutual interaction of technical control and reason, so that knowledge becomes inseparable from manipulating the conditions of the world.

These ideas were not confined to the natural sciences. The idea of using knowledge as the technical means of governing society gave rise to the social sciences—sociology, psychology and demography—and to the analytical tools that could rid the world of confusion, ignorance and ambiguity. Rejecting metaphysical ideas like "soul" and "natural impulse to perfection," sixteenth-century political scientists like Thomas Hobbes created a discipline, based on geometric precision, that would serve rulers to actualize justice, rather than merely dream of it. Two centuries of political thinkers who followed Hobbes accepted the proposal that there was no clash between selfish interest and the good of the commonwealth ("private vices, public gains," as Bernard Mandeville, the seventeenth-century social thinker, put it), between the pursuit of comfortable self-preservation and happiness, and between truth and imperial expansion over the entire globe ("the white man's burden," as Rudyard Kipling would say). From the same intellectual revolutions that would produce high confidence in scientific objectivity and methodic procedure as the means of saving the world from itself, emerged the liberal paradigm of individual rights, tolerance as the supreme virtue and limited authority.

The industrial order founded by early modern political thinkers and economists spawned a society requiring homogeneity in vast areas of social life. By the early eighteenth century, this society appeared, to many philosophers, artists and dramatists, as inhospitable to the human heart. By contrast to the new urban centres, "nature" became an enclave of spontaneous impulses that offered a return to "sweeter sentiments." This turn away from society is the essence of the intellectual and cultural resistance known as Romanticism. Again the university saw a transformation of the symbols "Christ" and "Socrates." From Jean-Jacques Rousseau to Marx, Christ and Socrates were interpreted primarily as individuals alienated from the world and as revolutionaries who were an inspiration to supplant the prevailing structure of power. Central to this reconfiguration was the new priority given to creative expression, the belief that there was a truth known only by the human heart, and the idea that there could be no reconciliation of the poet-scholar and society until the world was overthrown and then rebuilt to embody this new truth. Until such time, the only refuge from society's hypocrisies and deceptions was the satisfaction to be found in intimacy or among like-minded rebels aggrieved by the chill of the world. Throughout the literature of Romanticism lingers a longing for a lost unity and the search for a sentimental education to heal the torn heart. The alienation of those "in the true" has persevered into the twentieth century with the Existentialists.

Concern about the ravages of modern industrial society, and particularly the effect of the reigning scientific empiricism on the life of the mind, was not confined to Romanticism. The nineteenth century also saw a restatement of Classicism emerging from the German historical school and the British encounter with German Idealism. Many of today's disputes about the nature of liberal education have their origin in a lively debate between the New Classicism and the Scottish Enlightenment, which began with a series of articles in the *Edinburgh Review* beginning in 1809, then became focused on the value of the Oxford and Cambridge university curriculum and continued unabated until the close of the century. The debate had three dimensions—the relative merits of the ancient and modern curriculum, the one centred on Classical studies of history, philosphy and rhetoric, the other on modern literature, languages and history; arguments for the transcendent value of learning as opposed to learning as preparation for the world; and the relationship between religion and secular learning. Two works in particular are significant, partly because they played a large role in setting the direction that was to be taken in the United States (especially at the University of Chicago under the presidency of Robert Maynard Hutchins and the entrepreneurship of Mortimer Adler). These works were Matthew Arnold's *Culture and Anarchy* (1867) and Cardinal John Newman's *The Idea of a University Defined* (1873). Both writers defended a liberal education distinct from preparation for a practical life, and as a counterbalance to the commercialism and professionalization of industrial society. Arnold, however, appealed to the study of the "great tradition" of "the best which has been thought and said in the world,"[7] as the means of making humans morally virtuous and of perfecting the world. Newman, on the other hand, sought to make the entire world the student's university and saw liberal education not as a moral enterprise, but as the pursuit of universal knowledge for its own sake. The university, as a "place of teaching," Newman commented, did not aim at advancing scientific and philosophical discovery but at diffusing and extending what was known, with the benefit of creating understanding and tolerance for a world that could not be remade.

Arnold's work was written partially for an American readership and had its most powerful influence there, particularly sixty years later when Hutchins penned his *Critique of the American University* (1937) and commissioned Mortimer Adler to produce a definitive encyclopedia of "great books." This merging of the history of Western civilization and the history of its great books was one approach to American liberal education. Another arose out of the publication of Ruth Benedict's *Patterns of Culture* (1934) and Raymond Williams' *Culture and Society* (1958), which refused to give focal priority to a single culture and "taste," and saw ideas and values as derivative of, rather than determining, culture. "Great books" versus cultural anthropology does not, of course, exhaust the options experimented with in the United States. But the debate between Adler and Benedict/Willliams, and filtered through them, the difference in thought of Arnold and Newman, continue to define the parameters of the education debate. Allan Bloom's bestselling book *The Closing of the American Mind* (1987) harked back to Arnold and Adler, while Stanford University's controversial decisions to change its foundation course from "Western Civilization" to "Western Culture" and finally to "Culture, Ideas, and Values" exhibits the impact cultural anthropology, and somewhat more remotely Newman, had at that institution.[8]

One of the remarkable reorientations in the scholarly culture of the late nineteenth century was, to use the term of intellectual historians, the "linguistic turn." Language came to be seen as the primary object worthy of inquiry because it was argued that upon it depends not merely our perception of reality, but reality itself. Analysis of language, British philosophers in particular believed, would expose unfounded dogma and bring to light the ruses by which our grammar deceives us into believing that there are entities such as "causality" or "a subject." The "linguistic turn" has produced varied paths in the common project of overcoming ordinary language. Some philosophers, following the lead of Oxford philosophers G.E. Moore and Bertrand Russell or American linguist Noam Chomsky, have looked for a universal language lying below myriad human languages. Other scholars, particularly in literature and political thought, have adopted the deconstructive strategies of the French philosopher Jacques Derrida, who showed how an author's intention is often subverted by the very language he or she adopts. They used this insight to turn the common meaning of well-known texts on its head. Others have adopted the work of French critic Paul de Man and Duke University and Yale University professors J. Hillis Miller, Gerald Graff and Stanley Fish. They use Nietzsche's claim that language is no more than an "army of metaphors" to call into question the representational nature of any word. The benefit of this activity is an extensive unfreezing of dogma and an opportunity to reassess how our use of words like "normal" or "pure" have served various political agendas and have marginalized alternative ways of knowing.

The downside of the "linguistic turn" is the deepening of the gulf separating the scholarly culture and general society, reinforcing the idea that academics are aloof and disdainful of the world. Built into the writing style of many twentieth-century works is the unwarranted assumption that the humanities and social sciences will acquire the status of modern science only if they adopt its methods and language. The result of this assumption is a pseudo-scientific jargon that is nearly universally uninformative. The idea of the *intellectuel engagé* has, in the process, become perverted from meaning the responsible engagement of the scholar in humanizing the world, to the more dubious one of the distant academic who designs means to subvert the ordinariness of the world and re-engineer human existence. The vacuum between the two worlds has been filled with maverick scholars outside academe who are engaging the world with a clarity and directness nearly absent in academic work and thereby reinforcing the growing suspicion that the university is irrelevant.

The early roots of the university, as well as the layers of seven centuries of reinterpretation and transformation, are worth recollecting because they remind us of the breadth of human needs catered to by this institution. No period in the university's history can claim a legitimate monopoly on defining students' needs, and one could add that prudence should lead us to try to maintain the tapestry of invitations to encounters that its history offers. Many of the hot-button critics are ignorant of the university's roots and its evolving role. The singleminded desire to re-engineer the university adopts the unwarranted assumption that the West's processes of technological and social development are an unmitigated blessing. With its continued commitment to soul-leading conversation, the world of imagination, critical judgment and the unalloyed intellectual and spiritual journey, the scholarly culture of the university is the only true antidote to the anomie of our times and the locus of our hope for the renewal of our world. The university can serve these functions only if it can continue to enjoy detachment from society's urgencies and certainties, and if it is permitted to continue the leisurely examination of intellectual and spiritual possibilities that provide us with a higher idea of ourselves. Society should be responsible for protecting its intellectuals and scholars, providing them with a safe haven within which to advance culture. Scholars, in turn, should be accountable to society in their ability to give it direction and purpose. Society, with its concentrated focus on labour and consumption, and its reduction of leisure to merely entertainment and hobbies, permits few opportunities for individuals to book off time to examine themselves. The university is a counterweight to these propensities and particularly society's destructive tendency to precipitous action. We take for granted the value of the intellectual life, because its products have immeasurably improved our lives, but we forget that its value needs continuous revalidation so that its insights neither decay nor freeze into dogma.

Students' needs, defined and developed in history and through interpretations of significant symbols of order, are one component of the essence of the university. Now it is necessary to add the other half of the university equation—the scholarly culture. Like students' needs, that culture is neither uniform nor constant. Indeed, its two predominant animating principles—reading in the tradition of books and renewal by conversations—will appear as distinct motions.

The oldest tradition of the university is that of reading. The awakening, cultivation, and maturation of a student's needs, passions and longings happens largely through teachers fostering a communion between their students and books. As in other literate cultures, books in the Western world serve as the main medium for self-interpretation and exploration of meaning. They offer us the opportunity to enter a great dialogue spanning millennia and continents. It is a distinctive characteristic of our culture that it is defined by a pedigree of books, a continuous lineage that runs parallel to, and that has shaped, the history of our institutions and our social practices. The scholarly culture is an artifice that is an organized remembrance of this lineage.

In being given a selection of great literary and philosophic books, narratives of history, and works of art, music and drama, students are invited to encounter heroes and demons, saints and martyrs, fanatics and wise persons—the human condition in all its superlative virtue and all its depraved evil. The purpose of these adventures is to invite students to acquire the discipline of intelligence, to pursue intimations of wholeness, to cultivate a discerning appreciation of meaning, to fine-tune their moral vision and to learn how to respond to the contingencies of their existence with courage and hope. These encounters may be random and fortuitous. The experience of well-known CBC television producer Kevin Sullivan is a case in point. Although Sullivan was at the University of Toronto to study medicine, serendipity in the form of a brush against the Hart House Theatre took him to drama. The importance of adventures like these give the lie to efforts to "operationalize" teaching and to focus on "learner satisfaction." A genuine education is, in part, uncharted and unpredictable. Such an odyssey, quite unlike the narrow vocationalism being paraded today under the banner of "lifelong learning," is the only enduring education. Few teachers fail to be moved when they see their students transported out of the here and now, driven by an unalloyed intellectual curiosity and wonder, oblivious to daily matters. This brief and enchanted experience of self-sufficiency and independence from the business of the world that reading provides led Virginia Woolf to quip, "When the Day of Judgement dawns and the great conquerors and lawyers and statesmen come to receive their rewards—their crowns, their laurels, their names carved indelibly upon imperishable marble—the Almighty will turn to Peter and will say, not without a certain envy when he sees us coming with our books under our arms, 'Look, these need no reward. We have nothing to give them here. They have loved reading.'"[9]

Such an understanding of reading is markedly different from what is often debated in the increasingly sterile "canon wars," the dispute that is today's continuation of the debate between Adler's "great books" and Benedict/Williams' "other cultures." A canon is the traditional set of texts or works through which the most profound human achievements are recorded. The works worthy of our most serious attention are not just any inchoate expression of longing or desire; they are those that invoke a cosmos of meaning that speaks to our universal condition. There is no predetermined formula that guarantees the admission of a work to the canon. Included in it are works of philosophic comedy as well as of tragedy, texts that speak to our longing for wholeness as well as for recognition of our uniqueness, claims on behalf of community as much as of individual freedom, paeans to contemplation as much as to action. But when an author can elevate the particulars of his or her world and experience of it to the level of universality, presenting these events as part of a meaningful whole and thereby offering symbols of order to our complex natures, then we might assume that we are in the presence of a text worthy of being admitted to the category of canon. Acquainting oneself with the ongoing conversation of the canon is an invitation to participate in a great voyage of discovery and to contemplate the canvas of human vice and weakness. It provides us with stimulus to seek the good, while reminding us of our all-too-human nature.

It is so very difficult to say with any degree of precision or authority what exactly should be read. E.D. Hirsch has compiled a list of "what every American needs to know," whose mastery would give a person "cultural literacy." But like all things relegated to lists, compilations of books such as *The Dictionary of Cultural Literacy* impose too great an order on the life of the mind, rendering adventure into a pilgrimage, where one holy shrine after another is checked off. Been there, done that, seen that, as popular idiom has it.

Equally problematic is the compendium of foundational texts prescribed by Allan Bloom in his diagnosis of North America's intellectual ills. The series of texts is unassailable if one subscribes to the principle that our history is nothing but a search for rational order, and that Plato and Aristotle understood that search best. But it is as persuasive to suggest very different compendia. Where are the works of Cicero, Clement, Anselm, Peter the Lombard, John of Salisbury, Siger de Brabant, Erasmus, Hutcheson, Wollstonecroft, Macaulay or de Beauvoir in Bloom's intellectual history? These affirm our capacity for right action, spiritual obedience, governance by the rule of law, and spontaneous action—all equally compelling goals in human life. Lists of books are political instruments, and while affirming the possibility of an education that transcends politics, we would be foolish to deny that political power and knowledge have been interconnected especially at those historical moments when fluid experience has been transformed into doctrine and dogma. Selective histories built on the elevation of a single canon of texts and that promote one way of life—the life of the philosopher, to the exclusion of, say, the life of the saint—very often lead, ironically in light of the title of Bloom's book and his intention to open the American mind, to closed-mindedness.

On the other hand, it is a sign of the bleakest nihilism and abandonment of all criteria of preferment to think that no books may be prescribed and that there is no hierarchy among them. University education is about authority—the authority of compelling reason, the repeatable experiment, persuasive imagination—and acknowledgment of that authority arises from the ability to distinguish the higher from the lower, the better from the worse, the comprehensive from the parochial. Students undertaking the adventure that the university offers them should therefore have daily congress with the inheritance of enduring works that is deeded to them by Western and other cultures. In brushing up against these texts, students acquire the forms of cultivated humanity that permit them to become, in Michael Oakeshott's words, "civilized subscribers to human life."[10] But for that to happen a book must be taken up as offering a predicament that we do not presume to have already solved.

Above all else, we read to be given a narrative in which the contingencies and predicaments of our lives are given meaning. A book is a small cosmos that takes up the intimations, adventures and longings of our lives and sings them into a rhythm. As Newman says, the ultimate aim of education is a philosophical detachment that aims at uniting the disparate parts of the whole and recognizing the hierarchy that signifies their respective human significance. Students and scholars persistently express their revulsion at any process that makes the university, as Newman feared, "a sort of bazaar, or pantechnicon, in which wares of all kinds are heaped together for sale in stalls independent of each other."[11] The legacy of enduring books is an array of narratives whose contemplation endows our adventures with meaning and direction.

However great the array of small worlds created by books, we can identify the cardinal concerns we have as questioning beings to which the enduring books offer a map by recalling Immanuel Kant's statement that the questions humans will of necessity ask themselves revolve around three issues: freedom, god and death. Each of these is an ark filled with a multitude of human predicaments. For example, why is there something, instead of nothing? Why is what is as it is and not otherwise? How and why do things change? If there is order, why is there disorder? What is the end of desire? What is the meaning of finitude? What is our purpose? Is love or strife the basis of all things? What is it to be human? Not every lecture or classroom discussion resounds with questions as portentous as these. But they are implicit in the university culture, as much for students of the humanities as for engineers and scientists, and authors of enduring books have attempted to answer them. To understand why these questions are asked takes us far in understanding the nexus of student need and the scholarly culture. It also permits us to take positions on some of today's "re-engineering" schemes.

Let us take the question of freedom as an example. At the core of freedom is desire. Controlled by law, convention and habit, desire is nonetheless the potent force that percolates in every classroom. It is not accidental that when students in 1994 were polled across Canada about the hottest courses on campus, all five courses were on sex.[12] A seminar, in particular, can be intensely erotic. If we leave aside, for the moment, our North American "Puritanism," we can learn much from the

Mediterranean appreciation of how erotic human engagement is. Every conversation is a seduction, every search for meaning is a longing for reconciliation and completion. Students love to seek the extreme: they are drawn to the works of Rabelais, Boccaccio, D'Annunzio and the Marquis de Sade for the transgressions upon which they are invited by these authors. They take naturally to the postmodernists Foucault and Derrida for their iconoclasm, for their dissolution of boundaries, for their celebration of ambiguity.

But ambiguity is not the end of the matter: instead, this revelry gives rise to creativity. The music that students are attracted to is soulless only to those who see tyranny in every act of freedom and who distrust the redemptive possibilities of new beginnings and contingent actions. This is why there is something stifling about discipline codes and the tenacious administrative efforts to regulate the body. In principle, of course, "work and learning can best be accomplished in an environment of understanding and mutual respect for the dignity and rights of each individual," as the "Framework Regarding Prevention of Harassment and Discrimination in Ontario Universities" would have it, but to hope that "offensive materials" will never be used and that students will not enter dangerous territories, is naïve and contrary to the very meaning of the scholarly culture.[13]

The shock and dismay that McMaster University administrators registered when they learned that frosh, as part of their initiation rites, were required to simulate sex, was in great part banal and self-righteous. Native peoples have complex rites to celebrate passage from one state to another. The required acts are fraught with ambiguous sexual imagery, the coincidence of the sacred and the profane, and the mingling of terror and purification. As we are relearning, these rites are important to self-development and group identity. Granted, one major difference distinguishes aboriginal rites of passage from McMaster's frosh activities: traditional rites of passage are guided by elders who take on the responsibility of sublimating sexual desire. Left to their own abandon, the McMaster students may have been left, in the absence of authority, with no guidance as to how to satisfy their longing for wholeness in the future at a more elevated level. One should not defend the barbarisms of the hazing practices of the Airborne Regiment, but neither should one be overcensorious about the playful transgressions of young students. Such judgmentalism nearly always arises out of bureaucratic overzealousness, and it is fuelled by Protestant distrust of the body and the residual, though discounted, Cartesian view that mind and body are separate entities.

On the other hand, one of the great gifts of wisdom that experience brings, and that the scholarly culture can supply without the risk of direct experience, is that freedom is not immediate instinctual response. Nor is freedom denunciation of instinctual response. True freedom is the maturation of instinct towards the higher satisfactions that come from the exercise of moral choice and intellectual independent-mindedness. Student desire left to its own devices, and not invited to participate in the scholarly culture, will exploit the dangers of the in-between time it has been allowed the privilege of enjoying, and may become a powerfully disruptive passion such as lust for domination. When university managers are confronted with such wildness, their response has usually been to devise technical rules and codes to suppress it. The scholarly culture is thus badly served. The student is denied the pleasure of the higher forms of freedom, and the classroom no longer has the opportunities for ambiguous play that are necessary to the learning process. This breakdown of the university's civil association leads to a dangerous polarity of unchecked desire and technical regulation.

The breakdown has a historical origin. In a classic example of the sins of the fathers being visited upon the sons, we now have a generation of students taught by 1960s academics who believed that the lifting of all restraint and the release of all instincts—even "polymorphous perversity"—would usher in a new age of tolerance and reconciliation. Now, living with the effects of that teaching, where some students believe they can transgress all boundaries and vent the passion of the moment, we are compelled to exercise authoritarian rule by decree, thus vitiating the gains that were made by the generation that redis-covered the power and beauty of desire.

No less than freedom, the question of god arises in all areas of university culture. Fewer and fewer students are urged, of course, to reflect on the gods. We should probably not expect otherwise, given the reaction against the dogmatism that insti-tutionalized religion has imposed on the fluidity of spiritual experience. But students will admit and display their spiritual hunger in myriad ways. God is a symbol for the perfection and proportionality that students seek and scholars pursue, and if this symbol goes under the name of truth, awe, authenticity or self-examination, it is no less a meditation on god. More worri-some is the fact that if students are not encouraged to think in terms of wholeness and unity, their spiritual longings will become attached to surrogates. Consequently, they will develop unrealistic expectations of social reform or personal satisfaction. Fortunately, the present disenchantment with Western ways has brought about a revival of overt searches for perfection. Spiritual longing is evident in renewed interest in the cosmological visions and life-affirming rituals of Canada's indigenous cultures and the spiritual adventures of many non-Western peoples. Amidst our current university troubles and the widespread processes of deculturation in society at large, hope is offered through initia-tives like Trent's Traditional Peoples' Gathering and Lakehead's tribal elder counselling service. But the yearning is not exclu-sively evident in the curiosity for native ways. Large numbers of students are returning to Catholicism and the Church of England, in search of ceremony and spiritual exaltation, as they are experimenting with evangelical and Pentecostal communi-ties, whose focus is the spiritual bond between members.

Students today, as a consequence of television and the tireless portrayal of decay and destruction in the media, are confronted with death—albeit vicariously—more than past generations. This, of course, does not mean that they understand it better. Here, too, the scholarly culture informs and responds to the anxieties that accompany life's final chapter. The theme of death is certainly one of the most enduring and elementary concerns of literature, philosophy, history and religion. Why are we finite? Is there something beyond or within the finite that is infinite? What opportunities are given to us to immortalize ourselves? What is the meaning in the permanence we seek in perpetuating family name, building lasting monuments, exhibiting superlative virtue (in sport, politics or thought) to ensure our own remembrance? In asking questions of this order we inevitably encounter the omnipresent reality of contingency, indeterminacy and oblivion. In a convocation address at the University of Alberta, William Thorsell identified succinctly the importance of the institutionalized memory of the scholarly culture: "A university degree is a cure for the social amnesia into which each of us is born. When we die, most of what we know must *not* be allowed to die with us. Our universities ensure that it does not. Commencement days are society's fountain of youth, the antidote to mortality for our very civilization."[14]

What Thorsell does not add is that reflections on mortality have an opposite but equally beneficial effect. Before the reality of decay and chaos, all projects will appear vain and futile, especially those predicated on the assumption that there is "one best way" to order human life. This realization is nearly always a useful lesson, especially in an age where the actualization of extravagant dreams of perfection appears to be technically feasible, for it reintroduces humility and moderation. Reflection on the theme of death is a cathartic experience, purifying consciousness of pettiness and presumption by placing these dreams in the widest perspective.

By preserving a tradition of enduring books and works and inviting students to sample the worlds contained in them, the university provides a safe haven in which the concepts of freedom, god and death can be explored. This has always been part of the university's tradition. It is nearly always unfortunate to use the word "tradition" because it is most often seen as a death-dealing alternative to "progress"—and there are many instances where "conserving tradition" has been cited as a rationale for tiresome rearguard actions of reconsecrating a defunct past. Recently Professor Derek Allison won a fight for what he called "tradition" at the University of Western Ontario, when he persuaded the university to restore the use of "God Save the Queen" at convocation. He argued: "As such, playing and singing the royal anthem has been, until recently, a shared experience forging an unbroken link connecting all who have gone before—graduates, faculty, observers, as well as different monarchs and their representatives—to all who have come after. This is a precious thing, and I urge that we re-establish, reforge, this immemorial link, this small instance of shared experience that binds us and our successors with our alumni and predecessors."[15] While Professor Allison's sense of the value of partnership with a larger community is admirable, this nostalgic celebration of archaism is not what the university is. Such an antiquarian approach to the past is one example of how ideological posturing can be disguised as a defence of tradition.

The enduring books offer many answers to the grand questions in the form of propositions. More important than acquiring knowledge of the options of the past is the formation of a discipline of intelligence whereby the inheritance becomes a living present, an organic whole uniting past, present and future. An education true to its deepest meaning brings forth past and present forms of cultivated imagination and judgment, thus encouraging students to undertake renewal of the manners of human intercourse.

Conversations are the second vital component of the scholarly culture. However attractive it may be to focus exclusively on the bookish cultivation of longing and need, it is as important to recognize that what students will leave with at the end of their programs, is less wisdom and the aptitude to see the universal in the particular or the particular in the universal, than the art of pursuing intimations. The tradition of enduring works is the source of intellectual depth and breadth, but the continuous renewal of human purposes depends on the vital engagement provided through conversation. In Michael Oakeshott's terms, these engagements are "conversations." Parties to conversation are not presenting information, nor are they seeking to proselytize. They are engaged in what is beautifully conveyed by the Greek word for conversation, *psuchegogia*, or "soul-leading."[16]

Many parents wonder what their sons and daughters are learning, curious about the books and tales of classroom life they bring home. Their progeny often find it difficult to articulate what they have experienced and come to know. This is natural. It is nearly impossible to communicate or to state in propositional form the outcome of learning. F.R. Leavis once wrote that every moment of a university education is "a collaborative exchange, a corrective and creative interplay of judgments. For though my judgment asks to be confirmed and appeals for agreement that the thing is *so*; the response I expect at best will be of the form, 'yes, but…', the 'but' standing for qualifications, corrections, shifts of emphasis, additions, refinements."[17]

Yes, but…. No greater exactness can be expected when speaking of apprenticeship to the scholarly culture. There is knowledge, there are facts, there are data, but these are only approximations to answers. The answer to any question, as Northrop Frye once said, is just a way of formulating the next question, whether in the humanities or the sciences. The Church, not the university, is the place for certainties. This is why Oakeshott says that "no one can hope to say anything significant about the universities unless he understands that university education is neither a beginning nor an end, but a middle."[18] This is what lies at the heart of genuine conversation, and without it the scholarly culture would be a mausoleum. Often initiated outside the classroom in extracurricular circumstances, conversation is by nature will-of-the-wisp and inconclusive. Unlike chatter or information delivery, conversation edifies only indirectly. Uncertainty and hesitancy *are* the distinguishing characteristics of the scholarly culture properly understood. And they are a healthy antidote to society's unquestioning, obstinate position that it holds a monopoly on truth and freedom.

The university's culture, Oakeshott explains,

> ...comprises unfinished intellectual and emotional jour-
> neyings, expeditions now abandoned but known to us in
> the tattered maps left behind by the explorers; it is com-
> posed of lighthearted adventures, of relationships
> invented and explored in exploit or in drama, of myths
> and stories and poems expressing fragments of human
> self-understanding, of gods worshipped, of responses to
> the mutability of the world and of encounters with
> death.[19]

The danger arises when conversation is suspended by the
assertion of a single voice. "[E]ach voice," Oakeshott warns, "is
prone to *superbia*, that is, an exclusive concern with its own
utterance, which may result in its identifying the conversation
with itself and its speaking as if it were speaking only to itself.
And when this happens, barbarism may be observed to have
supervened." Matthew Arnold identified this danger particularly
with the distorting tendency of the "Puritan" who takes the task
of moral doing to an extreme.

> The Puritan's great danger is that he imagines himself in
> possession of a rule telling him the *unum necessarium*, or
> the one thing needful, and that he then remains satisfied
> with a very crude conception of what this rule really is
> and what it tells him, thinks he has now knowledge and
> henceforth needs only to act, and, in this dangerous state
> of assurance and self-satisfaction, proceeds to give full
> swing to a number of the instincts of his ordinary self.[20]

Arnold's point, like Oakeshott's, is that there is no *one* thing
most needful. We cannot definitively say what we are and
wherein our perfection lies, nor must we exaggerate the stability
or perfection of the past. We cannot, as a fellow traveller,

Hannah Arendt, once said, jump over our own shadow and refer to ourselves as objects, as we can of animals, plants and rocks. We are a "who" and not a "what." There is no final solution to the question of ourselves. The university is "a conversation to make us see" and to learn the manners of conversation. Nearly every good conversation ends in an "aha," confirming truths that emanate from the world of meaning conveyed in books, but like Homer's Penelope, who each day unravels what she has woven the night before, each morning starts anew with a "Yes, but...."

True teachers of tradition, as Frye suggests, are not dispensers of learning but transparent media of the world of culture. They may be explorers and transmit their discoveries, and they may find it useful to organize aspects of scholarship for clarity in teaching, but what they essentially convey is the complex tapestry of scholarship. Frye adds that "[the student] advances from 'taking' a subject to being taken up in it."[21] Student longing is often inchoate and dormant until it is awakened and guided by the patterns and interconnections of the scholarly culture. Models of "learner-centred" education are usually sterile because they assume that desire and need are already defined prior to the process of apprenticeship to the scholarly culture. But, at the same time, models that see a teacher as banking a deposit to be withdrawn later in life, fail to see the complex symbiotic relation between students and teachers. The teacher, as Plato's powerful image of the teacher as midwife describes, is one who draws out what is already intuited or nascently known and gives it an active presence. Genuine education, in which a student gradually acquires connoisseurship in discerning meanings within the scholarly culture, is wholly distorted by models that see students purchasing the services of instructors, acquiring information from talking heads or chit-chatting electronically.

Only through this ongoing apprenticeship to the scholarly culture will students truly experience the best that the university has to offer. Years of a genuine education can significantly change a young person's character, effecting a "turning around" as Plato wrote in his well-known cave allegory that tells of the soul's ascent to understanding. It is a metamorphosis, like the one Hans Castorp experiences in Thomas Mann's wonderful novel *The Magic Mountain*, where struggling through a blinding snow storm and in exhaustion, he finds a quiet hollow that allows "the great soul of which we are a part [to] dream through us, in our manner of dreaming, its own secret dreams, of its youth, its hope, its joy and peace." James Downey, former president of the University of New Brunswick and current president of the University of Waterloo, and someone who evidently loves and knows the university well, once said, "Every one of us, now and then, should experience an epiphany—a sense, a glimpse, a recognition—of the awesome wonder of the universe that is the essence of the university."

The intellectual and spiritual odyssey the university offers is, in Oakeshott's words, "a momentary release, a brief enchantment," preserving us, as Matthew Arnold suggested, from "thraldom to the passing moment" and from the "clamour of the immediate." The scholarly culture is an enterprise best understood as an odyssey that takes its members from the immediate and pressing concerns of their daily lives to worlds that speak to the plethora of their needs, if only to return them to their present lives enriched with perspective and understanding. This intellectual and spiritual odyssey is the hallmark of a true university and its translation into scientific discovery, social vision, moral decency and civic courage is the basis of our faith in the university. Many people see the activities of the university as distinct from the "real world" of commerce and industry, social obligations and bids for recognition. This image, however, is a threat to how we understand reality, for it reduces and condenses the range of needs and longings that humans experience. The university offers students the opportunity for a metamorphosis which has the great value of being an antidote to the reduction of reality to immediate urgencies. It is also an antidote to prejudice and factionalism, for it sows the salutary seeds of doubt and uncertainty in the midst of a culture blindly set on a single path of human development.

How powerful will the student's metamorphosis be? Even in the first year of university, many eighteen-year-olds will become permanently estranged from former high school friends, siblings and parents. A genuine education, as Socrates taught, is quintessentially the work of "corrupting the young," of bringing individuals to see opportunities that betray their own lives as provincial and limiting. The powerful myth of ancestral wisdom, of the authority of seniors, of the supreme virtue of continuity, will have been broken. This is what Harold Bloom means in his book *The Western Canon: The Books and School of the Ages*, when he speaks of the "uncanniness" of the great works: "their ability to make you feel strange at home." Having accepted the invitation to question and to uproot, students lose the innocence of early pieties and will experience restlessness, dissatisfaction and tension. They are awake to the powerful images of primordial wandering that will lead them to reject stability and continuity—a spiritual odyssey conveyed so beautifully in Bruce Chatwin's book *The Songlines*. But this exploration, tentative and vulnerable to so many false paths, will make them terribly out of sync with society's demands for certainty, continuity and order.

Not all of this dissolution and recreation will be comforting— some may be hugely unsettling and distasteful, and the process will include violent disagreement, confrontation and anger. It is precisely here that the university must exercise its most powerful responsibility, to tame and sublimate primordial longing. And it is especially here where the language of "empowerment" fails students. So much of the fault for the indecencies that erupt in university classrooms and residences lies with those who are happy to indulge their students to the maximum but then fail to take on the responsibility of maturing that newly released vitality and exuberance. When indifference to the need for guiding students on to maturity is justified by an appeal to "academic freedom" and the classroom is allowed to be a free-for-all, the scholarly culture has degenerated into a state of moral decay.

On the other hand, intolerance shown towards the young at

this time risks producing submissiveness or uncontrollable rebellion. Few university officials have much inkling of how to act towards students at this time. One would wish that university legislators and administrators would read Rousseau's *Emile* for its sage insights into the shaping of a young person's naturally irascible will, or Plato's *Symposium* for practical advice on how to weave together strands of human longing. Regrettably, most administrators have been weaned on the cynical teaching that the only relevant questions are "who gets what, when and how," as Harold Laswell once rather narrowly defined the scope of political inquiry. This is ultimately a teaching about power and how it is consolidated. Even at best, most university administrators have adopted the narrow horizon of some branches of contemporary psychology that sees humans only in terms of basic needs, the desire for recognition and a creative pampering of the self. Surprise and indignation follows when their students actually exhibit more potent passions such as erotic longing for wholeness, moral righteousness and political idealism, some of which will of necessity be foolish and reckless, but some of which are highly attractive and educable. Education's task is to engage them at this time in the serious reflection that guides these passions to their thoughtful exercise. Dating contracts, discipline codes, rights charters and other regulative devices are necessary only when and after the university has failed to forge the link between the scholarly culture and civil association.

The uncertainty of the university will, of necessity, be misunderstood. The university is a tenuous, vulnerable institution, its hesitancies misunderstood as indecisiveness, its scepticism as cynicism, its scholarly pursuits as nothing more than extracting sunbeams out of cucumbers, its latitudes and tolerances as irresponsibility. Yet, every year one hundred thousand new students sign up for the odyssey I have described, joining a community of one million students and thirty-five thousand scholars in Canada already launched on this adventure.[22] They have come and they stay not because they believe they can save the world from itself, or to find the elixir that will lead to their success in the world of power and utility, but to enjoy the interval that our society has believed, for its worth, its citizens should experience.

For the young men and women entering the university, this is the best of times and the worst of times. The virtual elimination of religious, race, gender and social class barriers in this century has made accessible to them the secret garden once reserved for the privileged few. Modest tuition fees, generous loan programs, the ease of admission, the variety of learning options, the general favour in which higher education is held, a generation of supportive parents who themselves attended colleges and universities, the growth of a knowledge-based society—all these conspire to instill great desire for the riches promised on campuses across Canada. Great books once owned only by the wealthy are now widely available for a few dollars. Freedom of access has reversed the practice still dominant in the 1950s where students had to have a certificate ensuring they were free of "mental problems" before accessing books like the Marquis de Sade's *120 Days of Sodom* or James Joyce's *Ulysses* that were on the "restricted shelf." Reproductions of great works of art and music can be found in all university libraries, and now increasingly on the worldwide web. Accurate documents chronicling world-historical events are at any student's fingertips. Laboratory equipment, once the reserve of a few research centres, is equally available.

But for young women and men entering university today, all is not well. They are the generation between times. They will miss out on opportunities available to the previous, wealth-sated generation, and while the necessity under which they labour may be the mother of many inventions, a spectre of foreboding is cast over all that they do. They are, as is often repeated, Generation X. They have fewer job opportunities. Their social world is gripped by many hatreds and divisions. Their debilitating spiritual languor, a torpor that often exhibits itself as physical and emotional restlessness, cripples them. Many leave their studies to travel, to work, to love, to escape themselves and their demons, though deep in their hearts they understand Horace's admonition that "they change their skies but not their souls who sail across the sea."[23] For so many of this generation, who only in passing are experiencing the magic that takes place when student need confronts scholarly culture, "the ideal of a university [has] become a myth, a vision, a meadow lark among the smoke stacks."[24]

But the source of their greatest disappointment is the fact that the university is not living up to its purpose. We need to understand this disappointment very precisely. Students complain about boring professors. They are discouraged when the university admits it cannot guarantee a better job or higher social status. They are demoralized when they learn that all the foibles, petty vanities, treachery and disloyalties that agitate society at large occur as much, and even more intensely, in academe. They are appalled by dilapidated facilities, book prices, food services and the indifference of administrators. As historical records as far back as the Romans demonstrate, these are inconveniences that inevitably accompany the scholarly life. However, when the university does not live up its *purpose*, then we have moved beyond the question of mere inconvenience.

The point of our discussion of students' needs and the scholarly culture was to give us a context in which to understand the great changes occurring today in the university. It should be obvious from what I have said that the scholarly culture, and the needs and expectations that animate its rhythms, form a polyphony of voices that offers a great richness of human possibility. But that richness is now in jeopardy and students are being significantly shortchanged. The threat to their experience comes wherever reformers generalize from the practice of the management consultant or the therapist and offer a simple scheme of resolution, thus flattening the modulations and syncopations that make the scholarly culture vibrant. These two sets of activists—the "managers" and the "therapists"—offer a semblance of continuation with the great primals of the university ("intellectual knowing" and "moral doing," to use Arnold's designations), but they threaten to sideline the subdued and nuanced activities of the university.

The university's uncertainties and tensions are easily seen as evidence of a vacuum. And fashionable certainty thus gives itself licence to step in. The first certainty is that of technical competence. Generalizing the success of mathematics and technical expertise from the laboratory and industrial realm of life, reformers would have us believe that the scholarly culture, repackaged and remarketed for "relevance" and "efficiency," would finally display the order that should be conspicuous in all human affairs. Now it is true that the scholarly culture must be ordered; without reason's steering hand it can become capricious and vacuous. But the current proposals to "re-engineer" or "rationalize" the university display an excessive and abstract will to unify the scholarly culture, threatening it with simplification and reductionism.

Other reformers propose to reconceptualize the university according to the charm of poetic awe. Generalizing the wonder and free-floating imaginative fancy that attend on poetry, these reformers would have us dissolve conceptual apparati, thematic associations, and identities and continuities of reason until there is nothing left but a kind of stupefaction before each discrete phenomenon. While undertaken in the name of liberation or of healing the scars of social regimentation (therapies of the self, consciousness-raising groups), these projects see triumph only in destruction, falsely identifying freedom with total emancipation and critical reflection with random thought. The immediacy they seek, the relentless negativity they employ and the indeterminacy they favour are all destructive instruments. Such fragmentation of the world would render both intellectual thought and moral action impossible; it is likewise capable of destroying the scholarly culture.

Neither the certainty of technical competence nor the charm of poetic awe give the range of students' needs its due. Nor do the supporters of these causes recognize that the viability of the university, and even their own projects, derive from a tradition that is continuous with the institution's origins, with all its inherent contradictions and tensions. The university has a noble pedigree of serving society by putting forward a higher idea of itself and of providing the vision to undertake the periodic renewal of culture. Yet instead of defending its own role, the university is largely ignorant of its historical roots, internally divided and an easy prey for those who would erode and destroy its unique position. A cacophony is developing across Canada, as outsiders and insiders shout solutions to perceived problems, drowning out the quiet and unspectacular processes that unfold in the university. Let us now look more closely at those who have sounded their discordant note in the midst of the university's healthy polyphony and at a muddled university culture that fiddles while Rome burns.

Chapter 3

Academic Privileges in the Spotlight

A little learning is a dangerous thing;
Drink deep, or taste not the Pierian spring;
There shallow draughts intoxicate the brain,
And drinking largely sobers us again.

Alexander Pope

Across Canada, university campuses are being thrown into the limelight, and in the process, becoming fractious sites where reason and power struggle, where one alarming and indecent incident after another erupts. Students are mobilizing and dividing, faculty and support staff are perturbed to the point of raising the spectre of nationwide strikes and academic administrators either wait with trepidation for the latest news in funding cuts and new regulative policies or resign to escape the growing fracas and palace revolts. Canada's university system, internationally acclaimed for solid and sometimes stellar research accomplishment, for teachers and scholars like Walter Gage, Northrop Frye, George Grant and James Doull, for Nobel laureates like John Polanyi and Sidney Altman, and for dedicated service to the community, is now like a supernova that, after a heady ascent, is exploding over the sky. Tempers are short, anxiety deep and rash action widespread. Old cleavages are reopening: professors versus the "big boys" of administration, unions versus management, junior versus senior faculty, tenured faculty versus sessional instructors, the universities versus government.[1] New cleavages are forming—the rainbow coalition of feminists, ethnics, gays and lesbians versus the white patriarchy, neoconservatives versus

59

postmodernists, academic freedom versus political correctness, tradition versus inclusivity—and the claimants for one or another of the dwindling entitlements see themselves as engaged in a zero-sum game.[2] Meanwhile, students are heading south: eighteen thousand Canadians now study in the United States, and the number grows yearly.

Amidst this battle there is misguided zeal, silly idealism, shrewd pragmatism, paralyzing cynicism and intractability. Journalists have been quick to zero in on the imbroglios. Swift's well-known caricature of the academy in *Gulliver's Travels* is mild satire compared to the stinging cartoons and editorials found in the last six years in the nation's newspapers. We are led to believe by some of the most outspoken protagonists that the fundamental crisis is one of fiscal constraint. That is not the case. The true fiasco is the moral and intellectual vacuum in leadership—the incapacity of academics, outside observers, governments or the media to retain or generate a vision of the university's genuine purpose and its future role in a country known for its decency and balance.

We have an abundance of mission statements, talking-head conferences and fervent manifestos, but many of these are little more than smoke and mirrors. Rarely do we see true statesmanship (the few exceptions are the presidents of the University of Toronto, University of Waterloo and University of Manitoba—Robert Prichard, James Downey and Arnold Naimark, respectively). The few academics and analysts who actually write about the university in this country, outside the "task-force" mill of the professional university associations, often have their noses so close to the grindstone that they don't recognize the intellectual and moral principles at stake in today's debate, and they dismiss fundamental questioning as the stuff of convocation addresses. The leadership vacuum, however, is being filled.

"Invent a crisis," Ontario Minister of Education and Training John Snobelen was widely reported to have told senior education bureaucrats in a training video in July 1995. "Creating a useful crisis is part of what this will be about. The first communication might be more negative than I would be inclined to talk about, emphasizing the need for change rather than talking about what those changes might be. We need to invent a crisis—and that's not just an act of courage, there's skill involved."[3] Snobelen continued by suggesting that the Ministry of Education and Training should paint a much bleaker picture of the current state of education than was in fact the case. Then, the ministry's subsequent actions would be applauded and seen as saving the education system.

Snobelen's statement is symptomatic of the debate on education in this country. The history of the last five years in Canadian education is a history of solutions looking enthusiastically for problems. The pundits all say that the university has a "perception problem"—to outsiders and some insiders alike the university appears archaic and inefficient. If perceptions reflected reality, the universities unquestionably would be in deep trouble. Yet polls suggest otherwise. In December 1992, an Angus Reid poll revealed that 83 percent of respondents felt that universities were doing a good or very good job. Further, 84 percent of university students polled in the same year by a *Maclean's*/Decima survey said they thought the overall quality of their university education was good or excellent. The true crisis is the bedlam that has broken out on Canada's campuses as a consequence of a legion of schemes and scenarios intended to "re-engineer" the university. Problems exist but many of them have arisen as a consequence of universities being agitated by "solutions."

Of the issues that have come to comprise what is said to be the universities' "perception problem" none are more potent than the following: (1) tenure, (2) what faculty do and the relative status of teaching and research, (3) the litigiousness of the university community, (4) the *Maclean's* rankings, (5) university accountability and (6) the government-university chill and the growing bureaucratization of university education. In this chapter I will address the first two of these, pertaining to matters internal to the scholarly culture, and in the next two chapters I will discuss the remaining four, which relate to matters that have come to the scholarly culture from outside. Each of these issues has its own distinct history and it is not my intention to retell these narratives.[4] But it is important to see how, in the context of recent events, these issues have been woven together by the media and by various protagonists to create the so-called "perception problem."

"O, to have the job that lasts forever," goes the taunt against tenure. I have already made reference to Michael Harris's dismissive comments about tenure and his commonplace equation of this academic privilege with job security. The Canadian Association of University Business Officers has been equally blunt about the "deadwood" protected by tenure: "Angry taxpayers are demanding to know why professors should enjoy virtual lifetime security. Frustrated administrators are unable to reallocate scarce resources. And many people are asking whether tenure is an outmoded system that all too often serves to protect the mediocre and the incompetent."[5]

Academics obviously think differently. When Alberta premier Ralph Klein ordered collective agreements reopened to include new redundancy clauses and called for a removal of "inappropriate barriers" to the capacity of governing boards to "terminate academic staff contracts for fiscal reasons or if programs become redundant," Alberta university faculty denounced his government. When Mike Harris began his stint as Ontario premier in 1995 with the warning, "The tenured system as it exists today…is passé, is gone…. I'm saying that I don't think tenure makes sense today," the response from professors was immediate and fiery. The same brouhaha regarding the employment security of faculty underway at Mount Allison University and Memorial University has precipitated poisonous exchanges between faculty and senior academic administrators. Nova Scotia's Council on Higher Education, under Janet Halliwell, met with intense hostility from faculty opposing its new "rationalization" schemes. In October 1995, the University of Manitoba faculty initiated a strike in opposition to the university's bid to have the power to lay off tenured faculty for financial reasons and the flexibility to cut programs. In what must be a first, the Manitoba strike went on the internet in November, as faculty aired their grievances and solicited support worldwide. Supporters from as far away as Harvard University rallied with the cry that academic freedom had been lost at the University of Manitoba. Abolishing tenure, however, has become a hot button to the public—those who denounce the privilege are applauded for being on the side of fiscal responsibility and relevance. Tenure has come to be equated, at least in the public mind and among the gatekeepers of the public's purse, with unwarranted job security.

The first salvo in this debate has come from the faculty associations, those formal organizations of academics bound together legally by a collective agreement (in many, but not all, of Canada's universities). Initially formed in the 1970s to protect academic freedom but increasingly focused on job security, higher wages and equity, these associations have played a major role in creating an artificial and harmful polarization between academic administrators (management) and faculty (labour). On the issue of tenure, the faculty associations were quick in their attempt to take the higher moral ground. Emily F. Carasco, president of the Ontario Confederation of University Faculty Associations (OCUFA), offered a characteristic defence: "Tenure is a status granted to those professors who have demonstrated excellence in their particular fields after a five- to seven-year probationary period. As recent examples prove, tenure does not protect those who neglect their duties. It protects the right of professors to pursue research in what may be unpopular areas and publish their findings free from fear of reprisal from governments, corporations or other interests."[6]

There is basis, obviously, for what Carasco says. Tenure, while dating from the seventeenth century at Oxford and Cambridge, can be linked back to a set of privileges granted to scholars in the Middle Ages. The purpose of these privileges was to ensure their independence (relief from military and certain civic duties, guarantee of food and shelter, protection from ecclesiastical and imperial disfavour). In the modern era, these privileges have been interpreted as freedom of thought and expression. Tenure, understood primarily as academic freedom, arose in Germany in the late nineteenth century to protect scholars from reprisal by the reigning powers.[7] John Cowan offers a concise explanation of how tenure subsequently developed in North America in the 1940s:

> [C]oncepts of academic freedom in Canada owe much to the watershed joint AAUP/AAC declaration of 1940 in the United States. The four pillars of academic freedom set out therein are: (a) the right to teach without adherence to any prescribed doctrine (provided that one dealt with the subject matter in the senate-approved course outline); (b) the right to research without reference to prescribed doctrine; (c) the right to publish the results of one's research; and (d) the right to speak extramurally, which includes the right to criticize the government of the day or the administration of one's institution.[8]

The reality of the day-to-day expression of these rights, however, needs to be recalled. Cowan adds rightly that, unlike the days when Jack Pickersgill, and one might add George Grant and Frank Underhill, opposed government or social interests, today there is not a great deal of iconoclastic thought in universities. Indeed, "academic freedom" has shifted to a tolerance of personal eccentricity or, even worse, to turning a blind eye to those who believe themselves to have licence to offend, taunt, relate off-colour jokes, display arrogance, assert power and generally offend the practices comprising what is meant by a civil association. Some faculty fail to see that current versions of "academic freedom" are merely licence for misanthropy, stereotyping, innuendo, prurience and vicious griping about students, women and those who have chosen alternative lifestyles (not only in "the old-boys' network" but in a wide variety of in-groups).

We cannot pretend that all is well in tenure-land. There are faculty who have abandoned their early scholarly ambitions and now make no contribution to scholarship. Many are, as feared, laughing their way to the bank, with paycheques that add up to $90,000 annually. Regrettably, many of these same academics have also lost their enthusiasm and passion to teach well, and instead have turned to university and faculty union politics for stimulation. Others use and abuse their tenure to pursue frivolous intellectual pastimes which lead to nothing but self-gratification. During the time of their evaluation for tenure—on average, a six-year probation period of peer assessment—they suppressed their boredom or their fervour for the arcane, shrewdly calculating the need to conform to traditional canons of scholarship. Once the magic wand of tenure had passed over their heads, however, they abandoned all subterfuge. And there are academics who actively pursue or undertake extramural business enterprises, political offices, social activism and sexual adventures, all the while enjoying fully the privileges of life sinecure.

Meanwhile, throughout North America, there is a vast army of nonemployed scholars, usually young women, with significant publications and an enviable track record of teaching (usually carried out in exploitive circumstances), who have no leverage to initiate reviews of the incompetent. Universities, encumbered with pockets of unproductive faculty, are now starting to regret the 1960s boom in faculty hirings, where raw potential was often the only criterion of employment. Overly confident and ambitious hiring practices, driven by dreams of unending university expansion, have brought us to a state in the 1990s where the chances for renewal are slim. From the perspective of the many vigorous "private" (read, unemployed) scholars, whose potential can be measured by real accomplishment, tenure is a scandal. It is especially so when every regulation (closely monitored by the faculty associations) conspires to keep the unaccomplished in their sinecure. Tenure is a highly contested and controversial privilege, not only for those looking in, but also for those within the university, who find themselves in the middle of antagonism between junior and senior faculty, nonacademic and academic staff, those whose tenure has been granted for scholarly publication and those for whom university service or membership in a minority group sufficed.

But this is only part of the picture and perhaps the lesser part. Young faculty, faced with the possibility of the serious erosion of tenure and seized by the injustice that their older colleagues have enjoyed its privileges without question, have recounted with passion what it is to be an academic with tenure. As Mary Pavelka, associate professor of anthropology at the University of Calgary, writes, "It distresses me because I know there is a public perception that university professors are somehow underworked and overpaid. That couldn't be farther from the truth. What people don't realize is that professors are working all day, every day, weekends, evenings. It's never finished. [Tenure] only guarantees that you get to continue jumping through the hoops. Once you get tenure, the pace, the demands increase. The university expects more of you."[9] And it is the voice of these young, productive faculty, who look for their role models among highly accomplished senior faculty, that justifies the strong defence of tenure, even if it must be retained in a modified form—as outlined in my concluding chapter. In the hands of faculty associations and in the legalistic language of collective agreements, tenure has indeed become security of employment. But behind that narrow understanding of tenure lies a more complex situation. Lost in the discussion is a concrete expression of what faculty actually need to be protected from and a principled explanation of how important such protection is for our society as a whole.

The purpose of tenure is to preserve and nurture a scholarly culture where teaching and writing can proceed without *intrusive* hindrance from outside or inside the university. Standards of taste and prudence and decisions based on the canons of scholarship act as justifiable limits on academic licence, serving to elevate the right of expression from indulgence to genuine freedom. There can be no academic freedom to vent unverifiable opinion or indecent proposals. Neither can there be academic freedom where interest groups and the governments who broker their power impose the one best way, the standard line or the approved lexicon by withholding funding or diverting critical funding to nonacademic priorities. It is equally questionable whether there can be academic freedom when faculty are obliged to teach at times that reflect the schedule of the workworld or when curriculum subjects are expected to reflect a "normal" population distribution. The rigidity or infinite elasticity that follow from these designs can only scuttle the primary purposes of the university: books and conversations. At the end of the day, that culture may make inestimable contributions to the social purposes that render political action legitimate. But tenure is the shield that allows these "clamours of the immediate" (to use an expression of Canadian educator J.A. Corry) to be fended off.

Are academics truly in need of such awesome protection? On the one hand, professors love to embrace the fable that they are scorned and victimized by society. This permits them to claim that society at large is dogmatic, reactionary, inauthentic and alienated. A growing suspicion of society extends from Plato to Sartre. In the case of Plato, the philosopher needs to escape as if from a cave of unwarranted opinion and ignorance. In the case of Sartre, the adventurer needs to extricate himself lest the "gelatinous ooze" of the "they" engulfs him. Academic lives are filled with stories about work being misunderstood, vulgarized and trivialized. Governments, corporations, elites and interest groups are one, by these accounts, in their conspiracy to mock the university as an ivory tower. But these are phantoms, and in tilting at such windmills, academics often appear naïve and gullible.

Yet on the other hand, public indifference is once again turning, particularly in the grip of the rhetoric of "crisis," and the dangers of real outside intervention are growing. Recent invectives calling into question the university's "relevance," its "accountability" and its "value-for-money" all reflect contemporary society's need for instant gratification, its narrow view of what is useful and satisfying and its often precipitate decisions on priority. "Zero tolerance" for ambiguity and for the unassuming plodding that characterizes the rhythm of the scholarly culture jeopardizes particularly the speculative ventures of the university. Robert Moody, in an article entitled "Tenure and Research," eloquently argues that even within the ambit of contemporary society's priorities—specifically its love of gadgets—the university must be given latitude to conduct research that, at first blush, has no immediate use or purpose. The CD player, he notes, for example, resulted from research on lasers, microchip computers, error-correcting codes, Fourier analysis and digital wave sampling, the physiology of the ear and the technology of plastics and semiconductors. All these investigations were driven solely by curiosity, or by the "useless desire" to understand the world, rather than by their economic possibilities or specific applications. The atomic theory of matter, DNA and genetics, calculus, the discovery of Upper Cretaceous extinctions, the periodic table, plate tectonics and penicillin all have their origin in the same, often unaccountable, pace of the scholarly culture.[10]

The root of the word "schooling," the Greek *skole*, is the verb "to leisure." As our own modern leisure is filled increasingly with managed activities and the expectations of "quality time," the original meaning is being lost to us. But the original meaning does lie at the heart of the scholarly culture in the requirement that one "leisure" oneself. Martin Heidegger has suggested an apt metaphor for the apparently erratic circumlocutions and wanderings that characterize the thought and intellectual curiosity pursued in leisure: he refers to them as *Holzwege*, woodcutter's paths that meander through the forest apparently at random. There is a slow, incremental and sometimes imperceptible growth to the university's accomplishments, and without the privileges of leisure, independence and the liberty to question conventional wisdom, there can be neither CD players, cures for disease nor the cultivation of informed judgment. The scholarly culture is an antidote to the haste of the world, its hesitations and uncertainties a counterpoint to precipitancy and error.

But the intervention that professors have to fear most is from the academy itself. However vocal and ardent the chant of freedom and scholarly independence appears, the truth is that received opinion and approved methods of investigation exert powerfully conformist pressures on scholars who are being considered for appointments, tenure, promotions and grants. Bean counting of articles published and committee work replaces substantive assessment of contribution to the scholarly culture. The academic establishment itself designates which journals are worthiest, whose authority can legitimately be cited, what rules of logic prevail, what evidence can be brought forward in argument and what must be left unsaid. Much "scholarly" writing is less an exploration of the world of predicaments and adventures than commentary on commentary and witty repartee on "in" references and allusions.

Grantsmanship, the skill of schmoozing within the academic circuit, comes to replace serious intellectual enterprise. Teaching and research have become increasingly derivative labours often occurring within an academically incestuous environment. In his book *Profscam*, Charles Sykes writes with some justice that today's academics have only four faces: high priest, witch doctor, bureaucrat and hustler.[11] Many professors, he claims, have abandoned genuine scholarship and now singlemindedly produce unread and unreadable scholarship, thus keeping libraries full and careers flourishing. Camille Paglia claims, again with some justice, that most academics become "toadying careerists." Those who fail to keep up in the race are ignored and rumoured to be intellectual lightweights.

Why does this occur? I have previously alluded to the slow and incremental character of scholarly pursuit. Thomas Kuhn has offered a useful metaphor to describe the research culture. He writes that researchers typically work within a "paradigm," a model—be it Newtonian physics or New Criticism—that serves to organize data, establish research priorities and, to some extent, determine the outcomes of investigation. Over time, he notes, an increasing number of inexplicable anomalies threaten the paradigm and eventually shatter it, leaving a state where a new paradigm must be designed. Kuhn's idea has numerous implications. If he is right, the Romantic cult of genius—the lone researcher in his or her laboratory fighting the forces of ignorance—must be shelved, to be replaced by the idea of a culture of scholars, all contributing to, but also reinforcing, the web of orthodoxy. This means that there must be tolerance within the scholarly culture for the many wrong paths chosen, the errors, the misguided enthusiasms, because it is the overall culture and the total enterprise that give rise to advances, not the isolated work of individual professors. But more important, Kuhn's idea implies that powerful pressures currently operate to stifle the iconoclasts who focus on the anomalies and work to disrupt the reigning paradigm.

Tenure helps counterbalance this tendency by protecting academics from the creeping conformism that is a significant part of the scholarly culture. It protects those who work outside the approved canons of scholarship, who avoid the company of the in crowd and orthodox career paths. It protects those who do not leap into every passing fad. Consider the case of Thomas Pangle, a political science professor at the University of Toronto. Pangle was denied tenure at Yale University because his work (a book on Montesquieu that has become a standard reference) was seen by leftists among the Yale faculty as not on the "cutting edge" of political theory. He has gone on to publish one erudite book after another and has become one of North America's most acclaimed academics. Neoconservatives today apply as much pressure and caustic censure to those they call out-of-season "market-bashers." Without tenure, independence from the scholarly culture itself could never occur. It is the minority of rebel academics who must be protected, to recall John Stuart Mill's powerful argument from *On Liberty*, from the tyranny of the majority—in this case, their own peers.

Tenure's purpose, then, is severely distorted when it is understood merely as job security guaranteed by a collective agreement, or when it is used as a means of protection from judgment about competence and scholarly productivity. The serious aim of tenure is recognized and preserved by judicial interpretation and decision. In 1990 the Supreme Court of Canada ruled against the application of the Charter of Rights and Freedoms to universities, thus opposing the power to make the scholarly culture conform to any blueprint either from within or without. The court identified tenure as the mainstay of that independence:

> The policy of tenure in university faculties is fundamental to the preservation of academic freedom. Once tenure is granted it provides a truly free and innovative learning and research environment. Faculty members can take unpopular positions without fear of loss of employment. ... Tenure provides the necessary academic freedom to allow free and fearless search for knowledge and the propagation of ideas.... [Faculty] must have a great measure of security of employment if they are to have the freedom necessary to the maintenance of academic excellence which is or should be the hallmark of a university.... [Tenure] undergirds the specific and necessary ambience of university life.[12]

Such a high-principled defence of tenure has, regrettably, also been used by faculty associations to protect individual members from censure. On the one hand, it has been useful, if not particularly effective, that faculty associations and the Canadian Association of University Teachers (CAUT), the organization founded in the early 1950s to protect professors' interests, have supplied information to the public in an effort to correct current public misconceptions about tenure. They have explained, for example, that when governments express the desire to have greater flexibility in streamlining the university system and in having more influence over programming, they are not coming up with new powers. For over a decade nearly 85 percent of collective agreements in Canada's universities have had program redundancy and financial stringency clauses, making it possible to revoke tenure when necessary. Second, these same agreements explicitly give power to university management to fire tenured faculty for neglect of duties and incompetence. Tenure does not mean an academic cannot be fired. Thus, there is some truth to the common response of faculty associations to the criticism that their ranks are filled with "deadwood": "the practice of tenure cannot be blamed if academic administrators do not act to terminate incompetent faculty."[13]

On the other hand, the response of faculty associations is also flippant, and the powers that collective agreements confer on academic managers over faculty are in great part nominal. Were it not for the nearly inflexible security established through the associations' collective agreements, presidents would indeed have the power to fire delinquent faculty. Faculty associations do everything they can to preserve the privileges of the least accomplished and senior, the mediocre and the average—opposing serious merit evaluations, denuding teaching evaluations of real bite and using the inflammatory rhetoric of "faculty versus the 'big boys'" to present the appearance of unanimity. At the same time they dare to pretend that they are always on the side of the angels.

It is questionable whether a true understanding of the scholarly culture and the university's roots was behind the infamous case of Herbert W. Richardson of St. Michael's College, University of Toronto. In an inquiry into Richardson's vast entrepreneurial activities and his apparent neglect of university duties, the case was as much a trial by the media as an investigation by academic administrators. Confused expectations concerning teaching obligations, research productivity and the legitimate scope of activities outside the university clouded the issues on both sides of the case. The tenured professor of religious studies was, without question, an entrepreneur. It is clearly a matter of concern that an academic was able to find enough free time to engage in an estimated $2-million enterprise on the side: the Edward Mellen Press, Mellen University on the Turks and Caicos Islands and Mellen Communications. The press's annual sales alone are estimated at $1.4 million. He owns as many as seventeen properties in New York State and is exploring the possibility of opening a university in Kansas. Not surprisingly, students at St. Michael's complained of persistent absenteeism, lack of preparedness in class and strained classroom environments. The primary reason for the eventual termination of his tenure was the extent of his involvement in his press and open university.

As in nearly all allegations about behaviour, it is very difficult to render a judgment. "Essays and messages grew dusty in mailbox," "away on business, he had his wife show videos to his classes," "he treated his lectures like personal therapy sessions," "he was yelling and screaming at us," "he put his arm around me and kissed me."…. Such stories are inevitably cases of "he said, she said…" and difficult to corroborate. Other irregularities in his conduct and interpretation of university regulations suggest that Richardson may have pushed the envelope too far, especially in this time of intense public scrutiny. Richardson's career record, however, does not conform to the popular image of the tenured faculty member who is taking it easy. He is a respected mediaevalist and the author or editor of over twenty books. He supervised more than fifty master's and doctorate theses, and he was actively engaged in vocational testing and counselling. Former students, who themselves have gone on to distinguished academic careers, recall Richardson's drive during the 1970s, seventy-hour weeks "equal," notes Larry Schmidt, "to the rest of the faculty combined." If Richardson had a lower profile in the college in the 1990s, Schmidt added, he earned it: "No one could have kept up the pace he did in the 1970s."[14]

Richardson's extracurricular activities, however, were the object of gravest concern. How legitimate were these enterprises, and did his heavy involvement justify the lessening of his teaching obligations? While some have denounced Mellen Press as a vanity press, and Mellen University as a degree-mill, a closer look at these two enterprises reveals a different view and, arguably, the hypocrisy of critics. The Mellen Press boasts a stable of over eight hundred books, primarily on religion, spirituality and autobiography. Among these are monographs and textbooks that have become essential reading or teaching resources in Canada and the United States. As one example, a statistical methodology textbook—scorned by larger presses—has been the mainstay of a generation of students who have gone on to become senior directors of Canada's polling and survey companies. Mellen Press's books are not mainstream, because they eschew current academic fads, and yet many of them resonate deeply with the political and spiritual concerns of a growing counterculture of scholars, students and social groups.

Mellen University, at face value, is far more questionable. Billed as an "adult college" with a base in Lampeter, Wales, investigation results on its status in the United Kingdom are murky. Despite advertisements that promise "fully accredited British M.Phil. and Ph.D. degrees," the award of degrees occurs in the Turks and Caicos Islands. Eyebrows have been raised about courses on Robin Hood and Marian as part of a "parent-child college" program offered by the university. On the other hand, the university has laudable characteristics. Admission is based on demonstration of cultural literacy, creative expressiveness and multicultural sensitivity, as well as ability to live life in a rational way with religious and moral self-consistency. Given the fetish of high-school grades alone in current mainstream university admission, Richardson's requirements are refreshingly responsible, concerned as much with quality of students as with quantifiable indicators. Mellen University, with no campus and no fixed classes, puts its emphasis on individual research, the packaging of credits bought as services worldwide and recognition of nonacademic experience.

The Ontario Ministry of Education and Training mocks Richardson's initiative: "Its graduates receive 'equivalency' degrees in 'life experience' but must travel to the Turks and Caicos Islands in the Caribbean to pick them up." But that same ministry, both in its flagship education proposal *The Common Curriculum* and in its endorsement of the Caplan-Bégin Royal

Commission Report, "The Love of Learning," encourages precisely the same initiatives.

The case of Richardson is an illustration of why the scholarly culture must continually aim for a wisdom that transcends the world of politics. In that world, the Richardsons are gadflies and their insights are dismissed as "entrepreneurial" and "irresponsible." The case of Herbert Richardson demonstrates that governments and the university managers they direct have the power to break the awesome privileges of tenure by recourse to the Achilles heel of "persistent neglect of or repeated and unjustified refusal to carry out reasonable duties" or "gross misconduct," written into nearly every collective agreement.

Richardson was fired, the first formal dismissal in Canada in twenty-five years, but what this means is not so easily apparent. A fuller knowledge of Richardson's multifaceted academic career and a more balanced appreciation of how individual members of the academic community contribute to the scholarly culture is necessary before one judges a case as complex as this. Joyce Lorimer, president of CAUT, argues that Richardson's firing has nothing to do with the disintegration of the tenure system. One might beg to differ. Would Richardson have been thrown into the limelight were it not for the powerful perception that the university is a "system that pays senior professors...$100,000 a year on average to work a schedule that people in the private sector would kill for: teaching two or three courses a week, spending some time in the office, attending faculty meetings and devoting four or five months a year to research," as one opponent to tenure complained?[15]

If cases like Richardson's are more ambiguous than the trial by the media suggested, in other cases tenure is being abused in the most distasteful manner. It is an embarrassment to permit, by an appeal to an academic freedom preserved by tenure, the sliding logic that culminates in the indecencies uttered by Matin Yaqzan who wrote: "When a boy invites a girl to his bedroom, especially after meeting her for the first time, she should consider it as an invitation for sexual intercourse" and "If a promiscuous girl becomes a victim of an unwanted sexual experience, she might more reasonably demand payment for her "inconvenience or discomfort rather than express moral outrage." Even more embarrassing are the contortions made by the Civil Liberties Association, the Society for Academic Freedom and Scholarship and John Fekete in his book *Moral Panic* to defend Yaqzan's right to express these things in print.

Equally questionable was the response of the University of New Brunswick's faculty association when the UNB president wrote a strong opinion essay entitled "Date Rape Is Never Acceptable" and circulated a letter to the media explaining why he had taken the route of suspending Yaqzan. The faculty association complained of a "witch hunt"—for someone who wrote that regular sexual intercourse is a "necessity" for "boys"? Only more unconscionable are the unconfirmed reports that Yaqzan was given three years' full salary as a buyout. Michael Bliss, at the conference "When Rights Collide" held at UNB in September 1994 in the wake of Yaqzan's date-rape essay, argued that one should distinguish between offensive ideas and offensive behaviour. His argument was reinforced by Alan Borovoy, the general counsel of the Canadian Civil Liberties Association, who argued that freedom of speech was the condition upon which all other rights are based. If there ever was a time in the past when untempered thoughts or words were dissociable in principle from vicious actions, by no stretch of the imagination could one think that such a time is now. The distinction assumes a culture of trust, of civic friendship. But our present state is one of mutual suspicion. We cannot hang our cap on the liberal distinction between thought and action, in the absence of the moral restraint that ensured a civil association. As the meaning of tenure becomes increasingly identified with freedom of speech, the horizon of the scholarly culture is diminished.

Equally humiliating to the scholarly culture is, in my view, a 1990 publication by University of Alberta physics professor Gordon R. Freeman. In the notorious "Kinetics of Nonhomogenous Processes in Human Society: Unethical Behaviour and Societal Chaos," Freeman indulged himself with the extravagant thesis that ran: birth control is the source of the feminist movement, feminism leads to socialism, and feminism is to blame for the Marc Lépine massacre. He culled this absurd chain of inferences from conversations with students of working mothers whom he concluded had a statistically significant predilection to cheat on exams.[16] That the *Canadian Journal of Physics* permitted its publication, thus conferring the authority of science on such nonsense, reinforces the cry against tenure and for greater accountability. It is not a matter here of extending to academics a right that exists in society generally. The point is that academics, through tenure and academic freedom, are invested with an authority that confers on them a responsibility to express the most enlightened understanding of the predicaments and adventures of our lives. The confusion of tenure with the right to offend has hurt its cause, as much as the perception that universities are filled with deadwood.

One final point needs to be made here. The case of Gordon Freeman, not unlike the controversy surrounding the race research of Philippe Rushton, raises again the issue of the relation between the university and society. Debate on their scholarship has been nearly universally confined to the question of whether the data it presents are true. But there may be an additional question, one as old as Plato's teaching that societies need life-preserving myths.[17] We so rarely ask ourselves the old Platonic question as to whether the intellectual life and the culture of social life are fundamentally opposed to each other, mostly because we have a naïve Enlightenment view that knowledge worthy of its name is an immeasurable good. Plato, and one might add, mediaeval thinkers, had a more balanced view of the results of unfettered intellectual curiosity. Prudence, it was held, is the better part of wisdom.

The practice of tenure expresses society's trust in the apparent inefficiencies, unproductive leisure and inexplicable paths of inquiry that characterize much academic activity. And paradoxically, such transcendence of the mundane pressures of life makes it possible for the university to exercise its true responsibility toward society, for by creating a space free from the rash demands for certainty of purpose, the priorities of society can be discussed and evaluated impartially and within the widest perspective.

When expressed in a formula for the purposes of evaluating academics' performance, faculty work is normally divided 40–40–20 between teaching, research and service, respectively. According to a 1986 survey of ten thousand faculty members at fifty-two universities across Canada, an average faculty member puts in eighty-hour weeks divided into 49 percent teaching, 26 percent research, 14 percent administration and 11 percent community service.[18] The Ontario Council of University Affairs suggests a more modest breakdown, but reinforces how hard most professors work: the average university professor, it reports, puts in a fifty- to sixty-hour week: lectures and seminars, preparation time, grading, supervision, committees, conferences, writing, reviewing, raising funds and examining theses. In spite of such quantitative evidence, tenure is still perceived to be unwarranted job security and sabbaticals are seen as paid vacations by the general public.

In a "Letter to the Editor" in the *Globe and Mail*, former Toronto mayor John Sewell put forward a familiar complaint: "There's a widespread feeling that many university professors are overpaid and underworked." He followed this with a modest proposal: cut university costs by year-round operation and oblige faculty to put in regular working hours. "For my money, universities should require that all professors and other teaching staff work a 40-hour week.... There's no reason why staff wouldn't be expected to work a full year, or why universities couldn't function 12 months a year rather than almost closing up for five months over the summer...."[19] The apprehensions about professor's work, however, go much further. The *Globe*, with some legitimacy, mocks what passes as teaching for many in the university: "a distant figure behind the lectern before a packed auditorium. No contact, no interaction; no questions, no answers; a class without attention and a professor without enthusiasm."[20] Or as one Dalhousie University student complained, "The notes of the lecturer are transferred to the notebook of the student without ever passing through the minds of either."[21] Reports of professors slapping students, taunting them, passing out their own provocative creeds on a wide range of social issues, denouncing minority lifestyle groups as psychopaths, dereliction with regard to lecturing, office hours and supervising—all these have hindered the professorial cause.

Equal aspersion has been cast on research—the 1991 Commission of Inquiry on Canadian University Education headed by Stuart L. Smith concluded that Canada's universities were putting a misplaced priority on research at the expense of teaching: "Teaching is seriously undervalued at Canadian universities and nothing less than a total recommitment to it is required." Smith's controversial conclusion received an unexpected support a few years later by Harry Arthurs, who at the time was president of York University and had been retained to assess what had gone wrong at Concordia to create an environment contributing to Fabrikant's actions. In his report, "Integrity in Scholarship: A Report to Concordia University" (written with Roger Blais and Jon Thompson), Arthurs pinpointed Concordia University's "research-production culture" as one of the contexts in which the Fabrikant shootings erupted. Reform MP Randy White's brazen attack in 1995 on the research grant system is another familiar indication of serious misgivings about the publish-or-perish culture of the universities. "Here we go again," he said in the House of Commons, "these people still don't get the message. Do they honestly think the average Canadian agrees with handing out over $100,000 to an academic to do 'An Interactive Study of Video Games'?"

While 26 percent of all research and development in Canada is done by universities, particularly in the medical, agricultural and telecommunications fields, Canadian industry has little collaborative engagement with the institutions, and 74 percent of surveyed companies said they had no plans to contract with universities.[22] Of all the G7 countries, only Italy spends less than Canada on research, and the United States, Japan, Germany, France and the United Kingdom spend twice as much. While 83 percent of Canadians think universities are doing a good job, only 7 percent think the research role of the university is important.[23] Such hesitation reinforces the neoconservative argument that research is done best by the private sector and contributes to the case made by fiscal hawks that the university as a whole should be contracted out to the most efficient supplier. The Smith Report's "back to teaching" call has become a favourite rally cry for those wanting to revolutionize the university—another hot button that curries the public's favour.

The Smith Report is unquestionably the work of a sincere and concerned academic. It is Canada's version of Charles Sykes' controversial book *Profscam*. It sent shock waves through the university establishment, causing many academics to bristle and putting many noses out of joint. The Association of Universities and Colleges of Canada (AUCC), who had commissioned the study, gave it only teeth-clenched endorsement. In it Smith castigates both academic careerists whose status depends on graduate supervision and research alone and a university system that leaves undergraduate teaching to graduate students and part-time instructors. He is right to believe that teaching deserves far greater recognition—a reform advanced by some universities and by the 3M Corporation, which has established prestigious teaching awards.

The response to the Smith Report is as illuminating as the report itself, for all the critics intoned a single message: the status quo is working well, all that is needed is more public funding. The President of the Canadian Association of University Teachers (CAUT) retorted that Smith "has chosen the wrong road to get improvements. He has failed to understand the gravity of the current financial crisis." Smith, he said, should have highlighted the fallout on teaching of the financial squeeze of the last two decades. The AUCC chairman, Kenneth Ozman, complained that Smith "does not give adequate justification for giving us more money." The chairperson of the Canadian Federation of Students looked at Smith's proposal for tuition fee increases and reiterated the call for more public funding: "This proposal," he said, "is outrageous because it totally ignores [the fact] that most students are struggling to survive at this very moment." The president of the Ontario Confederation of University Faculty Associations (OCUFA) rejected the report's challenge to university research and defended, without qualification, the value of research. "Research," she said, is "vitally important to teaching: you can't be a good teacher if you're not on top of new knowledge and involved in its creation." Smith, by contrast to this special pleading and in his appeal to a return to quality teaching, must appear as a white knight in the eyes of a disillusioned public.

Yet the report also reinforced a prejudice that is superficial and deeply harmful to the scholarly culture—that there is no necessary connection between teaching and scholarship. Outsiders looking for a window of opportunity to question university privilege seized on the idea that faculty were doing too much research and not enough teaching, and that this was leaving an entire generation neglected and untutored. Smith's effusive rhetoric transports the imagination, but is ultimately unpersuasive. The vast majority of scholars are also devoted teachers. Only a small minority immures itself totally in research. Harry Arthurs, challenging Smith's claim that academics undervalue teaching, admits a truth that most academics don't: "I do it; we do it—because it is our profession and our passion, because we seek the cheap thrill of classroom applause, and the long chance of immortality which comes from trying to ensure that our ideas will live on in our students."[24]

Smith's solutions too are garden-variety musings. He proposed a version of the "two-tier" university scheme that seems to be aired at least once a decade: establish one stream of universities that teach, another of universities that do research. Smith's idea was to give professors within a single institution an opportunity to say whether they wished to be evaluated primarily as teachers or as researchers. Those who chose teaching would be expected to teach more hours—a minimum load of eight hours per week; senior professors would be expected to actually teach some undergraduates; and universities would conduct peer reviews of their faculty's teaching skills. Smith also gave a gee-whiz thumbs up to the "exciting" curricular progress being made in areas like co-op programs to meet the "changing needs of students and of society" and to Ryerson's match of academic programming with the needs of employers. Added to the equation were the demands for more accessibility, equity, distance-learning and, ironically, in light of his general argument against research, funding for research on higher education. The report incurred Arthurs' fitting dismissal of being little more than an "L.L. Bean catalogue of trendy American academic prescriptions."[25] Smith seems to know little about the scholarly culture.

What Smith understood as "teaching" is also questionable. His enthusiasm for distance education suggests that like so many others who have dismissed the university's tradition of learning and understanding through conversation and a vital teacher-student relationship, Smith sees learning merely as mastery of information. Education has been replaced by solitary acquisition of knowledge and a consumerist approach in the form of access to desired services. One of the more recent bastard-children of the Smith Report is a publication by University of Guelph sociologist Sid Gilbert.[26] The study, under the imprimatur of the Association of Universities and Colleges of Canada, reports that students prefer large classes and that class size as such does not define the quality of education. Student satisfaction, Gilbert argues, is in fact greater in large-class teaching, since there is less pressure, more of a sense of independence and anonymity—and more useful student-to-student contact.

Smith would undoubtedly question the prescriptive value of Gilbert's findings. It is another question with what kind of teaching he would replace Gilbert's large-class instruction. It is nearly always strange to listen to psychologists, psychiatrists and sociologists discussing teaching, especially when the models of student need with which they operate are limited to statistically relevant or empirically verifiable behaviours and the restrictive models of human nature that distinguish "cognitive" from "affective" spheres. Too often these social scientists miss the forest for the trees because their disciplines have adopted the modern bias of breaking down complex compounds (like the human soul) into discrete components that are believed to be measurable and controllable. In the process, the metaphysical attributes of human longing—such as the desire for wholeness and transcendence—are dismissed as mysterious because they are not "falsifiable." Despite one's expectations, neither psychologists nor sociologists are usually illuminating in discussions of the needs of students and the scholarly culture.

The Smith-Gilbert challenge reveals how the debate about the relative status of teaching and research has been skewed. The natural and symbiotic relation of an academic's teaching and contribution to scholarship has been polarized—research productivity versus teaching effectiveness. A 1994 OCUA paper, "Undergraduate Teaching, Research and Consulting/ Community Service," confirms the perception that research and teaching, like oil and water, do not mix: "The evidence accumulated in the literature over the past 25 years is in substantial agreement that there are no necessary links between effective undergraduate teaching and research. Excellent researchers may well be excellent teachers but there is nothing to suggest that one is a prerequisite for the other."[27] After citing one Carnegie Foundation study after another from America supporting the argument for the conflictual relation between teaching and research, the OCUA report finally offers "a Canadian perspective" from an instructor at Malaspina College in Nanaimo, British Columbia. He "argues in terms of *the deleterious effect of research and publication on instruction.*"[28] It is unfortunate that the Malaspina College instructor could not present his findings in person to scholars like Northrop Frye, George Grant and Charles Taylor, whose prodigious publication records and star teaching belie this self-serving cant.

The 1972 Bonneau-Corry Commission offers some much needed direction in the debate, and it is unfortunate that the insights of this report have been forgotten. Louis-Philippe Bonneau and J.A. Corry argued that attention to what scholars do must shift from "frontier- or discovery-research" to "reflective inquiry" research (in which one must include performance and exhibition). Their point was that frontier research leads more often to self-absorbed singlemindedness, while reflective inquiry demands a continuous engagement and dialogue with other scholars and students. Scholars, they argued, spend most of their time integrating scholarship and looking for new syntheses, or applying that scholarship to the world around them. Without such scholarship, their teaching risks being out of date and parochial, even operating outside the accepted and evolving canons of scholarship. A truism bantered around by academics is that instructors in front of a class can often say just about anything without being questioned. Regardless of whether a statement is true or specious, students will copy it into their workbooks. If students don't challenge instructors, then who will? Research and publication serves as the corrective to an individual scholar's natural fallibility.

Such "reflective inquiry" research is not about productivity, but about evolving understanding of the meanings negotiated within the scholarly culture. It is also distinct from the self-absorption of "frontier research," which *may* be "deleterious" to teaching effectiveness. (This supposed negative impact can also be exaggerated. Often the enthusiasm of the frontier researcher is what students remember best, for it inspires their own inchoate intellectual curiosity.) The Smith-Gilbert reports fudge the distinction between these two forms of research, with the result that the scholarship essential to good teaching and engagement with the scholarly culture is condemned by association with the researcher who ignores his or her students.

A similar rhetorical ploy is at work in the emphasis on teaching at the expense of research. Assessing teaching by "effectiveness" (usually by examining student ratings) is as sterile as reducing research to productivity. The value of teaching does not come from "learner-satisfaction" (often used to mean "client- or consumer-satisfaction"), but from the extent to which the teacher has succeeded in engaging students in conversation. The students themselves often do not know what their needs are or how they wish to fulfil them until they have been awakened and guided by a professor. Students appear to recognize this, even if "educational consultants" do not. Twenty-two-year-old Lakehead University student Duane Wysynski asks: "At 16 or 17 years old, do we know enough about what we want to do with our lives?" A student's assessment of "effectiveness" often says little about the quality of teaching. Moreover, thanks to the faculty unions, teaching evaluations are highly politicized documents that shield the incompetent from harsh judgment and make serious assessment of instruction nearly impossible. The issue here is not whether a teacher's work is "effective," but whether it is consonant with the scholarly culture and the needs of students. "Research productivity" may hamper "teaching quality," but in a genuine scholarly culture, the two go hand in hand.

Teaching without active engagement in the scholarly culture degenerates into mere information transmission or empty utterance of platitudes. But not all research is true scholarship, and it would be inaccurate to dismiss Smith entirely. Academic careers are built on the bean counting of publications. Healthy competition is transformed into shrewd entrepreneurship through grantsmanship. One of the more destructive directions taken in recent times in the evaluation of faculty performance has been the move from peer review to "objective measures" like citation analysis—a count of citations to an academic's work in all journals in that academic's discipline. Such analysis was developed for the hard sciences where its appropriateness is more evident. In the humanities and social sciences, however, citation counts say much about the composition of an in-group or the current fashion, but very little about importance. Even in the sciences, citation frequency may say more about in-group acceptance than the ultimate value of the research.

Many misconceptions about teaching and research persevere in the debate about what faculty do. For centuries students have complained of droning professors, aloof professors and boring lectures. Mark Twain defined the professor as a person who talks in someone else's sleep. D.H. Lawrence recalled his own professors as "small men, all wind and quibbles, flinging out their chaffy grain to us with far less interest than a farm-wife feels as she scatters grain to her fowls."[29] In the 1600s Robert Burton decried those professors who "lard their lean books with the fat of others' works."[30] Through the ages, professors have enjoyed the fool's freedom—but they have nearly always been called to account for it. There is nothing new in the ridicule of the "sage on the stage" or Reform MP Randy White's mockery of Social Sciences and Humanities Research Council (SSHRC) grants for apparently arcane faculty research.

More discouraging is the lack of response by scholars. Consider the issue of research. It is true that the lists of the Social Sciences and Humanities Research Council (SSHRC) and the National Science and Engineering Research Council (NSERC) grants of the last five years contain questionable research projects. But the reality of funded research in this country is that one is generally hard pressed to find research grants that are totally irrelevant. Here are some examples of studies over the last three years: "International Trade Policy, Nature Resource Management and Economic Growth," "Topics in Intellectual Property and Competition Policy," "Mentorship Strategies: Increasing Undergraduate Women's Enrollment in Core Science," "Vandalism: Scope, Explanations and Remedies," "Approaches to the Restoration of Italian Renaissance Paintings," "Gender Issues in the Study of Occupational Health," "Investigations of the Abusive Personality." In the minds of some, like Randy White, "Histories of the Carolingian Empire," "The Behavioral Energetics of Hummingbirds," "Galactic and Extragalactic Astronomy," "Information Processing in Pigeons," and "Kinships, Social Associations and Paternity of Richardson's Squirrels" appear to be luxuries, especially in this climate of economic panic. But to carp about the "lack of common sense and accountability in the evaluation process," as White did, and to complain that "While this government flutters along in a financial daze I challenge anyone to justify spending even one cent on studying the behaviour of hummingbirds," reveals naïveté and philistinism.[31]

Short-sighted thinking of this sort led CUPE officers representing clerical and service workers at the University of British Columbia to complain bitterly that in this decade of dire financial constraints and threat of job loss, there could be no justification for the university's commission of two paintings of the retiring chancellor and the president at a cost of $45,000.[32] Universities need maintenance budgets, support staff, library acquisitions; cities need food banks, shelters and myriad social assistance programs. But individuals also need a culture and a community that sustains its purposes, to give substance to hope and meaning to contingency. The crass materialism and the disingenuous finger pointing that characterize intolerance for the scholarly culture portend the death of Canada as anything more than a business enterprise and welfare agency.

There are indeed instructors who specialize in drab lecturing or empty posturing. There is research that consists of little more than regurgitated data or repackaged truisms. But to return to an earlier argument, the expectation that every lecture class must sparkle with the misty-eyed frisson of Robin Williams' performances in *The Dead Poets Society* and that every publication must contain earth-shaking discoveries stems from a myth perpetuated by Romanticism and Existentialism—the cult of genius, originality and creativity. This myth leads both to disappointment and to the growing obscurity of the scholarly culture. Yet a great juggernaut keeps driving the culture in this direction. Peer reviews of colleagues' lectures are built on the expectation of dazzling insight and power to electrify students. Graduate students are expected to publish four or five articles before graduating, applicants for faculty positions are expected to have published a book, faculty seeking tenure are expected to have produced two or three. Thomas Hobbes and Immanuel Kant were in their late fifties before they published a book but today's new Ph.D. candidates are expected to peddle their research to publishers long before the dissertation defence. SSHRC now reserves a special section on its graduate student applications for publications, and graduate students desperate to promote themselves find it necessary to pump up their publication numbers by adding colloquium and occasional papers and "submitted papers" to the list, even though few of these are "published" or will be published in any traditional meaning of the word.

A wrong tack was taken in this country when universities gradually turned away from the British university model, with its emphasis on the teaching of general culture and scholarship, towards the German university model expounded first by Wilhelm von Humboldt, which gave priority to frontier research. Humboldt, who in 1810 founded the University of Berlin, had urged that universities turn away from the ideal of cultivating the "whole person" of humane learning and be primarily committed to the pursuit of pure knowledge. Canada's early universities—King's College (1821), Queen's University (1840), Victoria University (1840)—were rooted in Anglican, Presbyterian and Methodist commitments to a person's moral and spiritual development through the intellectual life. By turning our universities into research engines, we risk sacrificing teaching, the formation of character and the building of the scholarly culture. The British, more sensibly, opposed the research degree—the Doctor of Philosophy—because of its overspecialization and its narrow focus on professional training in scholarship. Our modern "multiversities" (as George Grant called them) look to the research conducted in scientific and medical laboratories and generalize these labours across the university as a whole. This has contributed to the trend where research has become the predominant means of building academic careers. It has led to curricula built less on the model of organic unity than on pragmatic decisions allowing every professor to have his or her course on the books. And it has meant that every university has to have a university press to publish the overspecialized scholarship that no other publisher would risk publishing—even when the only way of breaking even was with publication grants from the public purse.

Through these expectations and feverish activities, the scholarly culture deceives both itself and the public to which it is accountable. If there is one thing in particular which must be recovered from the past, it is the nobility of the "underlabourer"—for that is what all scholars really are, if their vanity does not intrude. Northrop Frye remarked that learning is the product of repetition, habit and practice. If there is drudgery in this—against which the cult of creativity and authenticity rebels—there is also the promise of a gradual fostering of connoisseurship and discerning judgment, without which no true discovery or insight could ever occur. As Virginia Woolf astutely explained, "Masterpieces are not single and solitary births; they are the outcome of many years of thinking in common, of thinking by the body of the people, so that the experience of the mass is behind the single voice."[33]

Intolerance for this rather unspectacular activity has risen sharply. Lamenting the increasing age of professors, Edward Renner recently wrote: "I can remember the sixties when universities were really vital, on the cutting edge of social change. Now they're one of the most boring places to be." Renner bases his judgment on data that show 61 percent of today's faculty were born before 1945, 36 percent between 1945 and 1960, and 2.8 percent after 1960. What Renner doesn't say is that during the 1960s many professors did not have Ph.D.s (explaining their relative youth), that most academics reach their intellectual peak not at the age of thirty, but more realistically between the age of forty-five and fifty-five, and that "vitality" is not limited to revolutionary zeal.[34] Samuel Scully, provost of the University of Victoria, contributed to the myth formulated by Renner when he added that there were "good pedagogical and cultural" reasons that "students often just feel more comfortable with professors closer to their own ages."[35] Renner added that "old-time faculty simply don't share the attitudes of today's students," that they are out of touch with their students' desire for training.[36]

The obvious response to Scully and Renner is this, Why should everything be "comfortable" and "in touch"? The Trent University professors who affirmed their right to make students "uncomfortable" may be overstating the case, but if a seamless web connects "the attitudes of today's students" and the scholarly culture, then all academics may as well hang up their caps, for there are more efficient and effective ways than university education to prepare individuals for the workplace and for certain social roles. Renner is a typical result of the confused intellectual climate of the 1960s, which was fuelled by a desire to be contemporaneous with every fashion and to be simultaneously in permanent revolution against the powers-that-be.

We can go further. In his provocative book *Tenured Radicals*, Roger Kimball advanced the thesis that the universities are in the hands of "tenured radicals" who are continuing their projects of emancipation with "ideological posturing, pop culture, and hermetic word games." This rings true in part, but it is probably an overstatement.[37] Many of today's academics who were student radicals in the 1960s have, in fact, turned into defenders of the status quo. It is hard to believe that even Lloyd Axworthy, whose proposals for an income-contingent student loan program and the future of university funding are straight out of Milton Friedman, was, during the 1960s a member of the militant and enraged Students for a Democratic Society. What is more difficult to take than the possibility that the radicals are ruling the roost is the reality that some who were once the New Left are now neoconservatives and have joined the Reform Party. Indeed, while this may appear harsh, I would argue that the responsibility of many of the problems in Canada's universities can be placed firmly on the shoulders of the sixties generation that now occupies most of the senior administrative and faculty positions in universities across Canada.

The sixties generation entered the universities when they were flush with money, opportunity and an unfettered commitment to limitless growth. Specializations proliferated, graduate programs grew exponentially (some institutionalizing arcane research interests of the faculty) and grants were abundant and, as significantly, expected. Now, thirty years later, we have a sprawling university system, with programs that in some cases have few students and merely replicate identical programs available from Vancouver to Halifax—and the academics who run the show refuse to let a single thing go. When cuts need to be made, it is rare that courses or programs reflecting faculty interests are shut down. Instead, departments offer fewer sections, larger classes and increased student-professor ratios.

A generation lives in wonderland. They point the finger at greedy governments, the ruthlessness of politicians seeking re-election and the bogeyman of the corporate world. At the same time they ardently defend the status quo as they knew it in the 1960s and live as if there will be no final reckoning. Weaned on Frantz Fanon's *The Wretched of the Earth* and Paulo Freire's *Pedagogy of the Oppressed*, they continue to use the counterculture's overwrought rhetoric, but in order to maintain or increase their own salaries or protect their research units. In 1993, for example, when the Manitoba government under Filmon initiated clawbacks of 1.08 percent, faculty warned, with characteristic hyperbole, that Manitoba was in danger of being turned into a Third World economy as a consequence of the underfunding of universities. While this generation sits on its well-upholstered seats (and enjoys salaries fattened by generous increments), it whimsically takes the higher political moral ground in defending its institutionalized privilege and it wields its authority from within the thicket of university administration politics.

Younger faculty, meanwhile, who usually have a more realistic idea of where the university is heading, are being advised to leave academe or to prepare for massive downscaling. It is only because teaching and research have been gutted of most of their meaning that the issues of the relevance of what faculty do have become so volatile. Many of the 1960s faculty who are now in their late forties and fifties teach and research sufficiently well if we adopt the narrow understanding of teaching and research which they helped to create. But the real issue behind the current skirmishes regarding teaching and research is the unwillingness of this generation to confront the elementary questions pertaining to the moral and intellectual purposes of the university. This generation of academics is often fighting for deckchairs on the *Titanic.* They believe the threat "Clean house, or we'll do it for you" is an idle one and that the privileges they enjoy are not in need of major reform.

The Fabrikant affair illustrates my point remarkably, for apart from the atrocity of the deed, it raises issues of the university culture that are ordinarily an invisible backdrop to teaching, research and tenure. Fabrikant, like Lépine, was obviously a deeply pathological person, and his crimes should not be taken as symptomatic of deep structural causes or systemic problems in the university system. Such an analysis would only encourage rash proposals to "re-engineer" the university. "Systemic" and "structural" analyses nearly always simplify the complex interactions of the university, and they theorize away one of the most significant human powers: the freedom and unpredictability of individual action, the potential for radical evil and, conversely, the possibility of dramatic redemption (the "dawn of a new day"). In both reports commissioned after the incident, the authors—John Cowan and Harry Arthurs—did search for structural reasons to explain the occurrence. One should therefore take these diagnoses with a grain of salt, but both consultants raised important questions about university practice, based on their reviews of the specific circumstances of Concordia University's administration and its Department of Mechanical Engineering.

John Cowan's "Lessons from the Fabrikant File: A Report to the Board of Governors of Concordia University" is a bristling indictment of university administration. The absence of line-authority and the vast decentralization and compartmentalization of responsibility at Concordia, he charges, were the primary reason why Fabrikant's history of bullying and harassment was not nipped in the bud before it led to the tragic events of August 1992. Cowan starts off bluntly:

> [O]ne must understand that the majority of academics who become academic administrators do not like administration itself, do not think of themselves as administrators, have no training for their administrative roles other than popular television shows and modest on-the-job exposure, and are accustomed to work in a milieu where the exercise of authority is considered in bad taste. Indeed, most expect to return to the ranks of working faculty after a brief sojourn in administration, and all are steeped in the important university traditions of academic freedom, pluralism, tolerance of eccentricity and reliance on self-direction for setting tasks. Giving an order, even a reasonable one, is anathema to many.

Cowan sees the "collegial culture" of the academic community as contributing to the breakdown of decisive action in the long string of incidents comprising Fabrikant's case against Concordia. The mishandling of Fabrikant's history of abusive behaviour arose, Cowan believes, because academic administrators preferred not to take "behavioral" disciplinary action. Instead, they used "academic" punishments (delayed tenure and promotion), thus failing to exercise their individual authority and simultaneously shielding themselves from possible blame. Wrong signals and unwillingness to call Fabrikant up on the carpet plagued the period from 1989 to 1992. There had been a complaint of rape against Fabrikant in the late 1980s though, ultimately, no charges were laid. In 1989 Fabrikant talked about shooting people and, later that year, amidst threats and warnings from Fabrikant, the university's rector was given security protection. Yet, while Fabrikant was fighting with everyone—from a language instructor to the purchasing office—he kept getting merit awards, pay increases and contract renewals. At key points when his disruptive behaviour could have formed the basis for terminating his contracts, no action was taken, and his supervisors continued to write laudatory letters about his research and teaching abilities.

Cowan concludes that the reluctance of Concordia's administrators to act like managers arose from a fear of grievance that might have occurred if they were to judge Fabrikant on any other ground but academic merit. The response to Cowan's charge confirmed the most salient parts of his analysis. One key player after another responded by shunting responsibility to another colleague or by hiding behind academic assessments of Fabrikant as the excuse for not exercising management leadership. In one of the few exercises of genuine responsibility, the board of governors fired the rector, refused to renew the contract of the academic vice-rector and accepted the resignation of the vice-rector, finance.

H.W. Arthurs' report took a different tack, but reached similar conclusions, which rocked the university community. According to Arthurs, Fabrikant had alleged conflicts of interest, illicit claims of authorship and professional misconduct. The report demonstrated that there were grounds for the allegations in some cases and that in other cases the allegations were wholly valid. The Arthurs Report is a sustained indictment of the production-driven research culture of the university. "It appears to us that, in some quarters, ever-higher activity levels, ever-growing output, bigger and bigger grants and contracts, more and more equipment and facilities, higher and higher graduate enrolments, have become ends in themselves."[38] Practices developed that are "the almost inescapable pathology of the surrounding research culture."[39] In his analysis of the events that culminated in Fabrikant's murder of four colleagues, Arthurs highlighted the way that academics were being transformed into managers of businesses, causing conflicts between their duties as intellectuals and as bidders for resources to expand their research agendas.[40] He condemns the priority universities give to career researchers and to a culture built on expectations of more contracts, graduate students and research facilities. He blames the federal government for the unintended consequence of its policy to give priority to private-sector suppliers of research services—namely, conflicts of interest that grew out of the need for academics to incorporate private companies so that they could be private-sector bidders.[41] Arthurs questioned a system that permitted the padding of resumes by claim to joint authorship and the use of academic prestige for private gain, and that failed to demand compliance and integrity statements from scholars before their articles were published. He also condemned the university for making no effort to establish administrative controls over the new entrepreneurial activity—not even with a statement on professional ethics or standards of scientific and academic integrity.

Arthurs concluded with a call for a "culture change." That call may be tantamount to a whistle against the wind for two reasons that Arthurs himself acknowledges. First, the scholarly culture is being taken over by a powerful political and economic discourse that entrenches aggressive entrepreneurial activity. Secondly, governments are, as never before, demanding that university researchers contribute to the nation's ability to compete globally. Arthurs' plea was seen by some as a case of "market-bashing." But does the Fabrikant incident, at least on Arthurs' reading, not reveal the horror that may arise when we turn away from books and conversations, mortgaging intellectual growth and productivity to economic and technological power? While many young and older faculty continue to invest their passion in teaching and research, a middle generation fiddles while the institution burns. They welcome the new regulatory demands being placed on the universities because such demands swell the administrative offices they wish to fill. According to conservative estimates, there are 2,200 faculty currently in middle-management academic administrative roles.[42] All of them are mid-career academics. At an average salary of $90,000 (most are also top-level associate professors and full professors), the cost is at least $176 million per year, not taking into account the staff and budgets they command. The Arthurs Report was a serious indictment of a general malaise.

The Fabrikant affair exhibits so many of the dangerous tendencies threatening the scholarly culture. It shows how tenure has
been distorted to become the be all and end all of a university
career. It brings to light the aberration that has converted scholarship and contribution to a community of scholars with proprietary rights to research work. The affair opens up the complex
question of how a *civitas*, a civil and moral association, legitimately governs itself and raises the question of whether legalistic
procedure is the best means of maintaining such an association.
In the final chapter I will propose a number of reforms that
would strengthen the scholarly culture and diminish the force of
some of the factors that corrode decency and good judgment.
Nonetheless, as it pertains to the Fabrikant case, it may be that
human artifice is impotent in the face of radical evil.

One additional aspect of the affair sheds light on the collapse
of the scholarly culture. It is generally accepted that Fabrikant
initiated a sting, first getting his colleagues to share in credit for
articles he wrote alone, then blackmailing them into granting
him tenure and finally reporting conflicts of interest and false
authorship to the Concordia administration when he did not
get tenure. The question is: Why are the conditions in the university such that a sting could work, especially by a perpetrator
who does not appear to be particularly shrewd or cunning? The
answer may lie in the growing factionalism, fractiousness and
invidious judgmentalism dividing society at large and the scholarly community in particular.

Chapter 4

Growing Discord on
Canada's Campuses

*What is a cynic? The man who knows the price of everything
and the value of nothing.*

Oscar Wilde

E vident at nearly every key turning point in the Fabrikant
affair was the growing volatility of the academic community. Older faculty and alumni agree that there are two major
differences between the scholarly culture they knew even two
decades ago and today's prickly environment—the increase in
litigiousness and the desire to manage the university with excessive precision and certainty. The litigiousness is a symptom of
the growing divisiveness of society in general. Jean Bethke
Elshtain, who gave the 1992 Massey Lecture "Democracy on
Trial," highlighted the dangerous tendencies that were making
our own established democracy so much weaker than some of
the newer struggling democracies of the former Eastern Bloc.
Our current political culture, she noted, is increasingly characterized by distrust for civil public engagement and deliberation,
as well as the growth of cynicism, privatizing and acquisitive
individualism, and contempt for the rule-governed practices of
democracy. Elshtain's warning has been echoed more recently by
Christopher Lasch (*The Revolt of the Elites*), Conor Cruise
O'Brien (*On the Eve of the Millennium*) and John Ralston Saul
(*The Unconscious Civilization*). The idea of civil society, according to these thinkers, is being overwhelmed by the fragmenting

politics of sectarians and special-interest groups. In addition, they warn, technocratic management, which looks to efficiency and automation as a panacea for all human needs, is replacing common sense and the wide range of cultural practices through which human longing has traditionally been expressed.

The university community, too, is being shattered by today's political shifts. Today, the civil association has become a tight knot of rules and laws that only approximate the deeper purposes of forming moral character and fuelling intellectual curiosity and accomplishments. Only a pale shadow of the original moral and spiritual meaning of *civitas* and *universitas* remains in the contemporary interpretation of the primals "accessibility" and "academic freedom." These regulations empower some while giving others a politics to demand new entitlements. Given the high-strung nature of many academics, the mood of the university community is by nature often testy. But the tension that in the past has been the source of creativity is now fractious.

The tendencies to rash decision making and to looking for "silver-bullet" fixes arise from widespread confusion and extravagant expectations about the scholarly culture. The litigiousness of students and faculty is one symptom of these misconceptions. It is played out within the university, although increasingly outsiders—the legal profession, social welfare agencies and administrative tribunals, among others—have begun to play a more active role in governing the institution. Another symptom of the growing irascibility and narrowness of society at large is the hastiness of judgments that say one thing is excellent, while another is not. Many new "stakeholders" believe they have a monopoly on what "quality education" is and have not shied away from severe pronouncements on the relative merits of one university over another. The *Maclean's* survey of universities is only one such effort at ranking, though it has become something of a wildfire through the seriousness attached to it. The survey has some merit, but it has also contributed to the precipitous manner in which universities are beginning to be managed and made accountable to society. In this way, the *Maclean's* survey is one of the most visible expressions of how discord is being sown on campuses and among universities in Canada.

The fissures that are now appearing cannot be properly judged unless one simultaneously recognizes that the intellectual climate in universities today is tragically contributing to the discord on campus. The litigiousness of the university community and the projects to rank the university are not alien phenomena. It is also necessary to add the rise of postmodernism into the mix, for its potent contribution to the distortions of the scholarly culture has made the university a fertile ground for the forces fragmenting society in general.

The litigiousness of students is the most evident sign of deep cracks in the scholarly culture. Since the late 1960s, in many of Canada's universities, students have, by university regulation, sat on most university committees, the sole exception being those related explicitly to student files and tenure and promotion. In nearly all cases student representation has been an important addition to the discussions surrounding decisions on appointments, curriculum and programming, resource use and the university's extracurricular events. True, situations arise when student representatives are like Plato's proverbial "young puppies," who with shallow draughts of learning "misuse them as though it were play, always using them to contradict…like puppies enjoying pulling and tearing with argument at those who happen to be near."[1] But in this they have been no different from inexperienced faculty who, in their first brush with university management, are often truculent and despoiling, but who gradually mature into more useful contributors to university administration. Increasingly, however, students are becoming acutely disruptive, and their conduct has infected the student body as a whole. Every faculty member and staff administrator can recount many tales reflecting the effects of student "empowerment" over the last twenty years: many students believe and act on the belief that grades are negotiable, others see rules and regulations as being subject to personal review, still others think academic decisions are open to endless appeal.

In one sense, it is a healthy sign when students exercise their judgment, call error to account and assist in opening opportunities for fresh starts and new directions. For instance, in 1993, students at the University of Alberta were successful in deferring a plan for quota hiring, the critically antimeritocratic policy embodied in the proposal "Opening Doors: A Plan for Employment Equity at the University of Alberta." But students are now agitating for the power to determine what they are taught and feel that they are in a bargaining position with faculty ("You wouldn't be here but for us…"). They are opposing tuition fee increases with the zero-sum logic of "our tuition fees or your RRSPs." There are students who devote endless time to finding loopholes that permit their own designs to be furthered. There are those who hop from program to program, university to university, to avoid the final judgment that they have failed (or, in Ontario, they contribute to an underground Grade 14— namely, a year of repeating Ontario Academic Credits over and over until they achieve a satisfactory grade). Some hide or pilfer library resources to keep an edge over classmates. Some exploit by fantastic demands the sincere efforts by universities to assist students with "disabilities." Others are willing to sacrifice self-respect and dignity for a grade increase.

David Koulack, a professor of psychology at the University of Manitoba, offers a typical story:

> Then there is the more potent, regular and direct pressure you will most assuredly receive from those dissatisfied with their grades. Here's an excerpt from a two-page grade appeal of a student of mine. The Grade Appeals Committee took it seriously and I had to respond to it in detail. The student wrote: "My reason for making this appeal is because I believe the exam was unfairly difficult…. I knew I answered the first question wrong but felt very good leaving the exam…. I prepared what I thought was beyond needed [sic]…. I ended up doing

more than half as bad as I normally did [sic]." This is not an unusual reason for appealing a grade. And, not unusually, this student never came to see me to discuss her answers. She, like many other students, simply decided she deserved a higher grade. Perhaps she needed it to get into graduate school. Or maybe just to graduate.[2]

The same brazenness is being demonstrated when graduate students opine that the program requirements for a doctorate are merely a form of hazing and are willing to go to a human rights tribunal (as happened in 1995 in the UBC political science department) for damages.

What cannot be disputed is the growing tendency of students to use the law—labour relations legislation, equity legislation and the Canadian Charter of Rights and Freedoms—to deal with their disagreements with the university. As constitution scholars like Rainer Knopff, Ted Morton and Peter Russell keep pointing out, a record of judicial decisions is now accumulating that reflects the legal system's receptivity to "perceived" or "felt" threats and to supposedly "systemic" or "environmental" menaces to rights. This is turning us into a grievance society, where, in the words of Knopff, intrusive and extrapolitical "social technologies" are being used to forge order and stability. The threat of using the law, rather than the more pliant processes of mediation, is powerfully intimidating. Students have learned, to positive result, how effective that threat is. Let it also be said that while faculty grouse about the growing litigiousness, it is the support staff and administrators who are usually the frontline for verbal abuse, intimidation, anger and hostility.

Litigiousness is hardly confined to students; university faculty are resorting to legal proceedings in equal numbers. University of Victoria political science professor Somer Brodribb and the members of the "Chilly Climate" committee went to the B.C. Humans Rights Commission with their allegations of harassment.[3] The spectre of formal grievance and legal action hung over the departures of two disaffected female faculty members from the political science department at the University of Manitoba. It is not difficult to speculate that the alleged harassers in the political science department at UBC will sue the complainants for defamation and that both faculty and students might seek damages from the university.

If students and faculty have become more litigious, it is because they are following the lead of university unions. When Concordia University's Board of Governors fired rector Patrick Kenniff in 1992 over the handling of the Fabrikant affair, the faculty associations and CAUT immediately objected to the violation of due process. In a country whose principle of responsible government is built on the idea of ministerial responsibility, was Kenniff's firing anything less than upholding moral responsibility? Union bickering has contributed significantly to the poor reputations universities are acquiring. Faculty associations take pride in their forward thinking but at the end of the day their bottom line consists merely of the narrow interests fought for by the most aggressive of their members.

It is always difficult to identify what factors account for complex social phenomena. The precise cause of the growing litigiousness between the partners of the university community is difficult to discern. But one could certainly identify contributing factors. Among them are the Charter of Rights and Freedoms, which defines rights as entitlements rather than responsibilities, and thirty years of experimentation with student-centred education based on the premise that self-esteem is the highest good. University ombudsman and equity offices also deny that there has been a rise in "vexatious" allegations of harassment, but fail to acknowledge their contribution to a culture that uses regulations and the law to resolve discontent rather than promoting a moral culture that pre-empts it. Disability centres press for increasing accommodations and employ an increasingly expansive definition of disability. Numerous university devices like grade-raisers and supplementals, which were designed in good faith, have often been abused, and university technicalities permit students to be awarded the privileges of the university (like graduation), even though found guilty of fraud or other crime. Even new copyright regulations reinforce the idea that knowledge is a commodity. As proprietary rights are emphasized at the expense of "fair use," litigiousness is encouraged and research and teaching impeded.

All these and many more factors are generating an irascibility on Canada's campuses built on the desire for status and power, which expresses itself in self-righteousness—as in the case of so many other republics of virtue. One vivid illustration of this balkanization of the university community was the 1993 rebellion of students at the Université du Québec à Montréal against the requirement that students write a French language exam upon admission. The requirement was instituted after 65 percent of the first-year cohort of students failed. Students blamed the school system and subjective marking for the failure. They complained that English universities in Quebec weren't making the same demand. The tests, the UQAM student association griped, are "contrary to the most elementary social justice because they restrict access to education in the most shameless way possible." Up to this point in their argument, the students can be seen as raising an important point, signalling that the issue might legitimately be assessed using an alternative principle of justice. But then they added an ingredient that betrayed the deep cynicism that lies at the core of much student empowerment. They claimed there was a hidden agenda behind the tests, namely, to "eliminate those who do not sufficiently understand the jargon used among those who control society."[4]

One should ask from where this idea of society as a war zone of power, and its accompanying premise that language is the tool of oppression, stems. It is instructive to examine one key ingredient that has been added to the pot and that has, unquestionably, flavoured the rest of the mix with a distinctly potent flavour—the ascendancy of postmodernism as the defining intellectual paradigm of the day.

Postmodernism is a perspective on human affairs that grew out of continental European linguistic theory. In its restricted

form, it is an innocuous interpretation of language as old as pre-
Socratic philosophical speculation. Essentially, that interpretation states that language does not represent anything, that what
we take as reality is mere linguistic convention and that language's slippery metaphorical nature leaves us unable to say
what things mean. As heir to philosophical scepticism, this set
of propositions (however much it seems to contradict the evident experiences of living) has a credible, even highly attractive,
pedigree. However, an emerging company of French academics—Paul de Man, Michel Foucault, Jacques Derrida—who
helped inspire the May 1968 Paris student revolts and offered
endless postmortems on its historical significance, gave its
propositions a distinctly leftist interpretation by transforming
them into a radical teaching of revolutionary social emancipation. By identifying the social construction of meaning and
logic and rationality exclusively with the exercise of power, postmodernists have supplied their followers with a manifesto: go
forth and deconstruct.[5]

Postmodernism defines itself in opposition to, or as a liberation from, "modernism." In explaining such ideas one risks
wandering into arcane regions of academic discussion. Stated
simply, then, modernity defines itself by its faith in science as
the universal script of human action, in the power to master the
unknown through human freedom, in the individual's capacity
to reason and to be free and in historical progress. Postmodernism sees itself as exposing each one of these—universality,
freedom, scientific rationality, historical continuity—as myth.
And through its focus on "intertextuality"—the unintended
interconnections between different authors' works—postmodernism has not only opened up a creative opportunity for new
interpretations, but has also legitimately called into question the
Romantic myth of originality.

The postmodern method of "deconstruction" entails searching
for subtexts and counternarratives beneath the dominant meanings that define the everyday world. These alternate perspectives
can be found most often among those who are marginalized in

society for not fitting in well with the predominant ideas of nor-
malcy or productivity. For example, if a culture is predominantly
Anglo-Saxon, unassimilated immigrants may have a "counter-
hegemonic discourse" that defines their understanding of the
world, together with their experiences of oppression or subordination. Women, gays and lesbians, and people of colour are
understood to have a "voice" that has been excluded from participation in creating culture. Similarly, the mad, diseased and perverted have suffered at the hands of those who are the gatekeepers
of terms like "normal" or "healthy." In each case, the perspective
of the marginalized will acquire visibility only if the "hegemonic
discourse" is deconstructed and revealed to be arbitrary.

Deconstruction is unlike the Marxian tool of "demystifica-
tion," though there is some resemblance between them. When
Marxists "demystified," they questioned whether ideas like "right
to private property" or "impartial knowledge" were truly independent of the existing "material relations" in society—who
owned capital and who controlled government. By looking suspiciously at the manner in which meaning is "socially constructed," Marxists attempted to discover the points at which
arbitrary power had intruded and unjustly stacked the deck to
favour the bourgeois and property owners. For Marxists, once
the real relation between ideas and possession was understood,
revolutionaries could proceed by overturning existing social relations and work towards bringing about a genuinely just world (as
Marxists understood it). Postmodernists, similarly, want to
expose the play of power that informs all ideas and political relations, but they deny that there is a "true" or "just" state of affairs
beneath the evident falseness and injustice of the world. Even
"subtexts" or "counternarratives" are only perspectives for postmodernists—they too must be subject to deconstruction.

Taking the idea of the "social construction of meaning" to its
most radical conclusion, postmodernists abandon the idea that
there is a "just" or "fair" manner of ordering the human world.
To adopt the postmodern manifesto of deconstruction is to sustain a kind of permanent revolution against all things. This kind

of infinite negation of truth and meaning, and a rejoicing in total emancipation from authority of all kinds, is what links postmodernism to nihilism—the creed that there is nothing out there in the world that we can represent, fight for or speak about. Intellectuals are limited to a subversion of all ideas, actions and utterances. In light of the new radical thought of the postmodernists, traditional Marxism today sounds very conservative, for it continues to speak of the ideals of social responsibility and justice, and to believe in a human nature.

Postmodernism has, unquestionably, made interesting contributions to our self-awareness. So much arrogance and presumption lies behind the uniform models of development or ideas of high culture that have until recently informed our relations to the non-West or our programs of higher learning. Postmodernism, in line with a long and respected tradition of philosophical scepticism, has pricked our puffed-up certainty regarding what is essential to human life. Postmodern criticism has brought to light a new awareness of the richness of African and Indian literature, has revitalized or shed light on many old narratives and has recognized new worlds resplendent with rich imagery and suggestive possibilities. It is an unmitigated blessing that the writings of Ben Okri and Rohinton Mistry have been moved into "mainstream literature," just as it has been liberating to rediscover the intense spirituality in the practices and stories of aboriginal peoples. These realignments in our thinking about culture may never have occurred were it not for deconstruction.

Other implications of postmodernism's iconoclasm are more disruptive, especially in the context of the culture of the university. Postmodernists reject the naturalness or inherent rationality of hierarchical relationships such as mature vs. immature, high vs. popular culture, authority vs. power, truth vs. opinion. Thus, the markers that guide sound judgment vanish, leaving confusion as to the purpose or meaning of education. And since reality does not exist independent of the power that represents it, academic departments no longer constitute discrete domains of study. While this notion appears to encourage interdisciplinary work, in practice postmodernists end up ransacking the university's offerings and reducing the plurality of journeys and predicaments to one alone—the play of power. Words simply form texts and these texts do not invite us to explore the real world through literary or philosophical symbol but only to play with the signs of language systems. This means that words have no integral meanings, and the whole point of the traditional idea of liberal education (books and conversations) falls into disarray.

In some way, it is right to believe that postmodernism is simply a recycled version of age-old relativism. It is also true that postmodernism is not so much a closure of modernism as a logical extension of the modern suspicion of authority and its celebration of freedom. But postmodernism is a bit of a snake in the grass if one allows it to be seen as compatible with traditional queries about the human presumption to know the truth and harness the human will. Philosophical scepticism is a powerful affirmation of human plurality and, in the case of its modern form, sustains a deep commitment to relieving the burdens of man's estate. In postmodernism, by contrast, lies a pervasive cynicism about human purposes and a merely diffuse confidence in projects on behalf of total emancipation that one commentator has likened to an uninformed jump off a springboard into the void.[6] Its relentless deconstruction of our aims and purposes has a way of removing meaning from our actions and leaving us with a life that is but a ceaseless flow of happenings. Postmodernism does not even allow us the comfort that David Hume could still find in everyday life—though he may have shared some of postmodernism's suspicion about what we commonly call "reality."

If friendship, conversation and the sacred trust of stewardship between instructor and student are integral to the scholarly culture, postmodernism is a serious threat to the university community. In its hands, education can really be nothing more than agitation propaganda, thus ending the chorus of voices we commonly understand as conversation. What postmodernism puts in the breach is the trust and psychic maturity upon which conversations among friends depends. Where everything is power, and where academics no longer take upon themselves to mature their students' desires, what will prevent young people's desire for glory, lust for domination, longing for total satisfaction and proclivity to weakness and despair from overwhelming their desire for the beautiful and good? As Aeschylus warned, "In every tyrant's heart there springs in the end this poison, that he cannot trust a friend."

Postmodernism calls into serious question the traditional scholarly reading of books, and their iconoclasm has come to rest in the well-aired "exclusive versus inclusive canon" debate. The arguments are by now well known, having been amply debated by Allan Bloom, Dinesh D'Souza, E.P. Hirsch, Russell Jacoby, Stanley Fish and Gertrude Himmelfarb, and I will not repeat the litany of charges and grievances.[7] The discussion, however, is an apt illustration of how postmodernism has politicized the curriculum and backed academic rivals into opposing corners. In one corner are the defenders of the traditional, exclusive canon; in the other are postmodernists who claim that all texts have equal claim to be included in the canon. Can there be a canon that is exclusive without being elitist or static? Unfortunately, few discussions of this possibility are occurring in academe. In Chapter 2, I suggested that works which invoke a cosmos of meaning that can be elevated to the level of universality are those properly included in a refurbished, exclusive canon. The current stalemate will be overcome only if certain aspects of both the traditionalists' and postmodernists' arguments are accepted and synthesized at a higher level of analysis.

Many books, like any jotting, manifesto, or scribble, can be read for solace, empowerment or temporary diversion. The works of a canon are different. A genuine encounter with the canon is built on responsibilities that both partners must uphold. If a reader senses that the author is proselytizing, attempting to convert his or her readership to a creed, the reader will suspend trust and openness. Tracts that conceal the foundational experiences upon which the text is built and that thereby eclipse cardinal aspects of reality and prevent the possibility of rational assent, simply produce disciples or sceptics. No true conversation ensues. By the same token, if a reader is unwilling to trust an author who is not proselytizing, and to risk the encounter upon which he or she is invited, the text at best reinforces the reader's prejudices. Again, the engagement becomes a futile enterprise. A genuine encounter with the works of Plato and Kant, Sophocles and Dante, requires receptivity and a willingness to assent to experiences that often shatter the commonplace experience and conventional opinions. Such an encounter does not lead to mere rationalizations of the prevailing structures of power. On the contrary, the reader discovers that each of these thinkers offers distinct portrayals of human potential, depicting both opportunities for action and the limitations forced upon us by the human condition. The communion of reason to which a canonical work invites the reader requires what the Greeks called *pathos*—a suffering or receiving of experiences and truths at a primordial level of our being. *Pathos* depends on a renunciation of the self fashioned by the modern discourse of empowerment and doubt, and it seeks a higher form of intellectual and spiritual independent-mindedness that unites freedom and obedience.

The postmodernist will have none of this apparent passivity and submissiveness. Denying that any text can be authoritative, that an appeal to reason is anything more than obeisance to a dominant power relation or that the Western tradition represents a widely divergent, though not exhaustive, array of human options, the deconstructionist sees only "logocentrism," "phallocentrism" and "Eurocentricity" or, in other words, political crusades against human desire, women, non-Westerners and other designated victim groups. The traditional canon and pathos, postmodernists claim, are animated by an intent to control difference and play. For the postmodernist the Great Books simply reproduce the historical prejudices of Western culture, and reading these texts is synonymous with passivity and uncritical acceptance.

Postmodernism is not confined to the "ivory tower." It is an intellectual tool currently being used in various social sectors to rewrite history and to re-engineer the evident experiences of living. The United Church recently asked for forgiveness in a "confession" to the First Nations concerning the "Euro-centricity" of its pastoral work. This may have exhibited an excessive zeal for the appearance of egalitarian justice while destroying its substance. The request for forgiveness may be appropriate; the self-castigation for "Eurocentricity" is excessive. In it lurks the possibility that the United Church will repudiate the tradition that supplies the moral and spiritual ballast for its charitable works, and then, arguably, may be unmoored from any serious purpose for its activity. While the documented abuse of native peoples by religious missionaries is unconscionable and a sad aspect of our history, castigating the entire European tradition for this action results in a denial of Western civilizational achievements in science and medicine, theology and literature, politics and social practice. Many thoughtful Westerners are increasingly having doubts about the uniform models of development, industrialization and social order we impose on others as much as on ourselves. To believe, however, that all expressions of every culture are equally worthy and that nothing justifies our political interference or moral suasion can contribute to highly culpable sins of omission.

The facts and burdens of human existence inevitably necessitate the need for judgment, often entailing difficult, not to say tragic, choices. But the deconstructionist seems to believe that such judgment is either not necessary or that it is avoidable by deconstructing all the limits and events that force judgment upon us. If the deconstructionists' call for self-reproach at being "Eurocentric" is obeyed strictly, we will end by ignoring disease, violence, corruption, cruelty and abuse of the weakest members of society when they arise from specific practices in other cultures. Remorse for "Eurocentricity" is every bit as elusive and inchoate as the attempt to identify systemic discrimination. Rather than pointing to specific, verifiable acts of transgression, barbarism and injustice, the deconstructionist vaguely alludes to the oppression arising from policies without actors, texts without authors and governance without rulers. Is this not a recipe for smug inaction or for exaggerated zeal in bringing a wholly new age and a wholly new humanity into existence? In refusing to address the substantive fruitful aspects of Western culture, is there not a risk that the deconstructionist will reinforce and contribute to the trivialization of culture? One rarely hears a deconstructionist advocating the comprehensive study of the language and culture of other societies. Instead, the culture and literature of the non-West is scoured to find tales of oppression and victimization. Ironically, such intellectual plundering of the non-West is virtually identical to the imperialist activity for which the West was initially castigated by the deconstructionist.

An Ontario employment equity officer recently said that to distinguish among school graduates on the basis of degrees is to commit the sin of "credentialism." The equity officer who would determine employability without accounting for measurable scholastic achievement betrays the same unwillingness to make the judgments that the facts and burdens of human existence demand. Every dedicated teacher knows that grading and attainment of a degree are in themselves only imprecise measures of the understanding students have acquired. Teaching, like politics, cannot allow, as Aristotle rightly advises, of more precision than the subject matter allows. But if we abandon all measurable criteria, however imprecise, in favour of a vague sentiment of worthiness, we will undermine our sense of individual responsibility and the reasonable bases of authority and leadership.

I doubt, however, that the equity officer's view was based on this impracticable, though defensible, moral principle. The more likely interpretation is that the officer's views reflect the same sentiment that led the Ontario NDP in 1992 to declare that unequal result as a consequence of merit was "an institutionalized form of racism and classism." This is a sentiment reflecting discomfort with the human longing for perfection and the reality that individuals, given an equal opportunity to improve themselves, will end up at different levels of success. Some, indeed, will fail; but even if none failed, the outcomes would always be variable, since individuals have different potentials to start with. A society based on sentiments that discount difference in potential and excellence emasculates healthy competition, initiative and achievement, and risks promoting collective mediocrity and private resentment. It also saps itself of the incentives that unite individual pursuit of happiness with the collective good of the community. Ambitious and forceful persons will always be with us, and in the absence of a relatively benign system of conventional rewards for merit (public honours, economic gain, social status) they will find more indulgent and criminal means of excelling.

I have dwelt on these two examples because they are characteristic of the corrosive impact postmodernism has on balanced public debate. They reinforce the ill will and rancour that was sown by incidents like the "Writing Thru' Race" conference, in which public funding was used to hold a colloquium exclusively for "people of colour" outside the "hegemony" of the "dominant culture." Similarly the "Into the Heart of Africa" exhibition at the Royal Ontario Museum was interpreted by black activists as implying approval and complicity, although the stereotyping and discrimination were depicted only for the purpose of criticizing injustices committed by Western missionaries in Africa. Lurking behind these incidents lies a regression from one of the West's great civilizational achievements—the recognition of the autonomous and unique person. The consequence is a vulgarization and trivialization of human purpose and a climate in which "rageful proclamations of one's unassailable and unassimilable identity" prevail, where we lose the encounters of a free citizenry and face each other merely as aggrieved groups in distinct linguistic and cultural villages.[8]

This is what I mean by identifying postmodernism as a snake in the grass. Under the apparently benign guise of pluralism and an inclusive canon, it allows for no authority except the student's own empowerment. Students are thus left with the baleful conclusion that society is little more than a contest for power. As Gerald Graff, a prominent spokesman for postmodernist strategies of education, says, all one may do is to "teach the conflicts."[9] As a consequence, conversation between reasonable persons that has the potential to elevate their longings degenerates into a series of mere professions or declarations. The unwillingness to at least seek the elevation offered in conversation and friendship displays what Frye calls the "human resistance to maturity." If the tone of postmodernists was scepticism alone, they would belong to a tradition worthiest of our renewed attention—the one given its consummate expressions by Augustine, by the Protestant Reformation and later by David Hume in its stand against pretence and presumption. But in the hands of postmodernists, scepticism has become destructive cynicism and despair, its anti-elitism an abandonment of substance and direction. "Elitism," as Frye rightly says, "is the bogey word used by people to discredit those who take education seriously."[10]

This is to paint postmodernism in the bleakest tones. It would be a gross exaggeration to say that postmodernism in the academy will cause the collapse of the university, but it would also be inaccurate to deny that many "postmodernists," in the attentive cataloguing of modern excess, have contributed to serious questioning about uniform Western models of development, industrialization and social order. It is also futile to presume that we should or could close off the possibility of expanding the Western canon by adding new works. In the introduction to an important study of multiculturalism, the philosopher Amy Gutman makes the insightful point that the raging debate today between conservatives and deconstructionists is intensified "by the zero-sum nature of the choice between canonical and new works."[11] What we need, above all, is to reassess the canon without derailing into total deconstruction, and to open ourselves to the depths of our canonical texts without blindly submitting to archaic beliefs and customs.

Robertson Davies was completely right to suggest that the greatest gift the university gives is "a genial irreverence toward learning."[12] But he concluded, in a way that the postmodernists do not, that "from that irreverence love may spring." What postmodernism no longer wishes us to entertain is the possibility that knowledge and power, or knowledge and authority, are distinct. And in the process, postmodernists are dragging the university into the limelight, making its scholarly culture appear sentimental, uncaring and naïve. Leo Strauss once wrote that liberal education seeks the light, but shuns the limelight. As the light is lost, the university stumbles like one blinded and confused into the fierce glare of public opprobrium.

Heightening the discord on campus and the confusion regarding the purposes of the scholarly culture, is a plethora of new schemes devised to deconstruct and reconstruct the image of the university. These new schemes—accountability models, rationalization plans, partnerships with colleges and business corporations—are not linked directly to the litigiousness of the academic community and the swell of enthusiasm for postmodernism throughout the university. But they are linked indirectly because they reinforce the idea that the university as an institution, and the complex tension of needs and longings it embodies, is an utterly arbitrary artifice that can be re-engineered at will. Never mind that the university has a tradition of eight centuries during which its practices were refined to the present state. Ignore the fact that the university has persevered against innumerable attempts to suppress its commitment to nonpartisan inquiry and to deny the critical distance essential to independent-mindedness. Taking aim at only the surface, and apparently ignorant of the tangle of expectations that the university has traditionally attempted to meet, those who have decided to expose the university's affairs to public opprobrium and to "clean house" are contributing to the decay. *Maclean's* has led the pack.

In 1991 *Maclean's* offered its readers "A Measure of Excellence," a fifty-six-page ranking and assessment of universities, with commentary ranging from "the mood on campus" to "what makes a school great." The aim of the exercise was to "provide one of the most comprehensive pictures of Canadian universities ever attempted" and to make these public institutions "accountable to outsiders." The issue is reputed to have sold as many copies as the one featuring Prince Charles and Lady Diana's wedding. Some universities were thrilled by the results and praised the initiative—McGill, Queen's and Mount Allison took first, second and third standing—while others (Carleton, UQAM and Cape Breton, who ranked forty-fourth, forty-fifth and forty-sixth, respectively) called foul. In protest to the rating of thirty-third, Memorial University administrators sold T-shirts printed with the words "*Maclean's* Rankings: Just Say No." While some university officials made statements deploring the "consumer report" mentality of the ratings game, other university administrators decried its utility. As the director of public relations at Concordia University said, "I don't think the survey is worth a hill of beans in helping students decide where to apply."[13] In 1992 when the Université du Québec, a distinctive multicampus institution, found itself unable to answer much of the *Maclean's* questionnaire because of its unique circumstances, no approximate data was substituted, and the university was simply ranked in last place. When two universities refused to submit information for a third year of humiliation, *Maclean's* went ahead and reported on them anyway but docked them points for failing to provide data. Blackmail may have been too strong a term, but the frustration of Memorial University and Carleton University is understandable. Universities that did not supply data on any given indicator simply received the lowest point score.

By the time the fourth annual edition of the popular issue was being prepared, the Association of Universities and Colleges of Canada (AUCC) asked for a Canada-wide boycott, and fifteen universities withdrew from the survey. Some, nonetheless, took out advertisements in the same issue, a rearguard action that tended to backfire, raising more suspicion than confidence. In the fall of 1994, *Maclean's* rival *Saturday Night* issued a special insert on universities featuring information solicited by its editors from universities on their programs. The total cost of acquiring this data—$100,000—was borne by the AUCC. Indelicate questions were raised as to whether the *Saturday*

Night special was anything more than an "advertorial."
Remarked *Maclean's* assistant managing editor, summing up the
universities' reluctance to be ranked: "These people spend their
lives grading students. It seems some are not comfortable being
graded themselves."[14] *Maclean's* editors took the 1994 withdrawal as an expression of sour grapes. The "No-Shows" were
highlighted in a separate section of the 1994 survey in such a
way as to hold up their diffidence to ridicule. By 1995 many of
these universities had rejoined the survey.

The reason for their return has less to do with the universities'
confidence in the value of the ranking than their prudent recognition that perceptions count. The public assumption that non-
participating universities have something to hide is not to be
scorned. Perceptions, after all, are often more potent than truth.
There are other university surveys like the dry and idiosyncratic
Linda Frum's Guide to Canadian Universities and the jaunty, stu-
dent-produced *Real Guide to Canadian Universities.* Neither of
these has so dramatically changed Canadians' perceptions.
When Frum attached the new moniker "Last Chance U" to
Carleton University (because of its policy of giving less accomplished students a second chance) neither enrolments nor
alumni donations were affected. The fallout from Carleton's low
ranking in the first *Maclean's* survey, by contrast, had dire financial implications, and the university has had to learn how
volatile perceptions truly are.

The *Maclean's* survey came with the weight of the imprimatur
of the Canadian establishment—1,040 public leaders, chief
executive officers of major corporations and academic administrators. The universities' return to the survey is an apt illustration of how outsiders exercise their stranglehold over them.
Damned if they participated, damned if they did not, the dis-
senters had little choice but to submit or face the financial consequences. Be that as it may, those who bailed ship in 1994,
while concerned about the impact of their ranking on enrolment
and corporate sponsorship, also had principled objections to the
methodology used by *Maclean's.* Indeed, in their most honest

moods, officials from the "winners" share these reservations. None of Canada's universities have been comfortable with playing a numbers game.

The *Maclean's* surveys have undergone revision in response to these reservations, and it is a mark of the integrity of its editors that *Maclean's* made efforts to meet numerous objections to its ranking methods. The 1991 survey took four factors into consideration—student body, faculty, financial resources and reputation—and divided these further into twelve subcategories, ranging from the grade average of incoming students, to research grants per professor, to operating budget allocated per student. All universities offering general B.A. and B.Sc. degrees were ranked globally, regardless of their distinctive strengths or the profiles of their academic and professional schools. The relative weight of different indicators was, in great part, ignored. By the 1994 survey, universities had been divided into three categories: medical/doctoral, comprehensive and primarily undergraduate; the indicators had swelled to twenty; and differential weighting of these indicators formed part of the equation. The 1994 survey appears both more rigorous and more frivolous. Whereas the 1991 editors warned that "the survey does not— and could not—measure the degree to which individual students can be enriched by the school of their choice," the 1994 survey is more assertive, equating its compilations with the "time-honoured tradition" of a professor's grading. While the 1991 survey included somewhat sombre thumbnail sketches penned by university presidents, by 1994 it adopted a trendy format that included sections such as: "What's hot, What's not...." By 1995, appropriate to a time when sombre forecasts of financial crisis hang as a spectre behind reviews of all Canadian institutions, the *Maclean's* university issue read like an obituary, and the focus turned to the bleak employment prospects for this year's graduates. It remains for many university officials problematic whether the changes from year to year have substantially improved the ranking exercise.

There are, however, many commendable features in the survey.

Though the limelight threatens the complex processes of the scholarly culture, universities cannot afford to conceal information about whom it admits and why, and what finances it has available and how it uses them, who its faculty are and what their credentials add up to, what accreditation its programs undergo and what services its members enjoy. All is not well within the ivory tower, and the growing number of indiscretions of which the public has become apprised justifies some of the concern being expressed by governments and the media. *Maclean's* dared to do what the universities would not: it lined up statistics in an understandable format and offered potential students informed comparisons.

This is not to say the universities are unwilling to report the facts. Universities currently submit as many as ninety reports annually to government regulatory bodies, ranging from financial audits to enrolment forecasts, economic impact studies, academic program reviews and facilities maintenance assessments.[15] Each year more and more data are requested, as equity, safety, accessibility and curriculum inclusivity become targets of government scrutiny. These reports are on public record and readily available, if one is willing to wade through heaps of minutes of governing bodies, précis of course evaluations, research grant summaries, program calendars and operating budgets. While the *Maclean's* survey contributes nothing new to what is already publicly reported, its format has appeal and has certainly contributed to the perception that the magazine is a white knight that has broken the universities' resistance to transparency. The question is, however, whether the filter is best suited to represent the scholarly culture. The equally important question is whether the approximately $100,000 it costs each university to compile the specific data set that *Maclean's* requests is public money well spent. That cost constitutes an indirect tax on all Canadians and contributes to the profits of a private business venture.

Many of the *Maclean's* indicators are illuminating measures of where individual universities are placing their priorities and how the university sector as a whole is responding to the demands placed upon it. The difficulty arises primarily in the comparative nature of the exercise. While it may have appeared for years that universities had something to hide in resisting sector ranking, the primary reason for such resistance was that comparing one institution to another often amounts to relating apples to oranges. In 1991, for instance, the survey did not differentiate between universities that were predominantly driven by their doctoral research programs and professional schools (law, medicine, engineering) and those that considered themselves comprehensive institutions, and others that specialized in undergraduate teaching. Instead, performance measures and indicators of excellence were uniformly applied, setting up a bias against institutions that were smaller, that did more teaching than research, whose faculty did not win large medical research grants, and institutions that did not house the huge research laboratories of universities like Toronto, McGill, Dalhousie and the University of British Columbia.

Even when greater discrimination was introduced in 1992, so that each institution in a category was compared only to another in the same category, the same performance measures and indicators were used throughout the survey. This is indefensible. A predominantly undergraduate teaching university, to illustrate, should be gauged by measures appropriate to it: the resources dedicated to training of faculty, the mentorship programs it offers its new faculty, its greater numbers of female faculty, the range of experiences brought by experts (such as diplomats and policy analysts) appointed for limited terms, and the ability of the institution to accept mature students, part-time students and the sporadic requirements of the lifelong learner, to list a few. The *Maclean's* survey still uses a homogeneous set of performance measures that assume a uniform type of student, faculty member and undergraduate career in each of the categories of institutions, and in different regions of Canada. The *Maclean's* student is one whose academic potential is based exclusively on high-school grades, despite the vast growth in enrolment of mature students, whose more immediate life experience is often the basis of admission. The *Maclean's* faculty member is one whose aptitude for teaching and research is based exclusively on possessing a Ph.D. or a terminal professional degree, despite the significant number of civil servants, journalists, policy analysts, medical professionals, performance artists and career diplomats who have significantly enriched academic programs in many universities. The *Maclean's* learning path is assumed to be consistent and steadily paced, despite the myriad elegant means many universities have put in place to make their institutions accessible to a wide range of students and the increasing number of program switches made by students.

Even if one accepts these assumptions, the indicators themselves are flawed. Faculty members' achievement should never be based only on the Ph.D. in hand and teaching awards received. The richness that academics invest in their teaching is based far more on the scholarship they conduct that translates into noteworthy publications, community service, work on commissions and tribunals and contribution to pedagogical innovation. The survey reinforces a certain reading of the 1991 report of the Smith Commission of Inquiry on Canadian University Education: the health of a university is gauged by the effectiveness of its teaching machine, rather than by its scholarly culture.

Universities also receive no credit from *Maclean's* for breaking from the pack. Universities like the University of Manitoba, which for years have exercised fiscal frugality and not run up huge deficits like McGill, have lower ratios of operating budget per student, and this harms their ranking. Universities that encourage their faculty to compete for private foundation or corporate research grants and international funding are penalized if their draw from federal research granting agencies is consequently lower. For example, one of Lakehead's spectacular achievements of late was the receipt of a multimillion-dollar grant from the Rockefeller Foundation for the study of aboriginal philosophy. This coup would not even be noted by *Maclean's*. Innovative programs like Victoria's joint degree in engineering and fine arts and Waterloo's extensive co-op program cannot appear in the tallies because they conform to no statistically significant indicator. Universities that respond to the distinctness of the ethnic communities in their area—either by special library acquisitions or heritage language programs—receive no recognition.

If university initiative is not recognized, neither is the effect of political legislation. There is a remarkable naïveté about the *Maclean's* survey generally, as if the performance of universities takes place in a political vacuum. Universities hampered by government legislation in respect of differential fees for international students, or by pressure for greater accessibility and equity, will display data that reflect these political contexts, and their ranking is thus harmed. In Ontario, for example, the composition of boards of governors is politically regulated—in some institutions, over half the members are order-in-council appointments. This allows a wide range of community sectarian interests (business, ethnic, professional) to politicize important decisions, affecting issues like recruitment, admission standards, honorary doctorate recipients, funding priorities, international involvement and influence in provincial education ministries. Equally powerful is the political effect of "envelope funding"—provincial funding based not solely on student enrolment but on specially targeted political projects, such as access for the disabled or "education equity." Universities are increasingly becoming clearing houses for the myriad agendas comprising the political world, and objects of micromanagement by government regulatory bodies.

The gravest problem with the *Maclean's* survey, however, is its exclusive insistence on what can be quantified. One is hard-pressed to find in the survey any measures that distinguish Canada's universities from a generic university found anywhere from Auckland to Los Angeles. Far more profound notions of accountability could be designed. How accountable, one might ask, has Toronto been to the rich legacy of the political economist Harold Innis, Queen's to the philosopher John Watson and

Carleton to sociologist John Porter? Continuity with tradition enriches an institution, and yet the *Maclean's* survey assumes that if it cannot be surveyed, it is not important.

What does number of tenured faculty say about intellectual passion or ongoing engagement with evolving scholarship? What does number of library acquisitions amount to if it is all "research" that has padded academic resumes? What does the dollar value of research grants in the humanities signify if research projects such as election data analysis, with a shelf-life of no more than a few years, are not differentiated from forms of scholarship such as meditative exegeses of Hegel's *Phenomenology of Spirit*, where little cost was incurred, and yet which constitute major contributions to the scholarly culture? What does class size per tenured faculty say about the importance of what is taught, even when it may indicate something about the effectiveness of the teaching?

Many other questions could likewise have been asked: how many graduates were accepted into which graduate school and with what amount of awards, how many faculty come from world-respected universities, how many books were published by major world presses, how much of the library holding is requested by interlibrary loan, how many invitations to be keynote speaker are extended to faculty, how many post-doctorate researchers are at the university, what cultural and community events are scheduled by universities?[16] In their absence it is dubious whether a reader learns much about the fertile engagement between students' needs and the scholarly culture. The data may be interesting. It is another question whether they are important.

The word "excellence" recurs throughout the *Maclean's* surveys, but the reader is never informed what this means except for a brief reference to the OECD's use of the term "quality of life" in relation to the comparative advantage of nations. The Achilles heel of the *Maclean's* survey—"the survey does not—and could not—measure the degree to which individual students can be enriched by the school of their choice"—was acknowledged by the editors in 1991 but was just as quickly forgotten. Qualitative assessment has therefore been replaced by the trinity of status, reputation and recognition. The disproportionate weight given to the reputation survey—20 percent weight in the overall ranking (compared to 4.3 percent given to scholarships, 7 percent to class size and 3 percent to students with high averages)—is highly revealing. If one examines the 1994 "breakout" charts that show how each indicator worked, one learns that there is a very small differential between the number 1 ranked university and the number 12 ranked university on an indicator like the average grade of the incoming class, even though the overall ranking chart leaves the reader with the impression that there must be a significant difference—that university number 12 is very low on this indicator. Insofar as the rankings are highly volatile to even minor variations in numbers, it is astounding that as much as 20 percent of the ranking is based on an elusive phenomenon like reputation. This is a signal that the exercise as a whole is not a serious assessment of the universities, but rather an entertaining diversion that amuses those who are used to tabloid and television glosses on complex social institutions and practices. One indication that supports my harsh judgment is the weight given to the survey of corporate CEOs—three times the weight of the other indicators. No fellows of the Royal Society of Canada were surveyed, no opinions of artists, musicians or architects were solicited, churches were avoided, and the judgments of scholars of classics, literature, philosophy and history (the traditional gatekeepers of the scholarly culture) were granted no standing.

The responsibility for a deeper and more serious inquiry falls on students. The 1994 *Maclean's* survey included a feature absent from previous years—a wide-ranging, eight-page discussion among a group of university students from across Canada about students' expectations and the future of the university. The discussion is a fine, seminal exploration of the complex workings of the university and its scholarly culture. *Maclean's* editors must be commended for finally giving a human face to the statistics (beyond the talking heads of previous issues) and permitting the voices of students to rise up above the jargon of "learner-satisfaction" and "performance indicators." It is also hard not to be impressed by the wisdom that comes from these students. "The university," comments Ray Westcott, "is a naturally inefficient thing. It's inefficient to send a bunch of eighteen-year-olds to a place to talk about history and politics and the arts for four years. I happen to think it's a beautifully inefficient thing. And I would be loath to see it disappear because we've become too damned concerned with 'Is this a tool which I can use when I walk out the door?'"[17] Pat Fitzpatrick complains that "white male fifty-five-year-olds are telling university presidents 'The market force needs people who are hardnosed business sorts.' These idiots are pressuring the universities and the government into forcing people to be 'utilitarian.'" He also points out that "those who are shaping the company from the bottom up" are recognizing the need for well-rounded students.[18] The student conversation is about the best thing in the whole four-year run of *Maclean's* surveys, marred only by the licence exercised at its conclusion when an editor indulged himself with a smarmy afterword: "Ah, the Nineties: radical students with their business cards."

Whatever else can be said about the survey, the reality is that *Maclean's* has contributed to the perception that league ranking is a valuable exercise.[19] Indeed, Robert Sheppard, the *Globe and Mail's* Western provinces correspondent, goes further, believing himself to be reflecting the *zeitgeist*. Sheppard wrote an opinion essay mocking the Association of Universities and Colleges of Canada for calling a boycott. "If it's OK to rank cars," he asked, "why not universities?" He continued: "Like it or not, we live in a 'ratings society' where consumer choice has become the watchword.... Cars, TV shows and politicians are all ranked in one form or another. Why should universities be any different? ...[A]fter the recent university-commissioned report on 'integrity in scholarship' at Concordia University...I'm not sure Canadian universities are in any position to throw stones."[20]

As vulgar as Sheppard's view is, however concocted his judgment that the public is clamouring for rankings, and whatever suspicion he reinforces in some circles that *Maclean's* is more interested in sales than in sound public debate, the rankings game has reinforced perilous tendencies in the university. Litigiousness grows daily, especially as services are being cut, proposals for a two-tiered university system (the exceptional institutions versus the rest) are being vetted seriously, university closures and amalgamations appear imminent and faculty are feuding over curricula. If the public is starting to feel it is being conned in the use of public funds, there are good reasons for such sentiments. Apparently unable collectively to stem the tide of fragmentation dividing the university community and to give a spirited defence of the scholarly culture, the universities have finally bent to the pressure exerted upon them to be accountable. The proposal is enough to make a sensible person weep.

Chapter 5

Skirmishes over the University's "Perception Problem"

The first duty of a lecturer—to hand you after an hour's discourse a nugget of pure truth to wrap up between the pages of your notebooks and keep on the mantelpiece for ever.

Virginia Woolf

The initiative undertaken by the universities in the last five years to produce an accountability model did not proceed from a feeling of goodwill towards the media or governments. Highly publicized incidents and political capital amassed by political parties favouring one or another crusade did not change the reality that the public was not complaining. The stick, however, was funding: universities were told that if they did not tighten their governance and generate performance indicators, subsequent funding would reflect the "public's" disapproval. The range of do-gooders who have set their sights on the university on the public's behalf include the Centre for Quality in Governance (in which Hugh Segal, Brian Mulroney's former bagman, plays a prominent role) and the Canadian Comprehensive Auditing Foundation. Their message has been clear: account for yourselves or expect growing political interference and bureaucratic control.

Since the late 1980s the number of reports that universities needed to submit to governments has risen dramatically. In response, predictably, universities have resorted to their favoured privilege—institutional autonomy. But the more universities appealed to their charters guaranteeing self-governance, the more government has intruded. The *Maclean's* survey was not the first attempt to make the universities accountable, though it may have been the catalyst for the university's willingness to design performance indicators. There is a detailed history of government attempts to establish university-sector management indicators, and resulting university opposition. What is new is the universities' scramble to produce "mission statements"—not as principled assessments of their perspectives on education, but as documents that could be used to ward off the intrusion of governments and to set their own standards of success. In other words, they have a strategic value.

If this sounds suspiciously circular and self-referential, it is. Universities are willing to meet the demand for accountability halfway: they agree to produce more public documents on how they perform, but these documents will be self-assessments of their capacity to meet the expectations of their own mission statements. Such cartwheels of assessment avoidance explain why it is easy to predict that the *Maclean's* survey will continue to be popular for many years.

In 1993 the Ontario Task Force on University Accountability tabled its recommendations concerning how universities should be appraised in a document known as the Broadhurst Report.[1] In 1995 the Association of Universities and Colleges of Canada (AUCC), building on the task force's work, produced a primer on performance indicators that heralded the day of micromanagement of the scholarly culture by statistical analysis.[2] These two documents can be adopted as representative of today's debate, though there is also a wide-ranging academic and management literature, not to say library shelves of proceedings from annual conferences and colloquia hosted by the professional university associations that deal with prevailing models of accountability.[3] These associations include the Canadian Association of University Business Officers and the Association of Universities and Colleges of Canada. Political scientists, economists, psychologists, sociologists, industrial relations specialists and a wide range of other interested parties have also added

their perspectives and engaged the exploratory work on performance indicators being undertaken in Australia and the United
States. However, all the literature is closely interrelated, so the
Broadhurst Report and the AUCC's performance indicator
primer can be taken as typical.

The Ontario Task Force on University Accountability accepted
the opinion that universities have a "major perceptual problem
[sic]." It demurred, however, from praising the *Maclean's* survey,
preferring to see the responsibility for accountability reside in
universities' boards of governors. The resulting report particularly
criticizes the "omnibus methodology" of comparative indicators.
Systems of education across Canada, it reads, vary too much in
organization, in interfacing with schools and colleges, in funding
and in cultural and social expectations to permit national indicators to be used. "Accountability by comparison," the task force
believes, only produces the appearance of accountability. The
alternative is self-assessment. "Quality, performance, and responsiveness should in many respects be measured against institutional mission instead of against a presumed and unavoidably
artificial "typical" or "average" institutional model."[4] The task
force accents especially how important it is for individual universities to assess quality *themselves*: "Of all the areas in which universities are held accountable, quality is the one that requires the
least external stimulus. Universities are naturally concerned about
quality."[5] Yet examination of the model of accountability the task
force proposes, and whose cardinal features are then elaborated
in the AUCC's primer, may lead us to hesitate whether this
response to the call for more qualitative assessment is anything
more than another round of self-applause.

The task force's proposal consists of two parts. The first is a
plea to expand the term "accountability" from its strict definition as conformity to regulations governing the use of public
funding to mean responsiveness to constituent groups in
broader society. It would see, in a way the *Maclean's* survey did
not, excellence measured by responsiveness to the public
demand for accessibility, diversity of students and staff, linking

of curriculum with other educational sectors, and public access to university facilities and resources. The task force's recommendation is startling. To date, accountability has been restricted to demonstration of quality of faculty and programs, usually through peer and professional assessment. The task force would now have accountability include how social policy is fulfilled. The threat this poses to the principle of nonpartisan liberal education, and its reduction of the scholarly culture to the task of brokering social interests, seem not to have been considered by the task force. But the report goes further.

Breaking from tradition and practice, the task force supports the trend that sees "ultimate responsibility" for an institution reside in a board of governors that monitors the universities' adoption of objectives set by outside political appointees. For the majority of universities that have bicameral governing boards— an academic senate and a community-based board of governors— this recommendation is not palatable. Technically, decisions regarding academic content of courses or programs, admission and graduation requirements or qualifications for appointment to academic staff rest with senate; the board of governors, by contrast, maintains responsibility for financial planning and the fit between established policies and mission statement objectives. The task force's slant on university governance shifts this division of labour so that it becomes the board's responsibility to oversee the regular review of academic programs. The concern expressed by many academics is that this reallocation of authority risks politicizing key aspects of the scholarly culture, especially when the government of the day controls the composition of boards of governors through orders-in-council. (This control permits the political party in power to designate those members of society at large who will serve its partisan agenda.)

"Accountability," in this state of affairs, becomes little more than the means to bring universities more under the direction of government, because representatives of the academic community on boards of governors are deliberately kept in a minority. The task force, however, is highly alert to this danger and even issues an indirect warning to governments. It suggests that governing board members must be willing to express their commitment to the "broad interests" of the university. Secondly, it asks that members "exercise the care, diligence and skill that a reasonably prudent person would exercise in comparable circumstances." These reasonable demands, if they could be practicably implemented (an arm's-length academic council that reviews order-in-council appointment recommendations?), might thwart the danger academics fear. It remains a question, however, whether the rest of the document does not in any event erode the very possibility of commitment to "broad interests" and "prudent" judgment.

The second part of the task force's proposal is to adopt a model of input-output analysis. The bulk of the report is an elaboration of how inputs (faculty/student ratios, class size, unit costs) and outputs (graduation and attrition rates, income of graduates, research grants awarded faculty) can be measured. Not wholly unlike *Maclean's*, the report recommends looking at library resources per student, percentage of students holding scholarly awards, percentage of faculty with doctorates, balance of full- and part-time instruction, instructional load and allocation of resources, to assess the quality of undergraduate programs.[6] But unlike *Maclean's*, the success is to be gauged by the efficiency ratio of inputs to outcomes with respect to the university's own mission statement. The proposal is vulnerable to criticism on two counts: the value of input-output models and the value of self-referential assessment.

The periodic recirculation of previously debunked methods and theories is one of the most curious facets of the academic world. Unbelievable as it may appear, from time to time sociologists or business studies researchers adopt a school of inquiry and blithely proceed in the use of its models, apparently ignorant of a critical mass of scholarly rebuttal that sidelined that particular school—often decades before. The historical amnesia can only be explained by the fact that today's scholarly culture is perilously fragmented. A case in point is the use of input-output models. In the 1970s David Easton took a method of inquiry that was in general use in the natural sciences—systems theory—and formalized it so that it could be used to analyze political systems. For over ten years, mainstream political science journals were monopolized by systems analysis research. Then came a sustained and utterly debilitating critique of the approach, and now, fortunately, systems analysis has, in great part, been retired. There were good reasons for this.

Systems analysis takes apparently isolated phenomena and renders them into manageable units of analysis. Discrete phenomena—voting, institutional continuity, revolutions, leadership campaigns—are taken to form an environment comprised of inputs, responses, outputs and feedback. The environment is viewed as a system that can be measured in terms of its capacity to persist in the face of stress, its ability to maintain equilibrium, and its responsiveness and adaptability. A university, according to Easton's analysis of political systems, would not differ from a factory whose task is to take in raw materials and convert them into finished products. University administrators retain support and the power to convert demands into decisions by ensuring that the outputs satisfy the demands of society. They also socialize the university community so that it sees the allocation of resources as legitimate and the outputs as authoritative. When demands become excessive or support insufficient, no conversion into decisions can occur. This leads to output failure and finally to a drop in support. The major source of output failure, Easton determined, is cleavage—when internal dissension in the system divides authority and no possibility of output resolution seems available. The only answer to the disequilibrium is reconstruction: reshaping conditions and creatively adapting to the new circumstances. The feedback loop, like a thermostat, triggers this adaptive behaviour.

Today's latter-day Eastonites could learn a great deal from the late 1970s rejection of input-output models. The limitations and errors of Easton's model are many. Systems theory derives from mechanistic models of analysis that attempt to avoid any reference to causes, principles or purposes that are not quantifiable.

It ignores the soul of human institutions—the creative and intellectual passion that keeps them in motion. It explains events as if everything should be in equilibrium, rather than recognizing the irreducible persistence and value of diversity and even dissent. It claims that a system is a system is a system and fails to discriminate between politics, data management, home heating and digestion.

Even in the nineteenth century, mechanical models of analysis were under attack because they reduced reality to quantities, and the late decades of that century saw a burst of "vitalistic" models surfacing. Neither the mechanistic nor the vitalistic approach may be highly illuminating, since the former neglects the poetic aspect of life in its belief that all things can be mathematized, while the latter abandons all hope that the world can be ordered through reason, leaving us with mere awe before the predicaments that arise in our lives. The mechanical model, however, especially when applied to the university, is the more corrosive. It makes the faulty assumption that statistical data are the chief or only basis for a rational assessment of the scholarly culture.[7] Easton sees culture as a "black box" of values and processes that cannot be explained. What happens in the black box is perceived simply as conforming or reactive behaviour aroused by the need to ensure organizational stability.

There are two major flaws in these assumptions. The first is the problem that the model applies a wide range of data to individual cases. As I discussed in Chapter 2, the reality is that the scholarly culture is a continuous adventure undertaken in response to unpredictable conditions. Such adventures are marked by individual acts of freedom and reason that have no statistical significance. They are often acts that lead to the renewal of scholarship and to wholly new paths of discovery, disturbing the equilibrium and upsetting the prevailing authoritative set of values. Aggregate behaviour can tell us nothing about the singularity of these acts, yet what is the essence of the scholarly culture but these acts? The second problem is that while there can be no certainty about values, the engagements within the black box are coherent and intelligible (otherwise why would anyone be seriously entertaining them?) but only because they are supported by the idea that in principle, transcendent insight is possible. To push the contents of the black box into a category "values" (read: subjective, unanalyzable and arbitrary) is to miss what university education really is and to abandon the possibility of rationally guiding it. Indeed, the most important facets of the scholarly culture occur in the "black box": reading, conversations over contested perceptions of reality, the formation of civic virtues and leadership aptitude, the development of reasoned opinions and coherent desires, the maturation of judgment and personal responsibility. In the black box are true "broad interests" and opportunities for forming the genuine virtues of the "prudent person," rather than the sham surrogates of shrewdness and appeasing university pressure groups. The black box, not the measurable inputs and outputs, is what the university is all about.

It is increasingly questionable whether many academics and external observers are aware of these meanings and purposes of the university. The growing moral bankruptcy of the institution and the fact that there is no sound leadership either inside or outside the university can be seen, to cite one example, in the response to the news that one instructor at Ryerson Polytechnic University, Gerald Hannon, was a self-professed "male prostitute" and advocate of "intergenerational sex" (paedophilia by another name).

The day after the announcement, the *Globe and Mail* editorial read, "There is nothing unlawful about either his avocation ('escort' prostitution is legal in Canada) or the expression of his opinions (which is protected under the Charter of Rights and Freedoms)."[8] The editorialist continued by asserting that "Mr. Hannon is a man of ethics," that there is no connection between a man's "private life" and his "public accomplishments," and concluded with the insinuation that if "anyone should be 'hounded' out of the classroom, it should be those academics who purchased Mr. Hannon's services." There appears to be a moral vacuum here. Mr. Hannon explained in an interview with the *Toronto Star* that his prostitution was the source of "resourceful experiences." The choice of words was apt, for to speak of others and oneself as a "resource"—as available for pleasure and convenience to others—Hannon admits that human dignity is a good not beyond bargaining. A week later Hannon would add, "I enjoy being a prostitute... I sell my brain for educational services so I can't see why I can't sell my body for sexual ones."[9] Can anyone actually believe that a person's private life, and a character informed by a commodity view of sexuality that approves of the use of children for personal satisfaction, has no impact on their public role? The same *Globe and Mail* editorialist said nothing to defend Matin Yaqzan, who was suspended after remarking that women who visit men's bedrooms imply assent to date-rape. The Writers' Union of Canada and the university faculty associations (who made identical defences of Hannon's freedom of expression) also made no comment. In the wake of Yaqzan's suspension, in words that ring as true in the Hannon case, lone voices in the wilderness were left to utter what public leaders and professional university organizations did not: "Yaqzan's comments serve to destroy civilized life and for that reason, and only for that reason, deserve censure. His view justifies exploitation, degradation, and deception-within-a-context-of-intimacy. Civilized human society is not possible unless there is trust and trustworthiness, and if trust is to be found, it is in our most personal relationships that we will find it."[10]

As long as we ignore the "black box" and limit the assessment of the value of academics and the university culture to a model of accountability that sees the university primarily as "investments in, information and skills out," Canada's universities will continue to deteriorate and lose their relevance to the world. A sound model of accountability would be one that is capable of registering a university's capacity to offer an intellectual and moral vision that speaks of goods beyond bargaining and inconvenience. Not everything in life is negotiable. Gerald Hannon stated publicly that there was no difference between child sex rings and organized hockey. Many would beg to differ. By some obscure "value-free" and structural reading, the two may bear some similarity. But by the standards of common sense and human decency, there is a great *moral* difference. The university, properly understood, draws its moral and intellectual authority from its capacity to maintain criteria of preferment that stand above and inform society at large.

While the university is not a "system," it can be perceived as one, and effects can be generated by tinkering in such a way that its behaviour starts to conform to system activity. This will happen if the universities adopt the recommendations the AUCC offered in its 1995 primer on performance indicators. Citing approvingly the OECD's 1973 report Indicators of Performance of Educational Systems, the primer reads: "The most complex problem is not the calculation of valid indicators but the classification of concepts" and "The key policy questions have turned from 'how many?' and 'how much?' to 'how good?'"[11] With such statements one might expect the AUCC to continue by explaining what constitutes quality education and to justify why university education in particular must be precise and definite. Instead, it offers more of the same: an input-process-output model that sifts through all the statistical data: income levels of graduates, employment rates, publication numbers, time to completion, cost-per-student, test scores, size of staff and proportion of tenured staff. Then it adds what the task force also recommended—namely, responsiveness to social policy, such as representation of women and ethnic groups in the faculty and student body. Though the words "quality," "goodness," and "excellence," appear throughout, the primer suffers from the inability to differentiate university education from vocational training and the implementation of social policy. Furthermore, it claims to speak for what the "public" and students allegedly want.

The AUCC primer sides with prevailing views about the university as an "engine of growth": "University education is recognized as a strategic, human resource investment which should contribute to building a knowledgeable, creative, innovative and advanced labour force—capable of succeeding in global competition and generating economic growth in Canadian society."[12] Like numerous politicians, government officials, "partners" of the university community and the media, the primer claims that the university is not up to scratch: "[D]espite the high level of overall satisfaction with universities revealed by opinion polls, there has been growing public and government disenchantment with university education in terms of standards, quality, employability and skills of graduates."[13] And finally, apparently approvingly, the AUCC primer adds that "university education has become mass education. Removed from the exclusivity and elitism of the past, universities are now more prone to be held up to common yardsticks...." One may legitimately ask whose interests the AUCC is truly serving.

While this appears to be a manifest sellout of the scholarly culture, the primer could perhaps be interpreted more generously. After all, the history of university-government relations since the mid-1960s is one of proliferating regulatory bodies and accountability schemes designed by the universities themselves, or associations representing the interests of the universities, to forestall direct control by government. The 1968 Hurtubise and Rowat Commission on the Relations between Universities and Governments was a shrewd assessment of the universities' need to band together, even at the cost of institutional autonomy, to "develop a central machinery before the government develops its own."[14] The Ontario Council on Graduate Studies, which regulates all graduate programs and has the power to prevent the funding of new ones, was the mid-sixties product of a warning from Bill Davis, then Ontario's minister of university affairs: "You regulate yourselves, or we will regulate you." The 1966 proposal of the Spinks Commission for a University of Ontario to regulate all Ontario universities through a "master plan," though it was not implemented, was intended to pre-empt direct political control. Buffer agencies like Saskatchewan's and Alberta's universities commissions, the Universities Council of British Columbia and the Ontario Council of University Affairs were all formed to stem political interference and bureaucratic control. The new call for undergraduate review processes and demands for accountability and performance indicators could be seen as having the same strategic value of proactive, rather than reactive, response.

The primer reflects the approach of Bill Spady, America's prominent spokesman for "outcomes-based education": "It's a matter of what they can do when they exit the system," he writes. The test of good education is a student's ability in "doing life." In the Ontario Ministry of Education's recent implementation of outcomes-based education in the high schools, "doing life" meant acquiring the "values, skills, and knowledge required for success in a rapidly changing world."[15] Echoing three decades of the same refrain about the irrelevance of "traditional education," the ministry claimed: "Facts change; information expands; concepts are the constant." The construct of the world that underlies such pronouncements is one that starts with the integrating global environment. No one has questioned whether the world's growing interdependence is either necessary or good: the ministry has merely scrambled to come up with a way of conforming to the phenomenon.

Even though the accountability and performance indicator models miss the mark, there are those who stand to profit from them: accountability has served well faculty who have channelled their ambitions into university administration rather than community service. Committee work, vice-presidencies and deanships have come more and more to replace community involvement. Through community service, dedicated engineers, architects and specialists in English as a second language could translate their research into implementable projects, justifying the public's trust in the funding that goes to the university, while also providing a reality check on research. Service could also mean work in professional associations, such as the history association or art galleries and performance groups.

Now, however, academics are spending more time on the internal administration of the university. Pumped up by the demand for accountability, service on committees or service as any one of the 280 supernumerary vice-presidencies available across Canada (the prize goes to York University and the University of British Columbia, each with thirteen) have replaced community work. There are currently approximately 2,200 faculty in Canada without teaching responsibilities, or with significantly diminished teaching responsibility, "serving" the university. They are paid upwards of $100,000 a year to monitor the accountability of the university.

Whatever else accountability serves, indisputably it offers ample opportunity for government bureaucrats to micromanage the scholarly culture. Not surprisingly, a growing chill therefore characterizes university-government relations. One of the surprises in the 1991 report of Stuart Smith's Commission of Inquiry was the hostility towards universities he met with from senior civil servants and ministers: "The consensus was that universities have not kept up with changing societal demands, have not remained relevant and are either unwilling or unable to change. The words most frequently used to describe them were 'remote,' 'isolated,' 'elitist,' 'arrogant,' and 'naive.'"[16] The history of university-government chill has been told better by others and many more such narratives will undoubtedly be written in the future.[17] For our purposes, I will refer to just three expressions of that chill that illustrate zero tolerance and hot-button politicking: the control of boards of governors, the support of college militancy and the new "Pan-Canadian Protocol on Transferability of University Credits."

Government's power to use its funding stick to fulfill its own ideological purposes is in direct proportion to the increasing level of public funding of universities. Even where universities were successful in forming protection agencies to buffer direct government intervention, these commissions have become bully-boys for the party of the day (the Ontario Council of University Affairs under Bob Rae's NDP government was one such commission). Or, as in the case of Alberta's and Saskatchewan's universities commissions, or the Universities Council of British

Columbia, when these bodies became too independent of government will, they were abolished. Now that they have got their backs up over a history of encroachment and refusal to collaborate, both universities and governments are sniffling over trifles—to the shame of both. Universities in Ontario and Quebec have closed ranks about the disclosure of senior administrative salaries. Despite media and union pressure, MP Chris Stockwell's private member's bill calling for transparency, and the obsessiveness of the Ontario provincial auditor and the Public Accounts Committee on this issue, the resistance has been unrelenting. Peter George, former president of the Council of Ontario Universities, put the matter bluntly: as long as the Ontario Hospital Association and the Crown corporations did not release their senior administrators' salaries, the universities would remain mum. All that the universities are hiding are benefits of approximately $150,000 to $175,000 and a modest array of perquisites, drastically lower than the benefit packages of their executive counterparts in the private and public sector.

Universities have exhibited similar bull-headed resistance to the demand for "in-camera" university board meetings. While the demand may appear to university officials as a form of meddling, what is saved by acting as if there is something to hide? Anyone who sits through a numbing four-hour session of senate or board of governors meetings would soon lose their idle curiosity. The demand for in-camera transparency of university board meetings would vanish as quickly as the request for in-camera court trials.

The University of Manitoba's faculty strike over the government's desire to have program redundancy and fiscal stringency clauses included in their collective agreement exhibits a shameless arrogance—especially since 85 percent of existing collective agreements in Canada's universities already include the clauses. Universities' reluctance to relinquish a single graduate program, despite massive duplication (especially within cities that have two universities), arises from the mentality born in the 1960s when graduate programs were proliferating wildly. Then the prevalent view was that every department worth its intellectual salt had to have graduate studies—an academic argument that masks the reality of status seeking and higher funding opportunities. No university departments, and few faculty deans, are now willing to rein in their *amour-propre* or greed.

Governments, for their part, have been no less intractable and parsimonious. They have advocated new universities as engines of regional development—for instance, the proposed new university in Lévis, Quebec—despite the academic folly of such an enterprise. Provincial governments have tried to exclude the university sector from critical consultations. In late May 1995 in Montreal at the First National Consultation on Education, there would not even have been CAUT representatives had it not been for the CAUT's lobbying. (Representatives of the federal government were also not invited.) The Ontario government has shifted its funding to universities from "block grants" (unconditional funding) to "funding envelopes" (conditional funding tied to the university's ability to achieve political objectives). Provincial governments have made it evident that their priorities do not lie with universities. For example, when Ontario's new education minister, John Snobelen, announced that Grade 13 would be phased out, he indicated that any resulting savings would be directed to more vocational training and community colleges. In 1991 the Science Council of Canada tried to interfere with the objective canons of knowledge when it called for "culturally appropriate" science and technology for northerners who see mainstream science as a "foreign body of knowledge, with little relevance to the realities of community life."

Governments have abolished separate ministries of university affairs, placing university education under the supervision of superministries. British Columbia's "Ministry of Skills, Training, and Labour" is a hybrid of the advanced education and labour portfolios; Ontario has merged education, colleges and universities, skills development and the Ontario Training and Adjustment Board to form the "Ministry of Education and Training"; Alberta has set up a "Ministry of Advanced Education and Career Development."

But nowhere is government intervention so clear as in its drive to control the composition of university boards. The experience of Ontario's universities at the hands of their provincial government is a case in point. In the spring of 1992, in an echo of the Los Angeles riots over the police beating of Rodney King, Toronto's Yonge Street fell subject to looting and vandalism. Government response was swift. A few hours later, Stephen Lewis, former Ontario NDP leader who is known to be sympathetic to special interest groups opposed to government, was appointed as "Advisor on Race Relations" and asked for an analysis of what came to be called the "Yonge Street Riot." With the guidance of Gerry Caplan, NDP party strategist, and deeply affected by the anger of the Black Action Defense Committee, Lewis began his report by writing: "First, what we are dealing with, at root, and fundamentally, is anti-Black racism. While it is obviously true that every visible minority community experiences the indignities and wounds of systemic discrimination, throughout Southern Ontario, it is the Black community which is the focus." Lewis went on to say that "[t]here is a great deal of anger, anxiety, frustration and impatience amongst those with whom I talked in the visible minority communities" and he concluded with the statement: "It means, I think, that government initiatives must come soon, and they must be pretty fundamental."[18] What followed this call to action was a series of recommendations focusing on the education sector for equity policies, antiracism education and quota admissions. While everything should have been done to verify the truth of the allegations made by the black community, and the plan for antiracist education implemented if the allegations of widespread racism were true, no corroboration or further testimony was sought. Instead, the schools and universities were singled out to be the object of immediate bureaucratic action. The universities, Lewis said, would now have to re-examine their governance and see if it conformed to the antiracist campaign he intended Ontario to adopt. Instead of looking at the more refined ways in which the scholarly culture ensures that its members respect one another's dignity, the government chose a narrow representation model and an additional layer of bureaucracy to achieve its ends.

The order to comply came from Richard Allen, then minister of colleges and universities. Henceforth, there was to be an increase of external constituents directing the university, and university boards of governors were expected to be "representative" of "Ontario's changed society." Allen provided an "appointment protocol" to ensure gender balance and representation with respect to linguistic and ethnocultural differences. The government of the day, through lieutenant-governor-in-council appointees, could appoint as much as one-sixth of the total membership of the body. On a typical board of forty members, only three needed to be faculty members, and these might easily all be senior academic administrators.[19] It was not surprising that faculty—those in the trenches teaching, researching and serving the community—were outraged.

They were aggrieved partly because anyone with experience on such rainbow boards has learned quickly how easily university policy comes to reflect less a commitment to excellence than a hybrid of grievances. The directive therefore serves no constituency well. While some aspects of education are sensibly guided by public will and by the moral leadership of politicians, this guidance politicizes education when it is based on quotas or considered to be more relevant than prevailing scholarship. The public relations of government action is generally poorly managed, with the result that universities become dogmatic and governments become obstructionist. Throughout 1994 and 1995 the Nova Scotia Council on Higher Education and its chair Janet Halliwell made a typically bureaucratic bid to re-engineer the university system: a central university clearing house, the University of Halifax, where the provincial government would name all members of the university's governing board. It is unfortunate that in this and other government measures, officials have failed to see that more is at stake than successful political rule by brokering interest groups and setting priorities by the level of expenditures.

The second expression of university-government chill grows out of a rising college militancy over status and funding, and government's indulgence of that militancy even (or especially) when it comes at cost to the universities. Although that militancy is particularly pronounced in Ontario, the emergence of more and more "university colleges" in Canada, particularly in the West, disguises what is in reality a complex war of politics between universities and colleges fuelled by government intrusion.[20] Ever since the Thatcher era, British governments have been steadily converting polytechnics into universities. In the United States, this conversion is not taking place—partly because in America's largely private postsecondary sector, no public funding rewards follow from such conversion, and partly because the word "college" in America implies no diminution of status. In fact, American liberal arts "colleges" have zealously guarded their institutional designation, in order to distinguish themselves by excellence in *teaching*, rather than in *research*, which is paramount at "universities."

In Canada, we have taken our own tack, partly following the British conversion scheme and partly designing a new hybrid, the "university-college." It is a sign of confusion about where we are heading in Canada that hardly anyone refers any longer to a sector of "higher learning." All education after high school is "postsecondary," and debate increasingly is restricted to whether a binary postsecondary system is the most effective, as if the difference between college and university were only a matter of degree.

In one sense, it *is* actually a matter of degree. Universities grant degrees, colleges do not. Colleges, however, are no longer satisfied with granting certificates and licentiates; they now wish to confer Associate of Arts and Bachelor of Technology degrees. The colleges' relentless push to be given degree-granting privileges is characteristic of these institutions' hankering after status. Government's tentative, but evident, responsiveness to this demand reveals how corrosive credentialism has become in today's society where the difference between vocational training and the scholarly culture is apparently not appreciated by the new superministers.

Status is an important part of the game for designation, but there are other more potent reasons for college militancy. When Ryerson was converted to a full-fledged university, its grants for the next six years were increased by $18 million, and it was given the opportunity to develop a graduate program. As then president Terence Grier said, "We're already doing the kinds of things that a lot of the universities do, so we should be up on the same playing field."[21] Ryerson also acquired a university charter that grants it the full powers of autonomy enjoyed by other universities—to the envy of the province's colleges which are tightly regulated by the Council of Regents. Ryerson also now has the power to grant its faculty tenure, a privilege that colleges do not enjoy.

What Ryerson does not have, however, despite its unassailable record of superlative vocational training, is a critical mass of scholars engaged in scholarship. In 1992 the *Toronto Star* reported that five Ryerson faculty went to Hungary to lecture on technology and were awarded "university doctor" degrees by the University of Miskolc for their efforts. Ryerson then included these degrees as doctorates in its submission for university status. Currently, only about 26 percent of Ryerson faculty hold doctorates. A doctorate does not, of course, a scholar make, but Ryerson also does not *require* its faculty to actively engage in scholarly research. There is a difference *in principle* between learning within the scholarly culture and vocational training, between scholarship and research that advances vocational objectives.

The confusion between colleges and universities is, however, widespread. Nova Scotia Council of Higher Education chair Janet Halliwell may enthuse about the meshing of college and university—"The traditional distinctions are blurring between the technical colleges and the liberal arts education. We're going through a fundamental shift in the nature of knowledge and the approach to learning"—but the reality is that the most salient truths of our lives—the meanings we imaginatively create in response to contingent predicaments—are not forged in laboratories or in programs on recreology or building maintenance. Former Ryerson president Terence Grier may believe that "the world of work and society are [sic] calling for a wider range of skills which are more applied than theoretic. That's the main reason for the blurring of the distinction [between institutions]," but his belief does not change the fact that someone has to be thinking about first principles in the natural and social sciences, and about moral and political purposes in the humanities, tasks at which the colleges have not displayed any acute aptitude.[22] Both Halliwell and Grier seem to believe that we are going through a shift in the "nature" of knowledge, whereas common sense should lead them to realize that what we are observing is widescale amnesia. Without research that operates at the level of first principles, we would not have, among other things, the derivative field of applied electronic technology in which Ryerson and the colleges invest so much energy.

Sadly, college militancy for university status is reinforced by many of the activities of the university itself and by the new expectations imposed on them by governments, corporations and the media. While we may praise, for example, University of Waterloo's extensive co-op program, and many universities' increasing number of program partnerships in everything from child care and midwifery to business management studies, the result is to make these universities look increasingly like community colleges. As we create more and more university colleges—like the university-college of Cape Breton, which offers undergraduate degrees with technical diplomas and apprenticeships—we lose what is distinctive about universities.

Governments would like to commit the universities to "life-long learning." One way of doing so would be to follow the advice of Donald Baker, former vice-president, academic of Wilfrid Laurier University: "Life-long learning requires multiple entry points and integrated ladders of educational opportunity for students.... It is enormously wasteful for students to be forced to spend more time and the public more money because universities and/or colleges cannot agree on how to transfer credits or will not cooperate in creating bridges from one institution to the other." If universities follow that advice, they may gain a cost-effective and efficient unitary postsecondary education system (such as the new Seneca College–York University initiative of a college campus at the university) and thaw the relation between colleges and universities, but they will lose its natural and healthy tension.[23]

If universities follow the lead of Stuart Smith in focusing on teaching, then in appearance the difference between colleges and universities vanishes. If we encourage the universities to do more and more remediation, and accept *Globe and Mail* education columnist Jennifer Lewington's admonishment, "Universities haven't done enough, not by a long shot. In fact, universities are part of the problem in education, always pointing the finger of blame at the high school and elementary level," we simply become part of a process of skills-acquisition and become vulnerable to the scrutiny of accountants who consider only efficiency in their evaluation of the universities.[24] Universities are now scrambling to produce "mission statements," but these rarely distinguish them from colleges. We have made no progress from forty-four years ago when the 1951 Massey-Lévesque Commission, commenting on the soul of the university, noted the "neglect and distortion of the humanities."

The low calibre of the education debate in this country is epitomized in the single achievement pertaining to university education for which ministers of education can take credit in the last five years—the new "Pan-Canadian Protocol on Transferability of University Credits."[25] It is the final blow to the universities, ensuring that soon many of them may be little more than glorified community colleges. The protocol establishes a "pan-Canadian" recognition of all undergraduate courses. To be included are all the university transfer courses offered by community colleges and university colleges. In the case of Ontario, the transferability of university credits will be automated, so eventually no "idiosyncratic" local administrator can impede the process. It is true that past practice was inefficient: each university department laboriously scrutinized transcripts and university calendars, and exercised sole discretionary judgment. But it was done with an understanding of the distinct practices and culture of each department and university, and it was performed by someone who was accountable to the faculty for the decision. Academic integrity prevailed over ease of accessibility. The new protocol is a classic example of a growing trend to sacrifice scholarly principle to administrative efficiency, with the accompanying loss of sound judgment and personal responsibility.

Little opposition to the new protocol has been heard. Yet we need to take warning from its logic: that the greater mobility of students and the educational advantages of greater mobility, combined with the fact that individuals are returning to university during their work lives, entails that universities must be more elastic in their accessibility. There is a destiny in the protocol's logic: a future where university and college credits are one and the same. At present the transfer is restricted to university credits, and lip-service is paid to university autonomy in regulating program design and academic prerequisites. But, especially under the force of automation and the persistent enthusiasm of ministers of education for "rationalizing lifelong learning" (as well as the encouragement of individuals like Janet Halliwell and Terence Grier for the partnership of the two institutions), the end result can only be a seamless web between colleges and universities.[26]

What makes these skirmishes all the more potent is the historical context in which they occur. How sentimental and nostalgic it must seem to speak of education as the art of leading forth, to ask "what is worth leading forth?" and to see the universities' vocation defined by debates that address first principles. It must seem naïve to believe that the university must repeatedly ask itself the question: Should the institution focus its resources primarily on channelling the longings of the young, or inculcating social and moral graces, or preparing students for a vocation, or cultivating an historic, aesthetic or objective sense or preparing citizens. How quaint it must seem to believe there are perennial and elementary eternal questions and that it is testimony to the importance of these questions that the university exists as a scholarly culture! Yet without this orientation, the ship is rudderless.

Unfortunately, it is not lack of university leadership and increase in the politicization of the university alone that is leading to the eclipse of the scholarly culture. The world historical drama, with its distinctive constraints and dangers, has also contributed to the universities' demise. The twentieth century, and particularly the last two decades, has been a period of extraordinary transformation, whose scale is perhaps equalled only by the thirteenth-century disintegration of the mediaeval synthesis of papacy and empire, or the sixteenth-century migrations of the Mongols. The late-twentieth-century collapse of an international politics of two empires, the vast growth of a global economy, the re-emergence of ethnic nationalism and religious fundamentalism, spiralling national debt loads and bond-market volatility, the reversals and realignments of significant social movements like feminism and environmentalism, the mobility of political refugees and the labour force in response to political crisis and economic agreements—all these form an angry, dare-all atmosphere that is informing our current deliberation about the future of universities.

This is not the place for an analysis of the state of the world nor of the civilizational crisis into which we are moving. Others—like Leo Strauss, Hannah Arendt, Michael Oakeshott, Francis Fukuyama, Eugene Genovese, Gertrud Himmelfarb and Robert Reich—have offered such analyses of the darkness of our times. Be that as it may, what I do wish to offer are thumbnail sketches of two thoughtful appraisals of the world drama, drawn from the writings of the political theorist Jean Bethke Elshtain and the philosopher George Grant, which identify a pattern to today's vast alterations—namely, the uncanny, but potent, conjunction of two powerful forces: one of fragmentation, the other of homogenization, that should be cancelling one another out but which in fact co-exist and reinforce one another. Ours is a world, as Benjamin Barber explains, where Jihad and McWorld reside side by side, or as the new middle-class adage would have it, we "think global" and "act local."[27]

In her 1992 Massey Lecture "Democracy on Trial," Jean Bethke Elshtain suggested that while the countries of the former Eastern Bloc are struggling to define themselves as democracies, the older, established democracies such as Canada's are faltering. "More and more," she writes, "we confront one another as aggrieved groups, rather than as free citizens."[28] Polarized between vast administrative governments on the one hand and the proliferation of racial, linguistic, gender and ethnic solitudes on the other, each of which has translated its wants into rights, and often in defiance of common civility, our democracies no longer encourage civil public engagement and deliberation. We are also suffering from a waning of our ability to transmit democratic dispositions and dreams to succeeding generations through education.

Above all, Elshtain questions the fragmenting force of identity politics—gender, race and ethnicity—and its resulting political gridlock. The irascibility of this politics is fuelled by the decline of "representative" democracy in favour of populist devices like referenda, plebiscites and even proposals for electronic participation in legislative debates. These political instruments, Elshtain notes, reinforce our role as isolated consumers of political decision making, rather than fostering our virtues as political citizens. The answer to the terrible wars of Bosnia-Herzegovina, the alienation felt by our immigrant populations, the plea for tolerance by many marginalized people, is not to fragment our political community further, and reinforce what Robert Hughes has called our "culture of complaint,"[29] but to revive the attractiveness of political citizenry.

To Elshtain's haunting picture we can add that ours is also an age of unprecedented technological systematization. George

Grant has even suggested that Canada and the rest of the
Western world have become technological societies, arguing that
we are increasingly incapable of conceiving of a life outside of
technological control.[30] We enthusiastically see our future as
one where all facets of our lives are managed and optimalized,
where the interface of ourselves and our machinery is so "user
friendly" that we do not realize how enmeshed we are in its
imperatives: mastery and efficiency at all costs. Technology's
universalizing and homogenizing force leads to situations where
the once isolated Brazilian Yanomamo now sport Sony
Walkmen and Nike sneakers, where knowledge degenerates into
mere information and data, where higher education is made
synonymous with all other forms of learning, and where ranking
of churches, universities or political institutions actually makes
sense to people. It has made our world concomitantly more
available and its mysteries more inaccessible. Our powers to
make and unmake have rid us of many fatal diseases, but we
have also made radioactive waste and unmade the osprey and
the Tasmanian tiger.

Just as important for Grant is the question of whether purposes and goods once revered before our era of technological
management, such as the life of reflective thought or a life of
noble political action, or patience with the simple goodness of
life, have not been displaced in favour of more and more mastery of our human and nonhuman environment. Have we thus
diminished the range of human achievement? One need think
only of how the consumption of technological gadgets has
become a surrogate for intellectual longing for wholeness or religious hope. Finally, Grant cautions, we must ask whether in an
age where everything that is technically possible is in danger of
being considered morally permissible, if principles of justice are
still unconditional limits to governing how we treat each other
as persons worthy of respect, and especially how we treat the
weakest members of society—the unborn, the old and the sick.
Stepping back, even temporarily, from the dynamo of technological growth may lead us to be more spiritually balanced—less

inclined to think all mysteries are problems that can be solved, less bored and inclined to frivolous pastimes, more realistic in our expectations for contentment in life.

Elshtain's and Grant's analyses recognize that we are at a significant threshold of our history. Under the strange alliance of homogenization and fragmentation, the modest and decent middle ground is vanishing. We can add many observations to those of Grant and Elshtain. In the last few years, uncanny events have erupted on our landscape: the Oklahoma bombing, the Waco, Texas, standoff; the middle-class escape to guarded enclaves away from the social realities that generate the Million Man March; the Unabomber raspberry in the face of America; the Oka crisis; the growth of Vancouver and Toronto's inner-city gangs; the crumbling of Canadian support for national political parties; the well-recognized futility of further constitutional negotiation (either America's Equal-Rights-Amendment or Quebec's "distinct society" clause) and the proliferation of the underground economy. These events seem, as a pattern, different from "traditional" acts of opposition, violence and anarchism, because such actions tended still to operate within some general idea of the need for civil society.

The serious question concerns how we should respond to this world transformation. Accountability models and performance indicators reflect the global homogenizing tendency, while the university response of using their own mission statements as benchmarks is related to the social fragmentation that leaves us with many linguistic villages but no national or ecumenical vision. The growing government-university and college-university chills are also the result of exaggerated expectations that reinforce either further homogenization or fragmentation.

One additional pertinent point could be made about the "Pan-Canadian Protocol on Transferability of University Credits"—specifically, its name. Nothing is as persistent in this country as the unease with efforts to design a national education policy. More than ever, "national" is a dirty word, so the preferred term today is "pan-Canadian." What hampers our efforts to instill in university education a passion for excellence is simply turf wars: *provinces* that regulate universities, autonomous *universities, faculties* run like fiefdoms and unassailable *tenured faculty.* If one of the aims of a liberal education is to reunite us at a higher level of our humanity, one might have hoped that at least ministers of education might try to invoke an image of national and institutional unity. "Transferability of university credit" just doesn't seem to make the grade somehow.

As we discuss the future of the university, we must do so realizing that the doctrine and dogma of the past are dead but we must also realize that if we do not acknowledge the losses and deprivals accompanying our global fate—the rise of technological civilization and the evident and widespread alienation of our inner being from the momentum of the external world—we are shortchanging Canada's future generations. That is why Neil Postman's tenet of "teaching as a subversive activity" is an attractive one. We may be moving in the right direction, but it is nonetheless sound for us to repeatedly question and re-examine the premises of our actions, even to the point where we entertain their intellectual subversion. The university is the most obvious place where that questioning should take place. It continues too to be the one place where common sense and respect for human decency have traditionally been fostered, the surest guarantors of the balance we will need in the decades to come.

The squabbling and sabre rattling I have referred to with broad brushstrokes in these last three chapters have generated a rich and multitextured politics, the account of which still needs to be told by someone else. But beneath these specific battles lies a far deeper turbulence about what a university is, and the contenders of this war do not share the idea of the university I have been elaborating. Their projects, even more than those I have chronicled here, arise from the powerful homogenizing and fragmenting forces now realigning our world. The major protagonists in this drama are those who insist that the universities re-engineer themselves or have it done for them.

Chapter 6

The Corporate Right:
Ending "Business as Usual"

*I believe that students at postsecondary institutions have had it
far too good for far too long, and that it is now time to wake
up to the morning of a new economic reality.*

Brian Goehring[1]

"We need to rethink how we do things, not merely do more
of the same," Lloyd Axworthy proposes in "Federal
Support to Post-Secondary Education," his supplement to
Improving Social Security in Canada.[2] What this has meant,
whether the government be left, right or centre, is the massive
adoption of the free-market model. "Market responsiveness" is
the magic word these days, as the era of growing government
expenditures, increasing taxes and expanding deficits ends. The
perception is that universities have been too lavishly subsidized
by taxpayers. Now is the time for the rule of the fiscal hawks
and for taking universities out of the "fool's paradise" they have
been living in for three decades. As the *Globe and Mail*'s editors
keep repeating, "our university system is in need of a renewal, a
structural transformation."[3] The open market, they believe, is
the only true form of accountability. As the corporate right likes
to say, "business as usual" has ended.

A clarification of what I mean by "corporate right" is necessary. What I mean is less a uniform perspective held by private
corporations than a family-resemblance point of view that coa-
lesces out of the opinions of rotarians and chambers of commerce, professional business organizations, recent governments

of both left and right, the media, policy wonks at the Fraser Institute and the C.D. Howe Institute, and many university managers. It includes major players like the Conference Board of Canada and the Canadian Manufacturers' Association, but also the Canadian Association of University Business Officers and more recently the Centre for Quality in Governance and the Canadian Comprehensive Auditing Foundation.[4] It follows from worried attention to the recent World Competitiveness Report that ranks Canada fourteenth out of twenty-three. It is reinforced by Statistics Canada's recent collection of data on the employment of students in their field of study upon graduation, statistics that contribute to the expectation that universities should be responsible for job slotting.

It would be ideologically tiresome to claim that this perspective has derived solely from private corporations, when big businesses such as Magna International Inc., Mutual Life, Quaker Oats, Systemhouse, Motorola and Mouvement Desjardins, to name a few, have been outspoken defenders of the scholarly culture and have backed their statements with financial endorsement.[5] For many faculty and academic administrators the very idea of business interest is anathema to university education. The old bugaboo "university autonomy" is their unrepentant hideaway. I do not share that fear of business. What I mean by the corporate right is the parsimony that is most evident in those who go under the label "neoconservative"—the new "young bucks on the right," as the *Globe and Mail* once referred to them—including Andrew Coyne, David Frum and Bill Robson. I mean also the millennialism one hears from Canadian spokesmen for the management philosophy of Tom Peters and Peter Drucker who would have us believe we are entering a wholly new age—the knowledge-based economy—where education must change and where all the old compass points are ineffectual. But I also include others.

The corporate right embraces those who sit on government commissions like Duff Roblin, chairman of the Manitoba University Education Commission, whose 1994 report told

Education Minister Clayton Manness to spend more money on community colleges and concluded that universities were expensive and poorly managed. Invest in the electronic highway and distance education, raise tuition fees and charge foreign students double, teach more and research less, especially with regard to fields that do not contribute directly to Manitoba society, he added. Clayton Manness continued in kind: "I question whether or not our university community is totally in sync with the daily lives of a lot of Manitobans." Manitoba's three universities, he said, would have to direct their energies to stimulating "a strong understanding of the engines of growth which are so essential to the social fabric and a strong understanding of how they interrelate." Manness concluded by threatening to "close programs, departments, and even whole faculties" if they couldn't demonstrate a practical link to the economic reality, or fit within the restructured network of other social, employment and investment agencies unified in the service of economic development.[6]

From those who head our few national think tanks we hear statements like this one, made in 1993 by the president of the Institute for Research on Public Policy,

> Education is the cornerstone of our economic well-being, and in the current "information age," characterized by rapidly evolving technologies, it has never had a more important role to play. The heart of our wealth is the knowledge and skills of our population. Our economic development, measured both domestically and against the success of our major trading partners internationally, depends to a great degree on our abilities to harness our human resources. In light of the importance of education in a fast-changing global context it is not surprising that many of the assumptions of the past are being questioned.[7]

Editors at the *Globe and Mail* take a similar "bottom-line" approach in their unending jeremiad on university inefficiency:

"the university does not need only quasi-market discipline, it needs full market discipline."

The corporate right includes education columnists who one day are on the left and the next on the right, like Jennifer Lewington. She exhibits her evident intolerance for the universities as she gleefully reports on European governments reducing university funding, targeting research funding and undertaking conditional contracting and regulatory changes giving external constituencies a larger influence. The corporate right also encompasses many others who are telling universities what the public allegedly wants and who are contributing to Canada's hot-button politics. In a recent commentary entitled "Education Is for the Birds Unless It Offers a Good Return on Investment," *Ottawa Citizen* columnist Ken MacQueen offered his opinion that "Education is a commodity.... What doesn't sell any more, are old ideals of education for education's sake."[8] John Cowan offered his strategic advice in *University Manager*, the magazine published by the Canadian Association of University Business Officers: "If you need to reassure your faculty, tell them you don't plan to butcher the sacred cows, but merely to lead them into leaner pastures."[9] As Peter J. George, former president of the Council of Ontario Universities, rightly points out, "none of this has very much to do with the wishes of the public at large."[10]

Nonetheless, the corporate right is pressing the right hot buttons. It is leading Canadians to see education as an expense, rather than an investment. It has elected four governments committed to evolving the university to a price-competitive system with the promise that they will thereby become more accessible, affordable, responsive and accountable. The corporate right, of course, finds itself consistently on the side of the angels. In the new Alberta planned by the Ministry of Advanced Education (set out in its White Paper, "An Agenda for Change,") "learning providers will share performance indicators with students to support more informed choice among learners. Access to learning opportunities will be maximized in response to demand."[11] The vision of the corporate right continues: if students carry more of the cost of education (the thinking goes), they will demand greater efficiencies, as other consumers do. This will drive the real cost of education down. The focus on greater efficiency, moreover, will mean that student and employer expectations will begin to govern postsecondary education. Through "outsourcing" and "modularized curricula," universities will be able to buy courses from the best teachers in the world, all to the benefit of the institution and its students. Everyone wins, no one loses, according to the corporate right.

The wisdom of the corporate right is urged on the universities even by those who represent its interests. Claude Lajeunesse, former head of the Association of Universities and Colleges of Canada, in response to the call for "bottom-line" rationalization, commented: "Being aware of what's around you is not a loss of autonomy. It may be the opposite. It may be the only guarantee to retain your autonomy. Acting like a grown-up sometimes is the best way to have others respect your autonomy."[12] Some, for whom autonomy means more than being given leeway to run the university as a business corporation, might beg to differ.

The Ontario Task Force on University Accountability, to which I referred in the previous chapter, has also contributed to the view that universities must respond to the perception that they are inefficient and are hiding it. "For many outside the institutions, including those in government, universities are very mysterious places. For many inside the university, too much university business is conducted in secret."[13] The university, in other words, was now in the reassurance business, regardless of the cost incurred in fighting the phantoms of "secrecy" and "inefficiency." It is hard to resist the conclusion that the universities' "perception problem" serves many people's interests.

Nonetheless, there is an economic reality that we need to acknowledge. Let me start by getting "just the facts" on the table. There is no escaping the reality of a $520-billion national debt (with some estimates as high as $600 billion), the interest on which alone has made us the puppet of the bond markets.

Currently the interest charges on that debt swallow up 33 percent of government revenues. It is a fact of life that the "mutual fund" of Canadian social assistance—health care, the Canada Pension Plan and unemployment insurance—is putting us on the verge of bankruptcy, as the International Monetary Fund keeps cautioning us. Everywhere the purse strings have to be tightened. Canada spends $53 billion on education—the second-highest per capita ratio in the world. There is no escape from the fact that total expenditures on postsecondary education are now $16 billion annually, of which $11.4 billion is on universities, and that the government share of the total cost of universities is 84 percent. It is a fact that only $1.4 billion of the total expenditures, or 12 percent, comes from tuition fees and that a paltry $270 million is from gifts and nongovernment grants. There can be no pretending that McGill's accumulated deficit of $72 million, or a projected total university deficit of $150 million, is not a matter of public concern. We cannot close our eyes to the fact that student bankruptcies and loan defaults cost the federal government $90 million annually and that total bad student debts now amount to $1.3 billion.

And there is, without question, extravagance and waste in the postsecondary sector. Does Nova Scotia need thirteen degree-granting institutions? Why does the University of Lethbridge have a $450,000 athletic program in addition to its campus recreation program? Does Manitoba need three schools of music and three education faculties? Does nearly every university department, regardless of its strength, need a graduate program when graduate education cost to the public is four times that of undergraduate education? Do university presidents' perquisites make any sense in the current climate of 10-percent-plus tuition fee increases and major cuts to library acquisitions? (Some examples: UBC president David Strangway received a $250,000 interest-free loan to purchase a house on retirement; former University of Montreal rector Gilles Cloutier, it is rumoured, was given a one-dollar membership in the prestigious Laval-sur-le-Lac Golf Club that cost the university $30,000.) Are legions of supernumerary university vice-presidencies justifiable? Is there any excuse for the fervent desire of Quebec Education Minister Jean Garon to build a new university within his riding of Lévis, when the Université du Québec à Rimouski already offers courses in Lévis?

Why are university calendars not "on-line" when up to $60 million is being spent by schools to link up to SchoolNet, and universities, hit by spiralling paper costs, are spending over $3.2 million annually for printed calendars? Why are open admissions of marginal students, and the resulting 50- to 60-percent first-year failure rates, being tolerated when approximately $15,000 of public funds is being expended annually on each of these students? Why are universities expected to shoulder the burden of remediation as a consequence of the shoddy work done by schools in teaching students to read and write, when colleges can do so at much less cost because they do not have to fund research? When research libraries between 1979 and 1989 cut a total of 40,406 journal subscriptions, worth $4.2 million, did any serious consequence follow? As many outsiders and insiders note, tracking university expenses is an elaborate shell game. Amidst the waste there are signals of prudent and responsible leadership: rationalization schemes like University of Toronto's Plan for 2000, which proposed eliminating three-year degrees and many programs not rated among the country's top third, and Saskatchewan's 1992 University Program Review, which recommended that low-enrolment programs be closed and that doctoral programs be offered only where "there are nationally recognized faculty and the appropriate critical mass of scholars and students."[14]

It is also difficult to generate great sympathy, in our current efforts to manage the public debt, for faculty associations at universities like Dalhousie or Manitoba, Mount Allison and Memorial, who have grieved in the face of major cuts and their administrations' demands for greater flexibility to declare financial exigency and program redundancies, to employ sessional instructors and to increase workloads. Incredulous disbelief is the only response to the lament of Ontario faculty associations over the recent repeal of the former NDP's Bill 40—a bill that conferred vast power on unions to control governance and arbitration. It is pathetic to observe those who have become weakhearted at the prospect of 25 percent cuts in library acquisitions, when about that proportion of library holdings is "research" that has done little more than pad faculty résumés. Objections to library spending cuts are also curious, in view of the fact that, despite endless incentives, faculty persistently hold out against using an electronic technology that would make the libraries of the world and international scholars readily available to them. Public funding has sapped the universities of entrepreneurial spirit, and while university development offices complain of the stinginess of Canadian private philanthropy and the unfavourable tax laws on charitable giving, until recently the universities had no incentive to pursue private or corporate donors.[15]

Today's squeeze on finances results directly from the indiscriminate expansion of the 1960s, and the blame should fall on those who governed in the period from the sixties to the eighties. Lavish governments like those of John Robarts and Bill Davis, Peter Lougheed and Don Getty, presided over the great increases in universities and graduate programs, and followed the bad advice of the day: invest more and more in education, this will drive the engines of economic growth and wealth creation; the faster the economy grows, the more you can invest in universities. Indiscriminate expansion, through a proliferation of graduate schools, courses of study reflecting the trend *du jour* and specialized centres and institutes, came at the cost of unity and coherence in the university curriculum as a whole, and brought widespread program duplication. In many cases, expression of interest alone was sufficient to spawn new departments and degree programs. Such extravagance paradoxically fit the mood of many 1960s faculty who, gripped by the manifestos of revolution they found in Herbert Marcuse, Wilhelm Reich, Theodor Roszak, Paulo Freire and Erich Fromm, saw little point to traditional defences of the university either. Through their efforts, the intellectual and spiritual substance of the university was depleted.

David M. Cameron says that the "crisis" in the universities arose from the contradiction between government's sponsorship of burgeoning enrolments and demand for services during the sixties and seventies and the simultaneous drop in government funding.[16] He is right in identifying this contradiction as the source of the crisis. What he neglects to admit is that if the universities had not been flush with money and exaggerated expectations, they would have survived the government's reduction of resources much better. But universities hoped against hope that the abundant public trough would continue into perpetuity. Now what we have in this country is a corporate right, which with some justice sees itself as having a huge inefficient, nationalized industry on its hands, and it is, again with some reason, shouting, "Sell! Sell!"

The glory days of government funding were the fifties and sixties, after the Massey Commission recommended that the federal government give direct grants to universities for operating costs. In 1967, direct grants were replaced by a cost-sharing program with the provincial governments, although the federal government continued to cover 50 percent of the costs of postsecondary education. The new arrangement gave provinces more muscle in what was, after all, their own jurisdiction, and many pursued growth aggressively. But the switch came at a cost—the beginning of an erosion of federal power to act for the national interest. The retreat of the federal government was particularly evident in the Established Programs Financing (EPF) instituted in 1977, a federal-provincial financial agreement involving a block transfer to the provinces to be used for postsecondary education and health care, and the Canada Assistance Plan (CAP), targeted for social assistance. Federal transfers under the EPF were now no longer directly linked to the costs of postsecondary education. Other changes occurred: per capita payments were equalized, and the federal grant evolved into a mixture of cash and "tax points" rather than solely money.

The new arrangement was highly satisfactory to the provinces. The "tax points" are a good example. Given to the provinces as a right to use more of the income tax collected, tax points swelled as provincial economies grew—providing additional provincial revenue of about $3.8 billion annually. Today, as provinces haggle over the level of federal funding, they have greedily decided that since these tax points do not constitute a "direct transfer," they should not be considered part of the federal contribution to postsecondary education.

Tax points thus became an unconditional transfer that gave provinces fiscal flexibility in spending on health and postsecondary education. It also had the effect of diminishing the provinces' incentive to spend on postsecondary education. By 1985, for example, the share of five provinces' funding of postsecondary education was less than that of the federal government. In Alberta and Nova Scotia, the funds were apparently used for deficit reduction. Ontario made plans for a two-tiered university system. Manitoba, Alberta and Prince Edward Island began discussing program and university closure and differential fees for out-of-province students. The anticipated savings were to be diverted to other areas, such as health and social assistance. The effective power to ensure national standards was significantly eroding. Moreover, the federal government realized that under the existing EPF arrangement, it was getting little credit for postsecondary transfer payments, although it was subsidizing postsecondary education to the tune of $8 billion annually (half the cost), $2.6 billion of which was cash transfers.

Finally, conservative financial projections disclosed that the EPF was due to run out within the next decade. A series of task forces and commissions toyed with a system of user-fee-like voucher funding and with federal withdrawal from postsecondary subsidies. With attention turning to the growing costs of the national debt, federal support through per capita transfers began to decline dramatically in the late 1980s, and universities calculated that they were losing as much as $1.6 billion over the five-year period leading up to 1991. The squeeze on operating grants was the most evident sign of the new austerity. The response of university presidents accustomed to the availability of public funds was characteristic: "Who's going to fill the gap?" asked John Stubbs, president of Simon Fraser University, in all earnestness.

Bad news for the universities was evident already in the 1994 federal Liberal budget. The Liberal *Red Book* had assured the public that deficit reduction would be gradual and linked to job growth, but the February budget outlined sweeping cuts of $13.4 billion in two years. In broad brush strokes it outlined the need for rethinking federal transfers and hinted at the government's intention of downloading the national debt onto the provinces. Provinces would have greater flexibility in the distribution of federal funds, but they would also receive much less. Provincial response was fiery and predictable. Ontario's former NDP premier, Bob Rae, said it was a "savage blow" and that Ontario had been "kneecapped" and shortchanged by $3 billion; he lamented that plans for daycare and welfare reform would have to be shelved. In March a process of whirlwind hearings with the public began. Axworthy took to the road, talking about "national prosperity" being tied to a "learning culture" and the imperative of "accessibility of those traditionally underrepresented." The "new economy" would be "knowledge intensive." James Downey, president of the University of Waterloo, pointing to the evidently perplexing message emerging from government—produce greater accessibility and quality, yet do it with declining funds—commented "the government has to be prepared to go further than saying, 'We will reshuffle the deck.'"[17]

The government did intend to go further. Rumours circulated, which Lloyd Axworthy did not deny, that the $2.6 billion cash in unconditional block grants to the postsecondary sector would be cancelled and replaced by a loan program. The specific targets of the cuts and savings, though, were kept under wraps, and the Liberal government revealed that they would not be announced until the 1995 budget, after a process of parliamentary committee consultations with the public. Days before the release of the preliminary draft of Axworthy's report, however, the *Toronto Star* published a leaked briefing note from the Treasury Board indicating that, though unannounced in the February budget, the government planned to cut an additional $7.5 billion over the next five years. The briefing note also revealed the "rapid and complete phase-out" of federal transfers to the provinces for education and confirmed the suspicion that tuition fees would double by 1997. There were scheduled cuts to the Canada Assistance Plan, of $500 million in 1995/96, $900 million in 1996/97 and $1.1 billion in 1997/98. The briefing paper, not surprisingly, cautioned silence: "Axworthy and Martin have agreed that neither the Social Policy Review paper nor the Fiscal and Economic Update will make these new targets public."[18] The pledge of secrecy notwithstanding, "the truth will out," as "gotcha" journalists like to say. The public had the facts before the long-awaited Green Paper was released.

Improving Social Security in Canada, the Ministry of Human Resources Development's Green Paper, set out the program for reform of employment, education and social assistance within the central theme of "how to improve opportunity and access to jobs for Canadians." A supplementary document entitled "Federal Support to Post-Secondary Education" spelled out the government's mandate.[19] In that document, postsecondary education was recognized as a "vital component" to "the success of the individual in the labour market and to the overall development of the Canadian economy."[20] It identified universities and colleges as the "principal means" of preparation for the labour market and as the source of new knowledge and employment skills. The elimination of the cash transfer, in favour of an income-contingent loan program, was confirmed. A tuition increase of $2 billion was built into the plans for reform. When questioned by the Association of Universities and Colleges of Canada, Axworthy admitted that fees might rise by $2,000 per student. But he also argued that in light of the cash transfer fund's imminent depletion, his new plan of a five-year experiment with an income-contingent loan plan would actually inject an additional $10 billion into the postsecondary sector. The AUCC, questioning the claim that the cash transfer fund was running out, asserted that the projected depletion of the fund was a political decision and that there was nothing inevitable about it. The Liberals, the AUCC claimed, had merely decided to cap the Established Programs Funding. When the auditor general announced that the Axworthy proposal for savings from the postsecondary education sector would lop $1.5 billion a year off the deficit, the worst suspicions about how and upon whom the deficit was being shifted were confirmed.

Not surprisingly, students were the constituency most agitated by the news. The point was not lost on them that the $10 billion proposed injection into the postsecondary sector would come in the form of their debts. In November 12,000 students protested over the prospect of increased tuition fees and pelted Axworthy with macaroni. In a bellicose mood, the Canadian Federation of Students warned the commons committee of the consequences of high student debt loads: "We can safely predict a grim future for the state of the housing market."[21] On the road, Axworthy retorted with figures revealing that students were contributing only 12 percent to the $16 billion annual budget for postsecondary education. He taunted them for their "what's okay for me" mentality and their exaggerated claims of what he was doing to them, called them "pampered and privileged" and wondered why 80 percent of the population should carry the burden of the 20 percent at university. The New Brunswick Student Alliance responded in kind: "If our generation has to pay, why not your generation?" and proposed a tax on all graduates, past and present.[22] The Canadian Federation of Students persistently returned to the contradiction between the commitment to lifelong learning and the slashing of funding, and found an ally in the president of the University of Toronto. On November 30, Robert Prichard said to the travelling House of Commons committee that the plans would "betray an entire generation of Canadians"[23] and jeopardize the country's research capacity.

December was worse for Axworthy. The International Socialists held a spirited macaroni-eating demonstration in front of Axworthy's house.[24] Placards read, "Is Education Axe-Worthy?" Sharp words were exchanged between Axworthy and Ontario's Minister of Education, David Cooke. On December 8, Cooke, reacting to Axworthy's figures, declared that Ontario's loss would be $700 million. Ontario universities, he warned, would have to be mothballed, illustrating that the cuts reflected the combined support for the University of Toronto, York University and the University of Ottawa, or 90 percent of support to Ontario's community colleges. The proposed increases in tuition fees, Cooke added, would "irreparably damage" post-secondary education in Ontario. Axworthy angrily retorted that Cooke's response was "a big lie, to put it bluntly" and described the response as the "most appalling and degrading piece of political tactics I've seen in a long time." He also indicated that this exchange of words could influence his thinking on the changes to the Canada Assistance Plan.

Cooke then announced to the media that 100 percent increases in tuition were imminent. On December 14 Axworthy accused Cooke of mongering "exaggerated fears" and projecting "the extreme end...of a range of possibilities." Cooke, of course, had other irons in the fire. Four months earlier, his Ontario Council of University Affairs had put forward a highly controversial proposal for a new university funding mechanism, built around the contract-by-contract bidding for teaching and research services. If this proposal were accepted, acrimony and divisiveness between the have and have-not universities in Ontario would be inevitable. It served Cooke well to have a phantom—the evil nature of the federal government—as a means of maintaining the universities' unity. In a further shrewd move, he announced a hiatus in discussions about the new funding proposal until the spring of 1995—after the provincial election.

On the federal side, there was a continuing erosion of the

appearance of impartiality, open consultation and genuine concern for the three sectors (health, social assistance and postsecondary education) to be hit by the reform plans. On December
20, amidst allegations that his office had secretly orchestrated a
coalition of students to testify in favour of the increased tuition
fees to the House committee, Axworthy appointed a lawyer to
investigate. The allegation proved to have insufficient basis. At a
January 1995 student demonstration in Toronto the atmosphere
was poisonous. "People who paid 10 percent of the cost of their
education, are now telling us we have to pay 50 percent,"[25] students shouted. York University sociology professor Janice
Newson summed up the mood: "Students are being asked to pay
more for a product that's deteriorating."[26]

A January 1995 discussion paper confirmed that Axworthy
intended to cut out the $2.6-billion federal transfer payment
and replace it with a $2-billion student loan fund that would
have a $500-million start-up cost. The AUCC lobbied for a
more diversified plan of reform that would preserve the universities' research infrastructure and the government's power to
redress regional disparities.[27] But the February 1995 budget
speech effectively scotched that proposal. Finance Minister Paul
Martin revealed the government's desire to reduce the deficit to
3 percent of gross domestic product by 1996/97 and announced
the amalgamation of the current transfers of the Established
Programs Financing and the Canada Assistance Plan into the
new Canada Health and Social Transfer. There would be a cut
of $2.8 billion, from $29.7 billion to $26.9 billion, and the
$6.25 billion direct transfer earmarked for postsecondary edu-
cation under the old scheme would become part of an undiffer-
entiated pool (though Axworthy denied the provinces the
authority to change current levels of health care and social assistance). The projected further cut for 1997/98 was $1.8 billion.
The AUCC calculated that the aggregate result of the cuts by
1997/98 would translate into 39 percent less being available for
postsecondary education. Martin added one final blow: the
major granting councils like the National Science and

Engineering Research Council (NSERC) and the Social Sciences and Humanities Research Council (SSHRC) would have their budgets cut by 12.9 percent, as would federal departments like Statistics Canada, which contract out research. Also released was the news of cuts of 20 percent to the Canadian International Development Agency (CIDA) and the International Development Research Program (IDRP).[28] The total loss to the universities' research infrastructure was estimated to be more than $100 million.

Not denying the problem of the national debt, the universities were nonetheless quick to point the finger of blame elsewhere. Citing statistics showing that universities had for decades been the victims of declining operating grants and a reduced percentage of provincial budgets regardless of the state of the economy, they counterproposed that governments aim at the two sectors that had grown massively and unaccountably—medical care and social assistance. They illustrated the destructive impact of years of staff reductions, reductions in faculty research, academic support, central administration, maintenance of physical plant facilities and student services.[29] Universities, moreover, found it difficult to square the new "deficit crisis" with the memory of the fiscal swing of 1993 when there was a crush of students seeking admission, 80 percent averages were no guarantee of entry, universities could cherry-pick their students and there were record waiting lists.

Ontario universities, at least, had been prepared for the significant reform of the university sector. Since 1992 the University Restructuring Steering Committee in the Ministry of Colleges and Universities had been meeting to discuss the more efficient delivery of programs and services. It was given the mandate to make the postsecondary sector "responsive to the continuous or lifelong education, training, and knowledge needs of a modern economy and democratic society."[30] The committee's succession of interim reports throughout 1992 and 1993 were prolix on lifelong learning for the "knowledge-based economy" (more technological innovation) and enthusiastic about new interdisciplinary programs in environmental and women's studies. Its members were subdued on what might be entailed in preparing students for citizenship in a political community, not to say on what would contribute to their participation in a scholarly culture. The reports' sole gesture towards these substantive purposes was a number of motherhood statements about equity and accessibility (the need for equity databases), the learning climate and inclusiveness of the curriculum. Like the Smith Report, greater focus on teaching and instruction was urged. Their opinions form the context for the August 1994 document already referred to, the Ontario Council of University Affairs' "Sustaining Quality in Changing Times." The OCUA made clear that the funding mechanism had to be revamped. Three models were suggested, two of which largely made only minor modifications to the present system. The third model, however, a "purchase of service system," was infinitely more radical. The OCUA "objectively" set out the advantages and limitations of each model. The tone of impending crisis, informing the presentation of financial data, however, suggested that "Model C" was the option the OCUA wanted the institutions to adopt.

Model C works on the assumption that the university is a private corporation, free to develop according to its own mission. Like a corporation, it would maximize profits and be accountable to its shareholders. Funding would be provided on a contract-by-contract basis. Governments would identify the level of service they wished to purchase from the university in the form of teaching, research and community service. The terms and conditions of funding would be associated with the institution's "deliverables" of quantity, quality and conformity to the government's specified policies. In the words of one academic administration, the university would be in the "vertically integrated knowledge business," where knowledge was "packaged for the student and the general public as the knowledge consumers."[31]

The consequences to university education are not difficult to predict. While one of the OCUA's proposed scenarios sees the government regulating the market, given the OCUA's limited sense of the public good (access and equity) as well as its evident commitment to the vocational needs of the lifelong learner, the more likely scenario was a free market with government's role reduced to unclogging inefficiencies. Severed from the public good and the leadership of elected governments (not themselves particularly dutiful gatekeepers of the scholarly culture), university education would be at the mercy of market demand. Subject to the market, that culture would be commercialized and shrunk to fit the packaging that was most viable to the consumer. Model C makes the unjustifiable assumption that the consumer already knows what he or she wants and how to get it. It demands an efficiency that, as the student Ray Westcott suggested, is alien to the scholarly culture.[32] To effectively preserve the essence of the university, cuts have to be made with a fine scalpel, not a machete. What is deceptive about the OCUA proposal is how the public good and quality of scholarship are eroded in the name of "responsiveness" and "accountability." Nor is the proposal an effectual end to waste—there can be little question that Model C's implementation and running would require a whole new bureaucracy.

The faculty unions had their own complaints. They saw behind Model C a drive to segregate Ontario universities into two or more tiers, with faculty in the second-tier teaching universities prevented from researching and having to bear responsibility for instructing under increased class sizes and teaching loads. "Model C," said the labour educator director of the Ontario Federation of Labour, "would result in a situation where the 'star'—read research-oriented—faculty/departments/universities would siphon off all the research money, while the remaining faculty/departments/universities would process ever larger numbers of McStudent outputs. The implications for equity and quality of education would be frightening."[33] CAUT president, Joyce Lorimer, denounced the "intrusion into university autonomy" that would in the process transform most of Ontario's universities into community colleges.

Leaving aside the interests expressed by the various sectarians, there are two grave problems with the letter, though arguably not the spirit, of these proposals. The first is the divestment of public responsibility for collective goods. It may be said that such responsibility, especially national, under the existing constitutional division of powers, has never existed. But this is simply not true. Liberal governments under Louis St. Laurent, Lester B. Pearson and Pierre Trudeau, which put in place the system of federal support for postsecondary education, understood that a national industrial strategy focused on the contribution of universities to economic growth and a well-educated and highly skilled workforce was essential to prevent provinces from acting on only their own interests. National goals and national planning, with provincial support, ensured the creation of smaller universities catering to important Canadian communities—the francophone communities of Rimouski, Chicoutimi and Trois-Rivières; the northern communities of Prince George and Thunder Bay; and the Newfoundland community that benefits from Memorial University. Federal control in university funding has guarded against the American trend that turned many universities into research-intensive universities at the cost of teaching. It has acted to promote official languages, cultural development, international trade and cooperation, and literacy. It has maintained interprovincial mobility by vetoing proposals for higher fees for out-of-province students. To give another concrete illustration: the federal government has until the last budget sponsored the Canada Scholarships Program—a program of university and college scholarships earmarked for high achievers going into the fields of science, engineering and technology. Four thousand and one hundred students have benefited from the program jointly financed by the government and the private sector since its inception in 1988. In addition to the strong message of support for high achievers, data collected by the AUCC reveal that one of the consequences of the program was a 32 percent increase in the number of women enrolled in science and engineering.

Secondly, a market-driven model in which universities compete for customers and students determine university priorities through their demands is, unless carefully monitored, a danger to the scholarly culture—especially when its dynamics are, as Lloyd Axworthy likes to say, "consumer power" and "university responsiveness." Students do not commonly make cost-benefit analyses of their education by looking to the rate of return (job income) on their educational investment. Their primary anxiety is not the inefficiency of "underemployment," as if the purpose of university education were job skills alone. Such ideas, which are built into the proposal to have funding mechanisms built on employment success rates, blunt the contribution the scholarly culture actually makes—better citizens and better persons. Axworthy's account of the federal government's interests and the OCUA's Model C catalogue of "deliverables" says nothing about the university's purpose of creating an informed public and active citizens, who have a sense of history and the judgment to discern what is thoughtful public policy.

The corporate right could respond that these goods will emerge spontaneously or are unnecessary in today's "knowledge-based" global economy. But this is a pipedream and a dangerous delusion. While the fallacies of monetary policy are now clearly evident, it is a leap of faith to return to belief in the beneficent "invisible hand" that will automatically produce compassion and other humanitarian virtues through the action of free-market forces. If Jean Elshtain's and George Grant's dark reservations about the potentially lethal tendencies of fragmentation and homogenization in our world carry any weight, should we risk leaving the formation of civic virtue, and intellectual or spiritual purpose, to accident or destiny? The isolation and selfishness the market reinforces, combined with its reduction of quality to what can be ranked and commodified, cheapens our human potential.

The scholarly culture, even when compromised by lapses and misguided enthusiasms, has traditionally been a counterweight to these tendencies. Will it continue to be so? On whom will we rely for even the minimal public goods we need as a nation? How are we to understand the "905 revolution" in Ontario—

the revenge in the polls of the 905-area-code suburbs against the Metropolitan Toronto of Bob Rae in electing the government of Mike Harris? Is it not the expression of a class that sees itself as taxpayers, rather than citizens?

The problem of seeing no public good beyond individual or group interests is hardly confined to the lower middle classes. In his last book, *The Revolt of the Elites and the Betrayal of Democracy*, Christopher Lasch offered a bleak indictment of the class that traditionally has been the source of leaders and philanthropists—the upper middle and wealthy classes.[34] He reflects on the meaning of the escape of the well-off and the wealthy into guarded enclaves, pointing to their lack of dependence on or commitment to public services and their lack of concern with national decline. Adding to the accounts of fragmentation and alienation given by Elshtain and Grant, Lasch points out that these classes—traditionally the revenue source of goods ranging from defence to culture—have become international ones with no national obligations or attachments, no sense of place or historical continuity, and increasingly no philanthropic generosity. Our situation in Canada may not be as destitute as the America Lasch describes—we still have the Bronfmans, Reichmans, Blacks, Molsons, Tannenbaums, Desmarais, Jackmans, Dunns and Irvings—but what is the future? The Axworthy and OCUA proposals to run the university according to market demand risk intensifying the callous hard-headedness and ruthless ambition of some, the diffidence and cravenness of others—and they seriously threaten the institution as an oasis of serenity and mystery in the midst of the technological dynamo.

Chapter 7

The Corporate Right:
Taking Care of Business

The conception of culture as expendable luxury, to be taken up only after we've done all the really important things like polluting the environment, is particularly strong in Canada, because two centuries ago Canada accepted the ethic of mercantilism that the Americans revolted against, and devoted itself to providing raw materials for centres outside the country. If Canadian education is persistently underfunded, Canada will disappear from history and go back to being again what it was at first, a blank area of natural resources to be exploited by countries that are more advanced and better organized than we are because they've spent more on their education.

Northrop Frye[1]

Every generation finds itself in intergenerational conflict. The impending clash of two generations over the cash-flow crisis of the oversubscribed Canada Pension Plan is now being given a first run. When Lloyd Axworthy mocked protesting students as "pampered and privileged," forgetting his own university days as a member of the Students for a Democratic Society, a movement, ironically, working towards a total revolution modelled on the actions of China's "gang of four," he sparked a new round of "Generation X versus the Baby Boomers." He also gave them something on which to focus their resentment—the income-contingent loan program. Together with a host of other initiatives being explored to bring the university "into the twenty-first century," such as "outsourcing," "modularized technology," "alternative delivery mechanisms," and "for-profit contract servicing," the needs of business are being well served.

One solution to spiralling education costs and to the enlarged education bureaucracies that contribute to the growing debt is a voucher system. Popular in the United States, some limited experiments with the scheme are currently being conducted in schools. Vouchers are seen by some as an obvious corollary to the ideas behind charter schools (now being developed in Alberta)—schools that design their own "charter" and curriculum and operate in quasi-independence from education ministries. Lurking behind the scheme is the idea of privatizing schools and universities and "giving them back" to the public. The way it would work at the university level is as follows: where governments currently fund university education by transferring grants to institutions, under a voucher system a certificate would go directly to the student, who would then choose a school and surrender his certificate to it. The university would then submit the certificate to the government for funding. The idea behind the voucher system is that it overcomes the inefficiencies and sluggishness of universities by subjecting them to rational choice and the open market. The scheme is attractive to many of the corporate right who see it devolving power to the consumer and making universities more responsive to market demand. Universities would have to compete for students, and each university would have to create a market niche for itself.

The income-contingent loan program (ICLP), an idea now being proposed in the current round of social security reforms, is not a voucher system, but its principles are similar.[2] In brief, ICLP entails a switch from government grants to student loans. It is not merely a loan plan, but a university funding proposal that would have students supply a larger proportion of the university operating budget. The argument underlying the scheme is that since students benefit from university education, they should pay. ICLP is, in effect, a user fee since the student would now assume the debt load directly, where formerly the taxpayer paid for the university because the federal government was borrowing money to give to the provinces for university funding. Economists call this kind of scheme "privatizing the public debt"—in this case, the burden of the debt is being shifted from the past generation of students to the present generation.

Income-contingent loan plans exist in Australia, New Zealand, Sweden, the United Kingdom and the United States, although students in those countries keep asking why they should be paying today for yesterday's debts.

There are, however, justifiable grounds for arguing that since students benefit, they should pay. University students, as is often repeated, acquire skills that lead to higher income and consumption. They are the primary recipients of public funding. Statistics Canada reports bear this out: university graduates earn 70 percent more after two years at work than individuals with only high-school diplomas. The average salary of those with university degrees is $50,000, while it is only $25,000 for those with fewer than eight years of education. The 1991 Survey of Consumer Finance shows that over a lifetime, postsecondary graduates make $500,000 more than those without postsecondary education. Early in 1994, *The Economist* weighed in on the side of shifting responsibility to university students, offering a cogent and compelling argument: "Investing public money in higher education makes less sense in terms of equity or efficiency than investing it in primary or secondary education. The higher the stage of education, the more the benefits accrue to the individual rather than the society at large—not least because one of the main functions of universities is to screen people for elite positions."

The financial picture of the existing student loan program is another factor that enhances the attractiveness of ICLP. Since 1964, $8 billion has been lent to over two million students. In 1991/92, federal and provincial governments spent $950 million on student assistance, an increase of 62 percent since 1981/82. In 1993/94, the figure was $1 billion. The net expenditure was $350 million in administration, subsidized interest and defaults. Since 20 percent of student loans are not paid back, $1.3 billion is tied up in bad debts. Every year the federal government loses $60 million on student bankruptcies and $30 million in defaults on student loans, up from $20 million in 1990/91. Under the existing loan plan, the federal government also shoulders the interest on loans until graduation. The situation is far from satisfactory.

The current loan program has not been adequate for students either. Based on a needs-test that looks at parental income regardless of parental contribution, many middle-class students, while needy, are ineligible. Moreover, $165 per week ($105 from 1984 to 1994) stretches a student's needs very thinly. It is no wonder that 700,000 of the students enrolled in Canadian universities work while they study. Upon graduation, students have to repay a set amount monthly, regardless of income. Students are declaring personal bankruptcy, since the jobs they acquire on graduation do not yield an income sufficient to permit them to pay back loans. Such declaration leads to other problems, as graduates find they cannot buy houses or cars, use a credit card, or rent a house or apartment. While the average $7,000 debt on graduation is not great, students with low incomes struggle for years.

Originally an idea proposed by Milton Friedman, the income-contingent loan program is now, as its advocates say, "an idea whose time has come." The corporate right is attracted to ICLP like bears to honey. Axworthy's *Student Debt Management Strategy* is a creative expression of the corporate right's agenda. It is a multipronged plan of action, serving many economic, political and moral interests. In essence, it is a flexible loan program negotiated on a student-by-student basis between students and the banks. Family circumstance no longer constitutes a barrier. The repayment of the loan after graduation depends on employment, and the rate and schedule of repayment is contingent on salary. There is a threshold below which a graduate does not have to repay, as there are provisions for relief from unmanageable payments and partial loan forgiveness. There are also special grants for students with special needs, single mothers and women enrolled in doctoral studies, where women are traditionally underrepresented. Savings accrued by governments will go into student counselling on debt management and distribution of budgeting software to students.

On the plus side, the advocates say, the new strategy will give students more clout to assess the performance of the university and give power to their desire for innovation and efficiency. ICLP will also enhance student mobility. Overall, the new debt management strategy is a great victory of individual choice, though as Axworthy says, "This is not a privatization. It is a new form of accountability. The federal government retains its role in running the program."[3] For one, ICLP makes certain that money allocated by the federal government will actually be spent on education. But the federal government is not the only one to gain more control. According to the plan, nine chartered banks and credit unions will administer the program. For their reward in decreasing nonpayment to 5 percent, they will receive a premium equal to 5 percent of the total value of all loans. They will also use their traditional methods of ensuring repayment—collection agencies—and through greater involvement in credit counselling have an opportunity for long-term customer relations with students. If there are still defaults, banks can write off losses against their profits. Not all, of course, will see the bank's new muscle as particularly attractive.

On the clearly negative side, ICLP continues the abandonment of national and provincial direction, giving these over to the vagaries and instrumental logic of the market. The anxieties of students can also be brushed off, but they are nonetheless real. Students are not thrilled with the prospect of accumulating a $60,000 debt with no prospects of a job. They look unfavourably on a scheme that would have them pay university expenditures back directly and on schedule, in the form of loans, rather than diffusely and gradually through income taxes collected over a lifetime. They were not taken in by the words "income-contingent," alert to the fact that while the loan was not repayable until a salary rolled in, the interest on the loan kept accumulating regardless, to the profit of the banks.[4] The Canadian Federation of Students identified ICLP's regressive direction, in that poorer students would pay a greater cost of borrowing, since they would take the longest to repay the loan.

Students questioned whether there was a contradiction between the government's commitment to lifelong learning and the prospects of repeated debt. As Robert Sheppard wrote in his *Globe and Mail* column, ICLP is predicated on the idea that higher education will lead to higher-paying jobs, when the reality is that the market's requirement of retraining every four or five years means a potential "loan-debt treadmill," from which some students will never escape.[5]

No less a concern can be expressed about the questionable future of public standards. Will loans be portable and mobile? Will universities continue to be accessible? It is unclear, for example, whether universities under the banner of "university autonomy" will have the right to set their own tuition fees, with possible side effects on other universities, or whether this will be regulated by the provinces. National purpose could also be subverted when students are faced with paying the full cost of university. Many, justifiably, may choose alternate forms of education like vocational training over university, and that may be a good thing. But it also means that those Robert Reich identified as the growing class of "routine production workers," many of whom are women, are deprived of the advantages and virtues arising from acquaintance with the scholarly culture. One of the disadvantages, for example, may be the reversal of a trend monitored by Statistics Canada showing that the wage gap between men and women with university degrees is closing rapidly.[6]

Moreover, ICLP operates on a premise that many could question. As Axworthy keeps saying, the attraction of ICLP is that since a disproportionate number of wealthier students go to university, and since their projected lifetime income on average will be much higher than that of other Canadians, it is fairer that they, rather than a general public of poorer and lower-income families, should be paying. In this sweeping statement, Axworthy has neglected to take into account the fact that many graduates go on to leadership positions and contribute to Canada at a level disproportionate to the average public.

Advocates of ICLP see such contributions—an informed political citizenry, guardians of Canada's cultural heritage, a population with intellectual horizons that lead to more mature use of leisure time—only as externalities and not to be taken into the equation. The platitude that reads "since university students gain the benefits of higher education, they should bear the costs" rests on the most naïve understanding of how national unity, duties to community and sustained productivity in employment are formed.

One must add the legitimate concerns raised by the Canadian Federation of Students: "In the future, students in sectors which have a higher rate of unemployment such as arts and social sciences...might be rejected for loan requests, while students in high-tech such as engineering and sciences might be accepted."[7] What will prevent banks from making assessments of the link between defaults and field of academic study? And as universities rush to the market to sell themselves, using money better applied to good teaching and research, what incentive will they have to maintain programs that do not enjoy the market's idea of payoff?

The income-contingent loan program is also a Trojan horse, for smuggled within the efficiencies it promises is a plan for vast increases in, and even deregulation of, tuition fees. This is a break with the past, for previously, universities that increased tuition fees faced a corresponding cut to their provincial subsidy. Since tuition fees doubled from an average of $750 in 1981 to a range from $1,170 to $5,700 in 1991, and they are projected to rise from an average of $2,500 to $10,000 per year, student anxiety regarding the future is great.[8] Nonetheless, tuition fees cover only 12 percent of total postsecondary expenditure and only 20 percent of the operating costs of universities and colleges. With shrinking public funds, tuition appears the obvious candidate for reform. The editors of the *Globe and Mail* have been particularly enthusiastic about the prospect of higher tuition fees. They praise Queen's for its full-cost recovery tuition in the MBA and University of Toronto's full-fee executive training program. "The result of all this?" the editors ask. "Empowerment of students.

Self-sufficient universities. Higher-quality education. A stronger workforce. A more prosperous country."[9]

Michael Mancinelli, deputy-chairman of the Canadian Federation of Students, confirming the adage that statistics are the devil's work, responded that the reason why Canada in 1995 could boast a 20 percent rate of participation in university education, as opposed to 1951's rate of 5 percent, was that today's tuition fees comprise 20 percent of the cost of undergraduate education, unlike 1951's proportion of 38 percent.[10] Michael Stewart candidly summed up the students' outcry: "What students are angry about is the fact that the baby boomers, who racked up the federal debt in the first place and attended university in an era of low tuition rates, are now telling us and future students that the free ride is over and to pay up."[11] Ontario students, responding to the province's conservative government's pledge to cut middle-class taxes, said, "We don't feel like paying for a 30 percent tax cut out of tuition."[12] Jeffrey Simpson responded bluntly with an editorial headlined "Stop Whining about Tuition Fees and Be Thankful." Meanwhile, students hit by user fees for use of rooms, audiovisual equipment and laboratories have felt they were being nickelled and dimed. As student Ray Westcott summed it up tersely in the 1994 *Maclean's* survey, "We're becoming penny wise and pound foolish. There's a general small-mindedness: 'God damned kids, we aren't going to give them anything for free.'"[13]

The future for foreign students is equally bleak. The corporate right believes foreign students should not be subsidized because they do not represent a return to Canadian taxpayers. Full cost recovery, currently followed only in some medical schools and management programs, is now on the agenda, as is the universal adoption of the current Ontario practice of taxing foreign students on their teaching assistantships (an indirect way of subsidizing the education of Canadians). The thinking associated with these schemes is short-sighted, ignoring, among other contributions foreign students make, the fact that the sixty thousand foreign students studying at Canadian postsecondary institutions are adding $1.5 billion to the economy. In general, students have one question as they face the prospects of far deeper debt loads and point to deterioration of services, unproductive faculty, the unwillingness of senior faculty to retire and the "research-production culture": On whose back will the universities operate in the future?

Morality is always a bitter pill to swallow. Whatever else ICLP achieves, it is also a form of moral education. Since *there ain't no such thing as a free lunch*, the additional costs students will have to bear come with the benefit of teaching thrift and industry. ICLP may achieve what many baby-boomer parents did not teach their children: that one will have more respect for things for which one has oneself worked than for what one receives without work. The twists of the ICLP that may have higher earners paying a surcharge on their own debt to accommodate lower-income borrowers, or that would raise the cost of the plan to allow for the requirements of women with children, are worthwhile lessons in charity. ICLP may also have the effect of instilling moderation and prudence, not to say patience—focusing priorities, reining in wants and forming reasonable expectations.

Since such virtues are being formed less and less in the schools, and yet are essential for the moral attitude that lies at the core of intellectual life and political citizenry, the lessons ICLP will offer cannot come early enough. ICLP may also do what university policy seems unable to do—turn away those for whom university is not the appropriate vehicle for tapping their distinctive virtues. Above all, ICLP has the potential to hold this country back from further debt and thus prevent Canada from violating decency and responsibility by passing a crippling burden on to the next generation. ICLP should be, however, only one plank in a student's moral education. Beyond the virtues needed to live in a money economy, are the virtues of justice, impartiality and good judgment that arise through repeated practice of those habits in the scholarly culture.

The development of these additional virtues is the only thing that can prevent the lessons of thrift and industry from turning into parsimony and ruthless ambition, or avert charity from derailing into resentment or moralistic righteousness. This additional component of moral education is not, however, understood by the corporate right. And nowhere is this lack of understanding more evident than in the proposals for new teaching methods, or "alternative delivery mechanisms," as their idiom goes.

Since January 1994, students at the University of Calgary have been taking a course in forensic anthropology via high-speed fibre optics at the University of Edmonton. Classrooms at the two universities are equipped with large-screen colour monitors, a projection-television unit and directional microphones. Automatic cameras simulate classroom discussion. Professor Philip Haswell, one of the moving forces behind this experiment, comments: "There are 23 post-secondary institutions in Alberta and it's likely that many of them are teaching the same course. One possibility is that we could share those courses. And there are also specialists in areas that we would like to share." In the future, Professor Haswell enthused, computer-mediated learning will come with "asynchronous" delivery: "Distant students can access the classes as a form of video-on-demand, tuning in whenever they wish and contacting the instructor with questions and feedback by E-mail."[14] The University of Calgary is preparing a $276,000 Centre for Distance Learning and Interactive Technology that will bring in satellite broadcasts from around the world. It is dubbed the "broadband new era of education." Virtual training sessions in corporate boardrooms and virtual thesis examinations and conferences with faculty in six cities are already possible.

The University of Calgary's initiative, which has a twin in the new $1 million Electrohome Classroom/Guelph-Waterloo Education Link System project, coincides with the widespread subscription to SchoolNet, the nationwide data linkage that provides Canadian school pupils direct access to the global information network. "It's encouraging to see how excited kids get just by text-based stuff," muses Rachel Welsh, one of the corporate leaders heavily involved in SchoolNet, "but it's not the text, it's the content, the interactivity of it. This just knocks down the classroom walls. You can have on-line mentors in New Zealand, and the kids just love talking to someone in another country. And the teachers have just been fabulous, even though this is throwing them a curveball, in a way."[15]

It is one small step from these initiatives to "outsourcing" and "modularized curricula," the current buzzwords in education reform. These new experiments are already being implemented. A new undertaking, the Canadian Continuous Learning Initiative (CCLI), will comprise a virtual campus to deliver education and training at schools, colleges, universities and corporate facilities across Canada. Its electronic resources will replicate or simulate university facilities—libraries, discussion rooms and private rooms—while adding internet access, e-mail, file transfer, bulletin boards and remote testing. And CCLI will ensure that the right courseware (electronic learning materials) is readily available.

The future promises much more. Robert E. Jensen, professor of business at Trinity University in Texas, explained "hypermedia" teaching in an issue of the bulletin of the Canadian Association of University Teachers: "Education is in the midst of a monumental technological paradigm shift, one that will eventually change the way that all instructors teach and the way that all students learn…. There is little doubt among researchers and scholars, though, that technological plates are sliding in a way that will lead to the ultimate pre-eminence of what is known as *hypermedia learning*." Jensen adds that "multi-sensory learning," which makes "the best materials of the world's best teachers" available in student-centred learning, will "jolt us with comparative advantages."

The corporate right evidently agrees. From Ontario's 1993 Postsecondary Restructuring Agenda to Alberta's 1994 "New Directions for Adult Learning in Alberta," from St. Mary's new classes on Maritime Tel's worksites to Simon Fraser's Harbour Centre campus, from Athabasca's virtual "executive roundtables" to the Open Learning System in British Columbia and the Téléuniversité in Quebec, the language of self-directed learning, flexible delivery, learning networks and inclusive learning opportunities dominates today's discussions of the future of education. Noting the success of University of Western Ontario's Business School or Queen's MBA program, where experiments with videoconferencing and workplace-based training by means of electronic teaching and learning networks have reaped great benefits, the corporate right has ambitious plans for the overhaul of university education generally.

The 1994 Alberta Ministry of Advanced Education document, a plan for a major restructuring of postsecondary education, is a case in point. The Minister Jack Ady sets out a mission that will see "quality learning opportunities" matched with "demonstrable economic benefit."[16] The document sets out a plan for a massive decentring of public education. Taking "the needs of the learner" as the starting point, Ady looks with interest to "private learning providers" and the seamless web of all "learning opportunities." He encourages employers to play a greater role in program design, he urges the creation of "new knowledge" through university-industry partnerships and he looks with favour on the proliferation of alternate means of acquiring degrees at university colleges and technical institutes. Employing "key indicators" and tying funding to programs that recognize "the needs of the labour market," Ady adds, postsecondary education will be able to "respond to change more quickly." He makes clear that the day when academic achievement was distinguished from occupational standards and trade designations is over. *Sotto voce*, he also sees the end of tenure, in favour of "flexibility to be able to shift resources to and from programs, departments or faculties in order to respond to fiscal restraints, program rationalization and reorganization" where academic freedom is, nonetheless, protected under the charter.[17]

It is important to be measured in one's assessment of these plans for "alternative delivery mechanisms," contract servicing and a future of "virtual universities." If one leaves aside one's scepticism over the boosterism—"taking universities into the twenty-first century," "change as the key to Canada's comparative advantage"—one will recognize the potential for cost-effectiveness and accessibility. Take, as one illustration, alternative delivery mechanisms for library holdings. Between 1965 and 1995, the average price for journal subscriptions rose by 1,280 percent. As libraries cut back drastically on journal subscriptions, faculty and students were forced to use interlibrary loan, a costly and time-consuming endeavour that, among other things, breaks the natural rhythm of research, namely, serendipitous discovery and unchartable pursuit of thought-trains. The move to electronic databases and on-line journals, the creation of virtual libraries to replace book libraries, the opportunity for different "libraries" to build specializations available electronically across Canada instead of proliferating the same mediocre collections, comes as a nearly unmitigated blessing. Although start-up costs are high, long-term payoffs (in the broadest sense of the word) are greater.

Equally fiscally responsible and compatible with the needs of the university is the move towards cost recovery or for-profit contract servicing—where competition on a wide range of university services such as printing, parking, catering, photocopying, health care, computer facilities, bookstores, food services, counselling and other special needs would lead to improvement and, arguably, better rates. These, along with the myriad investments the university makes in laboratory equipment, computer facilities, residences and brick-and-mortar, are externalities to the scholarly culture and thus appropriately assessed by value-for-money and value-added auditing. Indeed, these audits are critical for breaking up the unjustifiable privileges, patronage, protection and indifference in the universities, about which legitimate concern has been raised.

While no one should be fooled that "rationalization" means anything more than cutbacks, it is the case that, as a consequence of the bloated budgets of the sixties and seventies, there is much fat that can be trimmed—but it will not be trimmed by using traditional accounting methods. Many aspects of the university are best handed over to professionals. One thinks of the university presses in this country, some of whom have learned this lesson by having been turned around by managers from the corporate sector. For example, the University of Toronto Press had losses of $4.4 million in 1990, and after major restructuring, showed profits of $1.25 million in 1995. What is essential, however, if one grants that a scalpel should be taken to the university, is the need to look at a university as a diversified portfolio. Neither the corporate right nor the universities themselves do so. The corporate right sees inefficiency or ornament—like convocation rituals and heraldic symbols—and will not indulge them at any level. The universities, for their part, fear "invidious distinctions" and will not tolerate the apparent discrepancy between supporting some programs by public funds, while releasing others to be "marketed."

"Alternative delivery mechanisms" also bring their benefits. While Luddites question all use of advanced technologies, conveniently forgetting that the Gutenberg press spawned the print culture and revolutionized communication, it is questionable whether the new technologies will actually cause a sea change in the scholarly culture. Unless one has acquaintance with videoconferencing, the internet, interactive CD-ROM technology and electronic mail, one has little qualification to speak, as some do, of the end of teaching and learning. The internet, for example, is, as some faculty fear, filled with much frivolous diversion and indiscriminate information. But it also contains hard-to-find documents of the Carolingian period, rare commentaries of St. Basil and reports of recent breakthroughs in understanding atomic particles—and it hosts rich international roundtables on topics as diverse as Renaissance iconography and enzymes. There is among many faculty a great reluctance to experiment with the new technologies, a reluctance reinforced by institutional inertia, which, once moralized, results in stubborn resistance to new opportunities.

Nonetheless, much more is at stake in these modest investments in recent technology, the social practices they demand

and the accountability enjoined upon the university by the corporate right. Even if we leave aside the connotations of their unfortunate idiom of "suppliers, consumers, clients and deliverables"—which is seen by academics as philistinism—there is something infinitely more troubling about "alternative delivery mechanisms" and "virtual university" schemes. Clarifying the future role of Alberta in university education, Jack Ady said, "The government will retain its role of consumer protection." And explaining the relation of computer instruction to everyday life, Robert E. Jensen concluded: "Real-world experience is not necessarily the best teacher. In the technology paradigm shift...simulations and virtual realities are often better teachers than real-world experience."[18] In examining these two points further, we can see in the unbridled and unreflective praise for the new technologies and the market model that supports them, that the corporate right is attempting to trump the scholarly culture with its own political agenda.

Whatever the corporate right may say, the process of understanding is unlike the management of information. The engagement of souls in conversation is unlike the transmission and processing of data. Facts can be relayed, feeling-states can be conveyed, and skills can be demonstrated by computers and video, but nothing can replicate the contact of human beings. The simulation of such contact is so sophisticated these days that one can even envisage a time when the technology itself will become wholly transparent and a person's idea of the world and experience of it will become one and the same (perhaps with lasers and holograms). But even such simulation will not replace direct human interaction. We can consume physical things, and arguably mental objects, but only by an indiscriminate use of metaphor and stretch of the imagination do we consume thoughts, sentiments, sensibilities, attitudes and virtues. This is not what the corporate right says, but inner reflection and the next conversation will confirm it.

Item one: Paul Beam, an English professor at the University of Waterloo, has recently put his entire course on literary criticism onto a computer disk, a 1992 issue of *University Affairs* relates.[19] His course can be interactively accessed—a student does not need to go to the library or communicate with others to successfully absorb Professor Beam's course. Item two: We could envisage a student sitting at home or out in the woods listening to the set of audiotapes and videorecordings of "Superstar Teachers" offered by The Teaching Company in its regular *New York Review of Books* advertisement. Item three: We already know of experiments in postsecondary education in which students contract with professors to provide a service and in which classes are held wherever space is available—in schools or restaurants. One such organization is the Greenvale College in Nova Scotia, which Janet Halliwell, chair of Nova Scotia's Council on Higher Education, believes is "innovative," and a "breath of fresh air," to be praised for its "benchmark standards."[20] Item four: We can all appreciate the data showing that the occupational half-life of a worker's skills is three to five years, and the future workforce projections that suggest that in the future there will be many contracts, but few careers. But does any of this justify the radical overthrow of a traditional liberal education? Are there not profound costs to employing a model that sees the university in terms of suppliers and consumers of services and the salient terms of reference as decentralization, choice and competition?

Selective sociological observations (and by no means the most relevant ones) and fanciful constructs of teaching and learning have been used to conceive the idea of the "virtual university." Too many important questions are avoided. Is it a healthy thing for students to learn in isolation? Many would say not, recognizing that the disappearance of public encounters and the loss of the checks and balances of public deliberation come with the risk of a proliferation of dangerous private fantasies bred in solitude. Others may wonder how civic virtues could form when classrooms are converted to passive video watching and electronic "chat-lines." Is there a deterioration in judgment and understanding when the complex scholarly conversion of opinion to knowledge is transformed into transmission of information and concepts? Again, some may relish the encyclopaedic mind so formed, but others will wonder if the result is not a "trivial pursuit" accumulation of facts that misses the forest for the trees.

Even if analytical skills are stimulated by a talking head on a screen, such reasoning is short of the synthetic and integrative processes of intellectual understanding that spring from the often individually tailored attentions of a conscientious professor. Genuine understanding is a process that needs an instructor whose passion can eroticize a classroom, for from such passion are formed the *pathos* and spiritual bonds of friendship that lie at the core of intellectual adventure. Mere cognitive assent to facts, or acquaintanceships formed by accidental combinations of "virtual" students, is not the same. Similarly, information retrieval is not reading as a habit, mode of judgment or creative engagement. Information retrieval is accumulation, a succession of information bits, left willy-nilly to the consumer's own designs and management.

Can videoconferencing offer a satisfactory simulacrum of the traditional classroom? One trenchant observer of the influence of televisions and computers, Neil Postman, argues persuasively that the whole array of new educational technologies, and the representations that signify the universities' new "responsiveness" to the market, merely divert us away from the mysterious engagements of psyches in the classroom towards a condition where we are just "amusing ourselves to death."[21] The trouble is that "real time" and "real space" may contrast unfavourably with the captivating new "cyberspace," although reality, for better or for worse, comprises our home, with all its real burdens, contradictions and paradoxes, complete with the humanizing virtues that are unnecessary in the ether (-net). Some applaud the disappearance of the need for face-to-face contact and the emergence of network chit-chat in a medium that permits them to overcome all inhibitions and restraints—but what are we losing?

Many more questions that follow on these reflections can be posed. Many students love the new CD-ROM interactive technology, for it even permits them to rewrite the ends of

Shakespeare's sonnets and the discomforting anti-Semitism of *The Merchant of Venice*. After all, that technology is seductively fun. But does this leave them with the conclusion that all the world is available for their mastery and control? Does this erode the healthy receptivity to truths which in their immaturity they have not yet reached and does it create exaggerated expectations that the many unalterable burdens of the human condition can be similarly overcome?[22]

Is it sound to bring together a selection of courses and instructors on an episodic basis, creating in effect a modularized curriculum that is not informed by institutional continuity and that lacks coherence, since it is the accidental outcome of the contingent needs and expectations of the market? The gain is efficiency, but the cost may be a significant narrowing of perspective and the loss of the rich tapestry of the university culture that arises from the organic unity of its elements. Consider, for example, the corporate right's outcry against duplication. The problem with this argument is that it is predicated on the idea that a given subject is the same everywhere. But this is not true, and it is a good thing that it is not. For example, through the superlative scholarship of historians like Donald Creighton, J.M. Careless and more recently Michael Bliss, the University of Toronto has wielded vast influence in the study of Canadian history. But there are other perspectives on that history that do not make southern Ontario the central fact. The potential for misrepresentation of Canada's history is redressed by a subaltern strike against Toronto's dominance, particularly in the very different narratives of Canadian history that have emerged from history departments in French Canada and western Canada, for instance. Public understanding and policy is more just and representative of the truth because of the addition of the subaltern's counternarratives.

The example can be repeated in nearly every discipline, except perhaps the professional schools, where training may indeed be more universal. The question one must pose is why the corporate right extrapolates from the training of medical, engineering and business schools to every program in the university. The "private learning providers" that Jack Ady praises are, in fact, "voucher vultures," who see market opportunity but have little appreciation of the multifaceted interconnections of a university curriculum.[23] Contracting out faculty work to "rent-a-profs" may contribute to "effective" training, but it will not lead to a sense of corporate membership and institutional responsibility, the minimal conditions for the trust upon which the scholarly culture relies.

And how well served is society by the cost-efficient technologies the corporate right believes are so critical to our future well-being? The corporate right's plans for the new relationship between "provider" and "client" follows a wide trend in banking, communication and the entertainment industry. It is easy to appreciate the speed and efficiency of the new service culture, especially in changes that have introduced technology-enabled self-service (like ATM's, telephone registration and video-on-demand). But what is the benefit when the new consumer-driven services reinforce the impersonality of our society and contribute to the justifiable anger we experience when we discover that no individual will take responsibility for error? Value-added audits may lead to the elimination of inefficient and idiosyncratic middle management, but who is accountable for the decisions made by a machine? Moreover, what is the cost to the virtues of tolerance or compromise when these services change our whole perspective from "what you see is what you get" to "what you want is what you get" and finally to "when you want it is when you get it"? It is not difficult to imagine some highly unfortunate applications of the new "consumer is king" consciousness—the legitimacy granted, for example, to jaded and corrupt taste or utterly frivolous pursuit.

As the corporate right urges the universities to divest and deregulate, abandoning their traditional authority to a nexus of "providers," "clients" and efficient technologies, where are the forms of community that refine and mature this relationship? The corporate right is silent. Illustrative of its utter insouciance about these issues are the facile views put forward in a November 1995 *Globe and Mail* column by Andrew Coyne. Mocking those who distinguish between "consumers" and "citizens" and who would naïvely believe that education's purposes transcend the interests of the market, Coyne claims that "When we speak of markets versus politics, we are talking only of two different ways of making economic decisions, not about philosophies of life."[24] No one of sound mind, he believes, would choose the way organized by coercion and exacting passivity (politics), when given the option of a market with free choices and competition. "It's hard not to see," Coyne concludes, "why the long-suffering citizen should be lionized by partisans of those institutions of statist economics from which consumers, given a choice, tend to flee. A citizen, you see, is a consumer who knows his place."[25] Yes, the citizen does know his or her place in Canadian society, distinguished from others by its principled commitment to care and equity. This place, a stake in which produces moral responsibility and impartiality, is utterly unlike the placelessness of consumers who flit from commodity to commodity, to satisfy their wants as efficiently as possible. And until recently it was the scholarly culture, with its goals of independent-mindedness and civic virtue, that gave this place its sense of purpose and spiritual depth.

The strange new hybrid of "virtual university" and vocational training centre is unquestionably de rigueur among the corporate right. While Clayton Manness sees the need to rectify the problem of universities being "out of sync," perhaps the bandwagon is not the best place for the university. Consider, for example, the model of proprietorial competitiveness the corporate right believes is so useful. The Arthurs Report on the Fabrikant affair is often cited by the corporate right because of its critique of a "production-driven research culture," a commentary that is seen to square with the corporate right's view that universities are no longer teaching and researching what is commercially applicable.[26] This interpretation of the report, however, is erroneous. Arthurs was actually referring to the government's policy of giving priority to private-sector suppliers of research services, which forced academics to incorporate themselves so they could be private-sector bidders. This led to the conflicts of interest that sparked Fabrikant's rage. One might ask whether the most useful role the university can play is as a counterweight to the isolating and narrowing forces of the market—which teaches about forms of solidarity above the market. Those with a constant eye on change cannot distinguish between the essential and the accidental, between what is important and what is merely interesting. Forecasting the direction of trends and mobilizing institutions to reform in light of possible outcomes is a mug's game, because crystal balls are always hazy. The dream of "virtual universities" geared to "engines of growth" bears the risk of mortgaging the scholarly culture to wildly concocted predictions and fantasies. More importantly, it devalues the critical independent-mindedness and distance that, above all, the scholarly culture seeks to cultivate.

The prospects for such distance will vanish if university-industry partnerships continue to be seen as the primary jewel in the crown. There are two aspects to these newly minted relationships. The first is the direct preparation of students for employment. The Council of Ministers of Education has resolved that there will be an increasing link between the university and the workplace, both in curriculum and in linkages with employers. The University of Waterloo obviously leads in this initiative with its extensive co-op program. St. Mary's University, responding to the needs of Maritime Tel, has even moved classes to worksites. Much of this new enterprise is commendable. Theoretical inquiry is given a practical form; workplaces are renewed through the innovative contributions creative students offer and are broadened by some of the culture the students bring with them. However, university education, truly understood, cannot be seen only as job training. It is an incubation which calls for some seclusion and protection from the harsh glare of society at large. Such education, as Northrop Frye says, must necessarily occur behind a closed door. No corporation will invest in these elusive processes and the inefficient techniques by which they occur. Yet if our society is to go beyond its current dreary and often stalemated politics of brokering interests, should we not continue to give our young the opportunity for laying a foundation of good judgment and intellectual passion beyond convenience and bargaining? They will not have such an opportunity if universities succumb to the demand for "relevance," as did the University of Manitoba when it instituted a six-credit program in cleaning and building management.

Elation about corporate partnerships has also bred some strange commitments. Nova Scotia Education Minister John MacEachern has proposed offering employers a warranty for graduates, as part of his plan for a more accountable education system.[27] The warranty plan would guarantee to employers that the student had the skills and training and, if this failed to be the case, postsecondary institutions would be responsible for retraining the student at their own cost. A similar offer was made to corporate partners at Holland College in Prince Edward Island. Ministers may hope that they will not be called on this pledge, but at Durham College in Oshawa four employers took up the guarantee, insisting the college should teach the graduates new skills—not because the training was inadequate but because their workforce requirements had changed.

The second aspect of university-industry partnerships takes the form of financial endorsements. At Simon Fraser's downtown campus, the evidence of corporate endorsement is hard to miss: the Fletcher Challenge Theatre, the Placer Dome Lecture Room, the Canfor Policy Room. The presence of Westcoast Energy, Xerox, Labatt, IBM, Canadian Pacific, BC Gas, Scotiabank, Trans Mountain Pipe Line, Paperboard Industries and Cominco is everywhere. Whose interests are being furthered here?[28] Although these partnerships are often expressions of genuine commitment to learning, there should be little question that they also serve corporate public relations well. Moreover, it is legitimate to ask whether such endorsements do not come with strings attached.

In the United States, they certainly have. Pennsylvania State University's partnership with Pepsi comes with significant financial rewards, but it has also translated into Pepsi's exclusive monopoly over vending machines. In Canada, more intrusive control has been exercised by corporate donors. *National Geographic*, after donating generously to Toronto's Royal Ontario Museum and Drumheller's Royal Tyrrell Museum of Paleontology, has kept a tight muzzle on recent dinosaur discoveries until it suits the magazine to release news on the findings. Similarly, Cangene Corporation has kept strict control of research it funded at McMaster University on a pet vaccine against fleas. These two examples are not major, but they signal the danger of restrictions to come. Corporations are not in the business of disseminating information that would lead to a loss in their comparative advantage vis-à-vis other competitors. The scholarly culture, on the other hand, thrives on the dissemination of knowledge.[29]

Nor are corporations inclined to public spiritedness, especially when others offer to improve their bottom line. We have ten "centres of excellence" in Canada that are engaged in collaborative research between universities and industry in areas of "strategic purpose." What excellent things do they do? Notable projects are efforts to prevent the yellowing of paper and the destruction of timber by insects. Federal funding of $240 million has brought together eight hundred researchers, thirteen hundred graduate students and four hundred and fifty post-doctoral fellows in these centres. Recently, $48 million has been set aside to create three new centres for excellence, of which one may be Simon Fraser University's proposal for research on technology-based alternatives to the traditional classroom. With the evident payoff to our corporate "engines of growth," what has the corporate contribution to these initiatives been? In 1992/93 industry provided $4.3 million to the collaboration—less than 2 percent!

Private-sector bidding. Income-contingent loan plans. Alternate delivery systems. Market responsiveness. University-industry partnerships. These are all separate initiatives with different premises and different outcomes. But they also form a complete package—and a hot button that will further the political agenda of the corporate right. Let us not be deceived. Beneath the banners of "the public will" and "the morning of a new economic reality" lies a turf war.

On May 18, 1994, the *Globe and Mail* editorial read, "Universities must choose between what they do well and what they do less well, lest the government do it for them." The universities have been chosen to solve governments' deficit crises and advance their political causes. Citing the need for "accountability" and "cost effectiveness," government commissions in Nova Scotia, New Brunswick, Alberta and Ontario have all used the opportunity of assessing the postsecondary education sector to extend their micromanagement of the university. Value-for-money audits, for example, have been windows of opportunity for control by education ministries and provincial auditors. In Ontario, after a value-for-money audit of Trent, Guelph and Toronto in 1988 to 1990, the Ontario Task Force on University Accountability was formed and its forty-seven recommendations all justified increasing outside intervention. The Ontario Council of University Affairs' increasingly regulatory role made it the strongarm of the NDP government, especially in its recommendations for targeted funds, which would advance the government's ideological agenda.

Increased intervention has led to more political games inside and outside the university. The Ontario Public Accounts Committee, for example, has an interest in painting as bleak a picture of university inefficiency as possible, because it can thereby embarrass the ruling government. The peccadilloes it believes it has found can in turn justify increasing interventions by the provincial auditor. Faculty associations can use the auditor's data to mobilize faculty against university management and raise the accusation of "fiscal mismanagement," especially when relations between them is frosty on issues of mandatory retirement or voluntary redundancies. University administrators can fall back on the argument that their governing boards are responsible, because the membership of those boards (legislated by the government) pursues myriad conflicting social agendas. Even "university autonomy" can work its political effect, providing the opportunity for local "stakeholders" to control the university, rather than have its governance regulated by independent public authorities. As a result of government policy, boards of governors are increasingly not trustees to the idea of the university, but a body of delegates from the constituencies whose interests they represent. Few of the "rationalization" schemes are untainted by the jockeying for power.

What a tangled web we weave once we decide the university should be re-engineered! And all the while, the university is made poorer and poorer. The idea of public goods and community—trumped. The idea of education as a social benefit—trumped. The idea of the university as detached but nonetheless powerfully capable of informing social policy—trumped. The idea that the deeper satisfactions individuals seek need to be sustained by public validation—trumped.

What the corporate right does not recognize is the huge gap between our inner selves and the technological civilization it is building around us. It cannot see that behind social disorder and widespread anomie is something more than just another technical problem that can be solved. Essential human experiences are being blunted and diverted into surrogate, but potentially lethal, satisfactions by unconditional faith in technological progress. George Grant had a much more balanced understanding of our difficult times and cautioned us about our rush to embrace the technological dynamo. He also hauntingly described the essence of the university's beneficial spiritual and intellectual distance from the world: "It would be immoderate and uncourageous and perhaps unwise to live in the midst of our present drive, merely working in it and celebrating it, and not also listening or watching or simply waiting for intimations of deprival which might lead us to see the beautiful as the image, in the world, of the good."[30]

The corporate right's opposition to what it calls "business as usual" assumes the institution is a business. In some respects it is; in many more it is not. By extending the analogy of a business corporation to all university affairs, the corporate right has given itself the leverage to trump all that is essential in the scholarly culture. But the corporate right is not alone in exhibiting zero tolerance of that culture. It has found an unlikely ally—one which does not even share its political convictions, but which has been every bit as effective in trumping genuine education with its own brand of hot-button politics. That strange ally is the cultural left.

Chapter 8

The Cultural Left:
Gender Politics

We're afraid to walk the streets, afraid we'll be killed, afraid we'll be raped. We're afraid to go into non-traditional fields or try new ideas.

Glenda Simms

Like the corporate right, the cultural left is mesmerized by change. Its argument runs: since universities now have more women and more students from diverse ethnic and racial backgrounds, and since in the past none of these constituencies were represented anywhere near their sociologically representative number, and since there must be a reason, and since that reason is one alone—namely, discrimination—there must therefore be a sea change at the university. That change entails more than simply providing room at the table for the newcomers. As the keynote speaker said at the 1995 conference of CAUT's Status of Women's Committee, "The inclusive university is not about adding to our knowledge that which has been left out of the university curriculum; rather it is about transforming the entire 'dysfunctional curriculum,' which rationalizes the oppression of all groups in society.... Knowledge is positional."[1] Not only must the university itself change, the cultural left says, but it must, in turn, be the leading force in the next wave of even more radical reform.

Comparable to the corporate right's expectations of the university as an engine of economic growth, the cultural left has expectations of the university as an engine of social change. Where the corporate right sees the university as a business enterprise, the cultural left sees it as a social welfare agency and change agent. Much like the corporate right, the cultural left sees the universities at a watershed. We are, as the *Globe and Mail*'s education writer Lesley Krueger recently wrote, at the "crucial stage... grappling with our self-definition as a multicultural, egalitarian society."[2] Or, as a speaker at a recent education symposium speculated:

> [T]eachers and counsellors of the future will require a specific set of intercultural skills and strategies. The culturally encapsulated teacher will become a dinosaur, hopefully an obsolete and dying breed.... [T]eachers and counsellors must take on a futuristic vision of what their classrooms will be like in the year 2000 and prepare themselves to cope with an increasingly global composition.... There is also evidence that there is a universal drive to be in synchrony, harmony, and congruency with our environment and with significant others....[3]

The cultural left sees the world situation in much the same way as Jean Bethke Elshtain and George Grant do, but interprets it very differently. The fragmenting forces that Elshtain identifies in confrontations between aggrieved groups rather than dialogue between free citizens are viewed by the cultural left with relief as the forces ensuring the death of the Western experiment. Today's potent facts for the cultural left are the disintegration of European dominance, the destruction of high culture, the end of white patriarchy and the ascendancy of the marginalized. The homogenizing forces of technology and consumerism that Grant sees as reducing culture to commodity and depriving us of compass points in matters of justice are seen as opportunities for liberation—as long as the "backlash" of antiprogressivism can be prevented.

The cultural left was once fighting on behalf of equality and social justice. Its members were *intellectuels engagés* in the noblest sense of the word. At that time, the paradigmatic events around which they rallied were the 1960s ban-the-bomb and civil rights demonstrations and the principled resistance to the Vietnam War. In their opposition to ignorance and prejudice, and in their appeal to equal rights and a politics of respect, was born a proud, new feminism and an awareness of human dignity. Their work was an important contribution to the ongoing attempt to make our societies more just. While a few of that left (once the new left, now the old left) remain, the majority have changed their tune dramatically, though they are still tilting at windmills such as the state, the rich, the propertied and the military-industrial complex. Today, the cultural left recalls only one event: the Paris student protests of May 1968, which they often dub "a revolution." But the truth is that while the students believed themselves to be the vanguard of the revolution, the rampage and rioting they engaged in—run by a motley group of *agents provocateurs* of Maoists and Stalinists—was not viewed sympathetically by the labouring class with which they sought alliance. The week of violence, while sustained by the myth of a General Strike, was unstructured, episodic and void of enduring political meaning.

This meaninglessness has continued to generate fantasies. Retrospective storytelling sees the protests as the glory days when dreams of new battles to be waged—"identity politics" and "social movements"—were born. The new battles, unlike those of the old left, are no longer being waged in society at large, but within the university campus itself. For the cultural left the battles must be found in the areas of curricula, academic hierarchy, university composition and the terms of academic discourse. Pervasive injustice must be tracked down, in *Eurocentrism*, *androcentrism* and *heterocentrism* (the apparent privilege given to European civilization, male perspectives and heterosexual relations) and under the new mantra of "race, gender and ethnicity." The cultural left's major contribution to the demise of Canada's universities is the pathologization of faculty and student behaviour, because in the empire of social work that the cultural left has built up at the university to "cure" students and faculty, the first thing dispensed with was the natural trust inherent in the scholarly culture.

It is not difficult to speculate why the left's battles have turned inward. At a time when the world is renouncing the politics of the left, the academic left, immured in the universities, has little more to do than flex its muscles on the only terrain left to it. Although the irony that they are castigating the privilege of the university while enjoying all its privileges is not lost on them and while their academic Marxism has won them the moniker "jacuzzi Marxists," they are no less lethal in their actions for living the contradiction of driving Volvos and preaching revolution.

Another major aspect distinguishes them from their noble parentage. The old left, while its members had their differences, was composed of decent, civilized intellectuals. By contrast, the cultural left has little charm and bottomless reserves of malice. What is particularly precious is the way this left turns on its own kind, like scorpions biting their own tails. Indeed, among today's many historical paradoxes, one that stands out is the vindictiveness of the new rainbow coalition of feminists, visible minorities, aboriginals, disabled persons, gays, bisexuals and lesbians, proponents of minority discourse and postmodernist Marxists, against the old left. The case of Reg Whitaker, a once well-respected left-wing professor of political science at York University, is characteristic. In an elegantly penned *Globe and Mail* essay entitled "The Cutting Edge of Ontario's Bad Law," Whitaker made a modest critique of the employment equity laws of Bill 79, pointing out the contradiction between the goal of combatting discrimination on the basis of biological traits and entrenching these traits as advantages for the groups involved. He concluded that the bill "aids victims by establishing new categories of victims. It does this because it confuses fairness in process with equality of results."[4] A short time after this article appeared, Professor Whitaker received a letter from York University's Status of Women Office, stating that he should no longer sit on hiring committees, as he had revealed himself to be biased against women and minorities. The self-immolation of the left—one thinks of the self-destructive antics within the National Action Committee on the Status of Women and the accusations of faux-feminism that divide the feminist movement—is not accidental. Common cause is not what the cultural left is seeking. It is not merely looking for a seat at the table; it wants the table dismantled and no table rebuilt.

While much academic dispute is wound a notch too tightly, the cultural left's rhetoric is particularly vitriolic. More disturbingly, it utterly flattens the political spectrum. The cultural left's attitude is "If you're not with us, you're against us" and anyone who opposes equity or inclusivity, as they conceive them, is denounced as sitting among the political right. "Conservative," it goes without saying, is now a term of abuse in academe, "a sign of moral failure" as some faculty at Carleton University recently said. The crude reasoning runs thus: if you are not on the left, then you are obviously conservative, and if you are conservative, you must be like American conservatives, with their enthusiasm for the free-market model, Christian prayers in public schools, the recriminalization of abortion, stripping homosexuals of civil rights protections and censoring school libraries. In short: safe streets, strong families and nonintrusive government.

For the cultural left, it is beside the point that many liberals, red tories and social democrats, to name a few other political options, may actually support the idea of reward based on merit, or a liberal education founded on persuasive reason, without subscribing to these other neoconservative priorities. It shields itself conveniently from concerns being raised by sensible individuals about reverse discrimination, the fragmentation of civil society and restrictions on academic freedom by declaring, as do Stephen Richer and Lorna Weir in their recent pedantic panegyric to the "inclusive university," that "PC [political correctness] is a neoconservative offence that has replaced anti-communist rhetoric and sustains the social hierarchy of 'white, male elites.'"[5] Sober and analytical conversation about the terms of this denunciation cannot proceed because the cultural left believes itself to have deconstructed once and for all the myths of academia: the myth of meritocracy, the myth of objective standards and neutrality, the myth of nondiscrimination and fairness, the myth of democracy, the myth of collegiality, the myth of liberalism and openness, the myth of the search for knowledge, the myth of co-operation and the myth of individualism.

Incendiary rhetoric, hyperbole and sloganeering is obviously not exclusive to the cultural left, but what they have achieved is the disruption of the healthy polyphony of scholarly conversation, leaving little more than a cacophony of voices. Moreover, despite the cultural left's avowed mission of releasing the natural voices of the "oppressed" from the tyranny of the "dominant voice," the language of these voices is one that fewer and fewer people can understand—*discourse, logocentrism, marginalization, signifier, inclusivity* and *dissemination.*

If this sounds like pseudo-intellectual jargon, it is. The cultural left has swamped ordinary language with obscurantism, permitting much political posturing but offering little constructive insight into the real sources of injustice. The disdain for ordinary language, however, is also calculated. As Henri Giroux and Stanley Aronowitz tell us, "It seems to us that those who call themselves progressive educators, whether feminists, Marxists, or otherwise, who make the call for clear writing synonymous with an attack on critical educators, have missed the role that the 'language of clarity' plays in a dominant culture that cleverly and powerfully uses 'clear' and 'simplistic' language to systematically undermine and prevent the conditions from arising for a public culture to engage in rudimentary forms of complex and critical thinking."[6] In other words, to politicize everyday life, or to put it slightly differently, to revolt against reality, a new language is needed. Words are reality or, to use the cultural left's language, all meaning is "socially constructed."

While disdaining ordinary language, the cultural left has also rejected the *petite politesse* of refined speech. Having abandoned accommodation through rational engagement, the cultural left's language of confrontation is intended as shock therapy. The tactic of subverting authority through vulgarity is, of course, common—in the fifth century B.C., Aristophanes used graphic imagery and bawdy language to ridicule the pretensions of those

who claimed to be "in the know"—and it was used with positive effect during the American student protests of the 1960s.
Seasoned academics often use the tactic themselves, trying to get
their students to overcome conventional euphemisms and the
social platitudes underlying them, and the occasions are usually
filled with great mirth.

The cultural left, however, goes much further than this. In
addition, their vulgarity is humourless. Aristophanes and the
students of the 1960s did not see all of reality as a great act of
rape writ large. The cultural left does. Acts of reason are "pene-
trations"; using the copula verb "to be" to imply a permanent
state of affairs, is considered to be akin to forced "copulation"
and, as a recent writer in *The Canadian Forum* wrote, commenting on a male instructor's disagreement with feminists, "He may
even have chosen to provoke 'the feminists' by metaphorically
'waving his cock in front of the class.'"[7] For the cultural left,
rape must be met by vigilante rage. The *Emily* at the University
of Victoria, the *Surface* at Queen's and innumerable new journals offer up the same prescription of confrontational misan-
dropy and localized resistance, and they make clear that all
communications between men and women, races or ethnic
groups, are acts of violence and counterviolence.

For all this excess, the cultural left is, nonetheless, heir to a
worthy tradition. While the university is commonly identified
by its intellectual aims and achievements, no less a premium
should be placed on its ability to provide the fertile soil in which
genuine moral criticism and projects of social renewal are formulated. If "Take Back the Night" marches (to express solidarity
with victims of male violence) and recovery and healing sessions
are two of the more maudlin of these exercises, this search for
forms of commonality, even when they exhibit the fervour of
Pentecostal communities, is a legitimate expression of the work
of the scholarly culture. There is a place at the university, as I
have noted, for "transformative" studies and the creation of corporations of solidarity, reflecting its function as a *universitas*.
And an environment that puts such an unrelenting premium on

intellectual achievement and genius, or on the demonstration of authentic solidarity, is bound to be filled with hyperbole, extravagance, silliness, ambiguity and play that is on the edge of decency. The antics of young men and women filled with vital energy are no less to be tolerated than the kind of free association of metaphor in which radical feminists indulge, as in,

> As a Black woman I can not separate my head from my hips nor can I separate my facial lips from the ones that surround my vagina/ As a black woman my head is seen as an empty void that needs to be filled because *racism* names me inferior—*and...*/ My Black hole is the reservoir to which I retreat and if I do not take care to remain conscious of what fills it, I can lose sense of that internal source of awareness that keeps me whole.[8]

However uncomfortable to common decencies the celebration of lesbian writing as a revolutionary form, the praise of androgyny or the refrain that the "personal is political," beneath their passion lies a legitimate form of what the scholarly culture tolerates and should praise.

Moreover, while the university must, for the vitality of its scholarly culture, allow for a wide latitude of experiments and adventures, there can be no justification for the abuse of academic freedom that manifests itself in taunts and abuse, crude indecencies and belittling insensitivities. An evident case in point is the notorious 1988 case of Professor Richard Hummel who, equipped with snorkel and flippers, followed women swimming in the University of Toronto Hart House pool, staring (some alleged leering) at them through his mask. The indignity suffered by those women who legitimately advanced charges of sexual harassment is exceeded in distastefulness only by an ensuing appeal that attempted to have the ruling of guilt overturned because Hummel had not *intended* to create an intimidating and hostile environment. The case ended with Hummel being barred for a number of years from the athletic facilities.

Equal revulsion should be directed at the criminology instructor at the College of New Caledonia who assigned to his male students the homework of planning a perfect rape. These incidents and far too many more make deeply troubling the actions of the Trent faculty who signed a declaration of the right to be offensive and dared thereby to align themselves with John Stuart Mill's majestic words in defence of liberty: "If all mankind minus one, were of one opinion, and only one person were of the contrary opinion, mankind would be no more justified in silencing that one person, than he, if he had the power, would be justified in silencing mankind." These faculty forgot how circumscribed Mill's defence really is.[9] Mill, after all, argued that the exercise of liberty must not infringe on another person's liberty, and he held that the evolution of liberal society depended on progress in social manners. More fatuous than the Trent faculty's declaration was a comment by Robert Fulford who praised the Trent professors as "true revolutionaries."[10] Some may say that the behaviour of university members is no worse than that in society generally. What a terrible admission! The university community ought to set a standard higher than the behaviour one observes in society at large, not one that merely mirrors it.

If we accept Oakeshott's dictum that "[we] sail a boundless and bottomless sea" and "there is neither harbour for shelter nor floor for anchorage, neither starting-place nor appointed destination," we could see the challenges posed by the cultural left as opportunities for a healthy renewal. But we cannot be so receptive because the cultural left does not also embrace Oakeshott's prudent conclusion that our task is "to keep afloat on an even keel," recognizing that "the sea is both friend and enemy; and the seamanship consists in using the resources of a traditional manner of behaviour in order to make a friend of every hostile occasion."[11] To the contrary, the cultural left's *modus operandi* is to see only power struggle and antagonism in the world around us and to see its own task as promoting permanent revolution. "Racializing" and "engendering" history, politics and reason—the cultural left's way of saying that all events or historical periods must be understood essentially as struggles of race or sex—is a rally cry to deconstruct and corrode trust in the evident experiences of living.[12] It embraces all dangers and corruptions and fancifully imagines a future that has wholly overturned "traditional manners of behaviour," as in the following dream: "[Imagine]...if most political leaders were women, of colour, and lesbian? If Great Literature was almost entirely by lesbians of colour? If there were only goddesses and no major gods?"[13]

The cultural left abets mutual suspicion and scepticism and contributes forcefully to an insurrectionary climate and a tendency to revolutionary overthrow of all institutions. But the moral and spiritual vacuum is being filled—by the political clubs that seem to accompany all revolutionary times. These clubs— the National Action Committee on the Status of Women, the CAUT Status of Women Committee, the Canadian Association against Sexual Harassment in Higher Education, the Society for Academic Freedom and Scholarship—are contributing powerfully to the hot-button politics agitating Canada's universities. Among the most pronounced hot buttons of the cultural left is the politics of feminism—an issue we will examine here before turning to ethnic identity, the inclusive university and the infamous "zero-tolerance" policy in the next chapter.

In 1995, Jackie Stalker, a recently retired professor of education from the University of Manitoba contributed an essay to the *Globe and Mail* entitled "The Chill Women Feel at Canada's Universities."[14] The essay compared universities to harems, where "men are in the positions of authority, as tenured professors and senior administrators, exerting their will over women who are students, staff and even a small number of colleagues...a locker-room culture where they don't understand the game and have few or no mentors to turn to for advice." She complained of "entrenched and prolonged systemic discrimination" and a state of affairs where "the rules, regulations, curriculums, language, cases and support will not always make sense to female students either; they were developed sincerely and with the best of intentions, but by men and for men" and constitute

men's "hereditary privilege." "Entrenched and prolonged systemic discrimination," Stalker concluded, has led to "the 'chilly
climate' condition, created by the serious power imbalance, consist[ing] of hostility, discrimination, harassment, inequitable
treatment, violence and sometimes silent terror for more than
half the population in our male-dominated institutions."

The most unassailable component of Stalker's opinions is her
claim that in sixty-four years the percentage of women faculty
has increased only 2 percent—from 19 percent in 1931 to 21
percent in 1995.[15] The 1992 Statistics Canada analysis of
61,845 full- and part-time faculty offers an additional dimen-
sion that makes these statistics even bleaker—while 88 percent
of full-time faculty are male, only 12 percent of full-time faculty
are female. In society generally, as a 1995 Statistics Canada
report shows, there is progress in what women have achieved:
women represent 45 percent of the workforce and 43.1 percent
of management and administrative positions, and their wages
comprise 72 percent of men's earnings, with 91 percent
recorded in the age group between fifteen and twenty-four. In
universities, the distribution across ranks and academic administrative offices is not even remotely on par. The data reveal that
the higher the rank, the higher the percentage of men in
tenured positions: at the level of assistant professor 46 percent
are men, at the level of full professor 88 percent are men. There
are only nine women presidents in Canada's ninety-two colleges
and universities, and the proportion of women in vice-presidencies, directorships and deanships is equally dismaying.

The situation among students is not significantly better.
Women now make up approximately 54 percent of university
students, but their distribution is skewed along "traditional"
occupation lines: for example, in doctoral studies, 60 percent of
individuals enrolled in education are women, 46 percent are
women in the humanities, 45 percent in the social sciences, 43
percent in the health sciences, 33 percent in agricultural and
biological sciences, 18 percent in mathematics and physical sciences and 10 percent in engineering and applied science.

Such statistics can be duplicated *ad nauseam*, but the questions of what they mean and what should be done to change the situation are much more ambiguous. At the University of Manitoba, for instance, after months of agitation over women's marginalization, female faculty were given a 3.89 percent salary increase to compensate them for being traditionally underpaid. The ruling was based on a study showing that women on average received $2,215 per annum less than men. Male faculty complained that the raw data did not take into account other reasons for salary differentials—for example, differences between faculties and ranks, and the disproportionate number of women with higher salaries within some faculties and ranks. Female faculty did not take kindly to the complaints—the explanations often simply corroborated their allegation of unequal treatment. The clash between statistics and their political interpretation also created a ruckus at McGill University in 1994 when women discovered that a new pension plan, whose mathematics was based on actuarial tables, paid smaller monthly benefits to women than to men because women's average life expectancy is 7.4 years longer.

A balanced and conservative assessment of the data should lead to two conclusions. First, there are grounds for the concern expressed by senior women about an "academic funnel" that has meant fewer women at higher ranks and administrative posts and a "glass ceiling" that has prevented their upward ascendancy. (Data that show women earning 98 percent of the salaries of their male colleagues at the junior levels also show that senior women at the rank of associate and full professor were earning only 95 percent. It is also difficult to understand why only 9.8 percent of university presidents are women.) Secondly, the condition of junior faculty women is improving. The wage ratio in society generally of 91 percent of women between fifteen and twenty-four offers reassurance for the future; there has also been a 7 percent increase of hirings of female faculty through tie-breaking affirmative action policies. Nonetheless, efforts to redress the former injustices by accelerating the project of equity are fraught with perils.

Leaving aside, for the moment, concerns raised about the injustice of reverse discrimination, equity action is also producing numerous negative side effects for equity itself. Many women legitimately claim that because of the push to improve gender representation on university committees, tenure is more difficult to obtain. This is the result of a policy that stipulates that service on university committees carries less weight than research publication and teaching. Another peculiar side effect of current efforts to establish more equity occurs when larger universities, undertaking preferential hiring, compete vociferously and successfully for outstanding women, leading to a situation where there are fewer of them available for smaller universities. The more modest, and sometimes mediocre, hirings that occur at small universities legitimately raises the wrath of applicants excluded from fair consideration on equity grounds. However, following the practice of hiring only on merit does nothing to balance the proportion of men and women at smaller universities. Perils notwithstanding, Stalker's outrage has a core of truth to it, and it is to the shame of Canada's universities that the small steps being undertaken to recognize the rightful place of women are too little and have come too late.

Many of the interventions and compromises that needed to be made could perhaps have been carried out if the various constituencies of the university had not felt they were backed into a corner. Sexual harassment workshops, colloquia on forming an environment conducive to learning, lessons on the harm of gender-biased language—all are part of a larger program on the "traditional manner of behaviour" and all are geared towards improving the effectiveness of lectures and the excellence of research. These can hardly be seen as incursions on "academic freedom" or mischievous politicizations of the university. But the cultural left's rhetoric and its eye to political gains have presented these changes in such a way as to produce paralysis and intolerance on Canada's campuses. In recent years one precipitating event, and its interpretation by the cultural left, is responsible for a great deal of that intractability—the Marc Lépine massacre of fourteen women.

The 1989 Lépine massacre is of a scale that should lead any decent person to see it as an expression of "radical evil." Nothing can or should erase the memory of that singular atrocity. The only human option that we ordinarily have in the face of barbarity—forgiveness—and which is chosen only after extensive reflection and through resolute sacrifice, can, in this case, not be chosen without losing some aspect of our humanity. There are those who are outside the pale of humanity—Marc Lépine was one.

To move, however, from this terrible event to an analysis of "systemic" sexism in society generally, and the universities in particular, is an example of intoxicating rhetoric triumphing over reality. Yet such hyperbole is endemic to the cultural left's response to the Lépine massacre, and to the media, which flatters it. In their analysis of 172 *Montreal Gazette* stories about the massacre, M. Grenier and L. Hachey found that "the misogynous character of the offender...tended strongly to be generalized to men as a group and not particularized or restricted to one male or one type of male. In a word, what emerged was a fairly consistent image of the male gender group as being inherently misogynous." For a year after the event, media coverage of violence against women was thirty-six to forty-nine times greater than coverage of violence against men, despite the equal likelihood of violence against either gender.[16] The tenor of the analysis was reflected in the remark of one feminist: "Men have to look at the rapist inside of them." Lépine has become, in the hands of the cultural left, the most visible expression of pervasive, systemic violence against women. For example, in a discussion with students about violence against women, former Ontario Attorney-General Marion Boyd answered a question about a case of a student at the University of Western Ontario's law school, who had brought a charge of harassment against a professor who called her a "good girl." She suggested that it was helpful to think about incidents of harassment and verbal violence on a continuum, which in the extreme can culminate in the Marc Lépine massacre.[17]

When a Canadian Forces corporal opened fire in 1984 in the

National Assembly in Quebec City, nobody said there was pervasive and systemic discrimination against politicians. When a student at Brampton Centennial Secondary School in 1975 shot a teacher and fellow students, no one said there was pervasive and systemic discrimination against teachers and students. When an employee shot and killed two Du Pont executives in 1971, no one alleged that there was pervasive and systemic discrimination against corporate executives. Nonetheless, many, many expressions of hostility and indecency are directed at politicians, teachers and executives. To allege "systemic" discrimination against women and pervasive violence against women with the ardour exemplified by the cultural left following the Lépine affair, one must have already decided that all men are Bobbitts. The note Lépine wrote before the massacre explicitly linked what he was about to do with the shootings in the National Assembly, expressing regret that he had not conducted that attack. He may have had many additional murder campaigns in mind.[18]

In the aftermath of the Lépine massacre, the Royal Society of Canada sponsored a panel discussion on the "backlash" against women. Six men and two women participated. As the editor of the resulting book notes, the men's assessments were more "personal and perplexed" because they looked to individual psychology to explain the tragedy. The women, on the other hand, were "more analytical and wide-ranging" because they identified structural and systemic causes and thus contributed to a "women's studies" perspective that according to the editor was a genuine "intellectual inquiry," unlike the opinions of the men. The panel undertook, among other goals, to acknowledge "the disturbing recognition that universities may in some way be responsible [for the tragedy at Polytechnique.]"[19]

The discussion reached a peak in ideological assertion when Rose Sheinin, then vice-rector, academic, of Concordia University, stated that the massacre was "one event in a continuum" of the misogyny inherent in the "authoritative knowledge" of "Western thought." That misogyny, Sheinin argued, can be traced back to the ancient Hebrews and pursued all the way up to Freud's psychoanalysis. Her extraordinary chain of inferences flits from Aristotle's views on the inferiority of women, to the supremacy his writings enjoyed in the University of Paris and Oxford University in the thirteenth century, to the misogyny of Marc Lépine. Lépine, she concludes, must lead women to "confront some ten thousand years of misogynistic practice and theory."[20] Like most revisionist history, Sheinin's narrative serves the purpose of empowerment well, but serves intellectual clarity poorly in my view.

Kai Nielsen was also on the panel. An otherwise informative philosopher who has the virtue (unlike most professional philosophers) of actually engaging the world, Nielsen on this occasion went similarly awry. Pointing to some "No means now" slogans that appeared at Queen's University during a feminist "No means no" campaign, and to a "Shoot the bitch" banner that was waved at the University of Alberta in response to a female student's protest against sexist rites, Nielsen too acknowledged the "pervasive" sexual harassment in our culture. He bid us to "summon up the courage and strength to accept Marc Lépine as a brother, a sibling" of the "same toxic cultural environment and with whom we share a number of internalized values, beliefs, desires, and fears."[21] In a bizarre expression of cultural analysis, Nielsen concluded with the argument that the collapse of the John Wayne male-type has created a vacuum in which men's anxieties end up playing out "Rambo-like fantasies." Once again, anecdotal evidence took the place of hard fact, and assertion was permitted to triumph over argument.

Another panelist, Louis Courville, asked one of the few sensible questions raised by the discussion: how could an individual who appeared to be "rational, calm, deliberate" in behaviour be at the same time "mad and sick." Although not provided in the course of the panel, there is a general answer to Courville's question which might explain Lépine's actions to some degree. In her analysis of Adolf Eichmann (the Nazi who sent hundreds of thousands of Jews to their deaths, and who, when tried in Jerusalem by his Israeli captors, displayed neither remorse nor

215

understanding of his immoral deeds), Hannah Arendt has suggested that perhaps evil of this order was utterly "banal." It was occasioned not by immoral hatred but by a pathology that welcomes disconnection, isolation, social fluidity and historical amnesia at the cost of narrative unity and responsibility. Eichmann on trial, she observed, appeared incapable of recalling his actions in anything but episodic and fragmented fashion, of recognizing emotions except in evident isolation from one another or through a self-indulgent association of circumstances with feelings or perceptions. In her book *The Origins of Totalitarianism*, Arendt offers additional explanations of how the Eichmanns (or Lépines) of the world develop, suggesting that psychic fragmentation is reinforced by political environments that prevent public engagement, isolate individuals in their own subjective fantasies and treat concrete persons as abstractions or a bundle of reactions to stimulus.

The scanty evidence left in the wake of Lépine's terrible actions does not permit a thorough diagnosis. But it seems clear from his notes and letters that Lépine suffered from syndromes not unlike those of Eichmann, and it is obvious in his evident isolation from the world, that he was rarely in a situation where his perverse (but strangely internally consistent) logic could be held up to the common sense of genuine public debate and deliberation. If Arendt's general analysis is of any use in the particular case of Lépine, we should beware of any teaching that urges on its subjects a radical dispossession, that would uproot individuals from the common world where their perceptions and perspectives are held up to public debate, and that praises the everyman (or everywoman) who lives in a subjective fantasy more certain and consistent than the ambiguous common world. Yet what does the cultural left utter but the postmodernist opinion that all human life is structured by nothing but relations of dominance and subordination and that, as a result, no civil engagement is of any value?

A restoration of the "commons," and its accompanying common sense, cannot be expected if we follow the recommendations of three other feminist offerings from the cultural left. "The Chilly Climate for Women in Colleges and Universities"—a video produced by the University of Western Ontario's Caucus on Women's Issues—is widely distributed in Canada for use in the classroom. It is also one of the most emotionally manipulative forms of agitprop the cultural left has produced. It begins with a parade of older white males filing across a stage while the voiceover of Dr. Glenda Simms, president of the Canadian Advisory Council on the Status of Women, expounds, "Education can be a deadly weapon. It will always be a tool of oppression when it is used as such by one culture, one race, one sex, or one religion." The video continues with anonymous testimonials by faculty, students, and support staff of an environment "chilly to the point of toxicity"—women who speak of their pain, their exclusion, their silencing and their disappointment. At one point a woman expresses her frustration that her male colleagues do not invite her for lunch, but complains that when they do invite her, the lunch has the tone of a date. By some baffling linguistic wizardry, the event is interpreted as resonating with the Lépine massacre.

A recurring theme of the video is that male truths masquerading as objectivity and neutrality are merely thinly disguised power plays. An audience might expect an equally robust account of the form that just relations between men and women should take. Disappointment is in store for anyone with such expectations. Simms finally comments that "equity must become part of the ideology of the university" and with that admission the chickens come home to roost. If the university is no more than "ideology"—read struggles of power, brokering of interests and ideas furthering dominance—then by virtue of what is the duty to respect others to be entertained any more than the right to exercise one's power? When everything is a contest of power, what is the status of the principle that distinguishes just power from unjust power?

The answer appears to be—just imagination. In a mawkish ending, lamely evoking the memory of Martin Luther King's famous "I have a dream…" speech, Simms intones, "I have ideal-ism, let idealism live."[22] The young women, and one might add the young men, of Canada, to whom is left the difficult work of composing the new world where men and women of many races and cultures are accorded a principled recognition and respect deserve much more and much better.

The video "Inequity in the Classroom: A Video for Professors and Adult Educators" produced by the Office of the Status of Women at Concordia University, also in wide use across Canada, suffers from the same faults. Power, the narrator says, is in the classroom all the time. A typical classroom is one where men are always interrupting women; instructors are ignoring women and treating them abruptly; and sports analogies, com-parisons to machines and sexual innuendo prevail. In short, women are patronized and men dominate. "The hero of schol-arly life," claims Dorothy Smith, a York University professor, "is always a male" and so men are given higher-order questions and receive more praise and attention. Women are powerless and their male teachers have all the power. The narrator of the video concludes with a lament that men use academic freedom only to reinforce the status quo and fail to recognize the truth "that knowledge has always been tied to power."

One might wish to differ with this perspective. What status, pray, does this analysis itself have, if we are all systemically oppressed and playthings of power? In a 1995 letter to the edi-tor, after months of heated exchanges in the press about the alleged sexism and racism in the UBC political science depart-ment, Anne Vézina made a compelling point about the systemic nature of sexism: "It cost UBC $237,897.68 but at least now we know that sexism is not rampant in the political science depart-ment. In sexist societies, women are not paid handsomely to scrutinize the behaviour of their 'oppressors.' In sexist societies, accusations of discrimination don't make front-page news."[23]

One could add that in systemically sexist societies, how-to manuals for feminist revolutionaries like *Lifting a Ton of Feathers: A Woman's Guide to Surviving in the Academic World,*

are also not supported by public funds. In 1992, in the wake of
the Lépine massacre, Paula Caplan was commissioned to produce this survival guide for women in academe. The resulting
book is predicated on the idea that when women fail, and falsely
believe they are themselves at fault, the truth is that their fate
has been sealed by barriers within male university culture.[24]
According to Caplan, the university culture is fraught with sexual harassment, sexist language and jokes, and barriers to
women's progress, all reinforcing the general "maleness, racism,
and heterosexism of the environment."

Caplan's portrait of Canada's universities is not flattering. Even
if her general indictment is exaggerated, her lively depiction of
loutish and boorish male behaviour is, lamentably, not wholly off
the mark. The premium that universities put on freedom and
unconventionalism does generate excess and indecency. If
humour is not crude, it is nonetheless biting; if opposition is not
physical, it does, however, strike deeply in the soul. However, is
Caplan right that women are singled out particularly for abuse?
Her evidence is, at first blush, persuasive. Pointing to the double
standard that applies to men and women, she notes that when
men are ambitious, this is praised. When women are ambitious,
this is aggressive and their behaviour is seen as bitchy and grasp-
ing. When men complain about procedure, it is seen as constructive criticism; with women it is seen as nagging. Yet, when
women's behaviour is more pliant or dramatic, it is rejected as
emotional or passionate. Men are usually treated as individuals,
while women are treated as a group. A man is a bad administrator, while a woman is another example of what happens when
women are made administrators. When women make an effort
to socialize, their intentions are interpreted as sexual. Can many
men deny they have judged women this way?

It is hard, though, to resist a tit-for-tat. When men praise one
another, it is "the old boys' network," while if they praise women
they have ulterior motives. When men raise procedural issues,
they are seen as closing ranks, while when women do so, they
are viewed as overcoming barriers. When men resist equity

policies, they are impeding justice, but when women rig employment practices, their courage is applauded. When men question motives, they are stereotyping, but when women advance the thesis that they are surrounded by a culture that systemically (even invisibly) oppresses women, they are theorizing. But to engage in such tit-for-tat is to fall victim to the very traps that Caplan's study sets—pitting women against men in a zero-sum game, and offering a seductive, but doubtful, thesis that all tensions and predicaments can be structurally explained.

The latter argument is one of the most disingenuous features of Caplan's guide to women. She takes ordinary occurrences that strain the lives of everyone, whether men or women, and elevates them to "women's dilemmas":

> I know I'm supposed to play the academic game, use the jargon, make political moves, etc., but I really, desperately want my work to speak for itself.... I also feel torn between feeling I should be tough on students in order to prepare them for graduate school and giving them grades for opening their souls to me.... I feel I have to be on guard all the time, careful not to say anything about my private life in front of male faculty, because otherwise they will find it hard to take me seriously....

Caplan finally places the blame for women's anxieties and disappointments firmly to rest on prevailing female socialization and rampant sexism in the university.

More dubious than this conspiracy mongering is Caplan's advice on countering the structural sexism in the universities. She starts out modestly ("create a savings bank of support for your self-esteem") but then adds three far more controversial recommendations: "Do not assume that those who have the power to evaluate your work at any point are objective or correct," "Learn to recognize how much clout you really do have," "Ask yourself whether you really *want* to be like 'them.'"[25] Just as in the Concordia and Western Ontario videos, the ultimate message is power against power, ideology against ideology, interest against interest.

Authors like Caplan might try a different tack if they sincerely wish to arrest the growing deterioration of relations between men and women in the university. Instead of dwelling on women's victimhood and feeding paranoia about structural intentions to thwart and hurt, Caplan and the professional university association that sponsored her project might wish to put together an anthology of women's exemplary work in literature, science, art and the social sciences. For too long now we have invested greatly in the project of creating human bonds on the basis of pity and resentment, encouraging the unleashing of the lethal and corrosive passions of envy and revenge. Would we not dignify the world that must be redesigned, where women and minority groups gain their rightful respect, if we looked instead at our excellence and our virtues?

Unfortunately, this is not the tack being taken. Instead women are getting, especially in women's studies programs, platitudes like "Women's Studies are those studies which place women at the centre of the process of researching and writing for the purpose of establishing women's realities."[26] Or they are being given assignments, as happened in a Women's Studies program at the University of Victoria, in which students were asked to pair off and act like lesbians on the university campus. When a female student launched a formal harassment charge, complaining that lesbianism was being pushed onto students in the course, the department head, Jenifer Waelti-Walters, gave the assignment an unqualified defence: "The idea is to get our students—many of whom are white, heterosexual and middle class—to have some sense of what it's like to be in other people's skins."[27] This form of pedagogy, made infamous in the quasi-Maoist values-clarification exercises and gestalt-therapy techniques popular in the 1960s, has outlived its welcome, having been seen by most psychologists and professional educators as ineffective in encouraging respect and profoundly lethal in the hands of those lacking common sense.[28] Perhaps it is time to propose a women's studies program that puts women's intellectual achievements, spiritual journeys and moral acts at the centre, and thus focuses on women's contributions to human accomplishment.

Finally, it is eye-opening to examine a document produced by the CAUT Status of Women Committee in a 1994 supplement to that organization's bulletin. In an article entitled "Academic Freedom *is* the Inclusive University," authors Janice Drakich, Karen Grant and Joyce Forbes question the absolute primacy given in universities to "academic freedom" and justifiably point out that civility, respect, sensitivity, understanding and tolerance are equally important to the health of the institution. But then their argument goes off kilter, as they posit the same tired complaint that "traditional education" and "canonical subjects" repress the heterogeneity of identities and experiences that deviate from those of white males. The solution the authors recommend is to have a more appropriate gender, race and ethnicity representation in the curriculum.

The inclusion of non-Western, nonmale and nonwhite scholarship has great potential to enrich university offerings. The problem lies in the ensuing commentary by Jill Vickers, which offers an idea of the "representation" the cultural left has in mind.[29] Reflecting on an occasion when an aboriginal student expressed concern that a text presented as fact the theory that aboriginal people had come to North America over the Bering Strait from Asia, as opposed to that student's view that his people were indigenous to North America, Vickers enjoins her readers to acknowledge the importance of teaching "parallel 'belief systems.'"[30] Parallel teaching, without a value judgment, is to be followed even when, as Vickers admits, the aboriginal student had acknowledged that the primary purpose of his alternative thesis was to oppose the argument that native peoples had no more claim to their lands than other groups who came to North America. Being "inclusive" for Vickers is evidently more important than being factual and moderating ideological zeal.

In the April 1995 *CAUT Bulletin* "Status of Women Supplement," the argument for an "inclusive university" went further. The university, its editors wrote, must have an "equity culture": "our universities and the curricula we teach reflect the experience of all who are (or would like to be) a part of the university." The CAUT Status of Women Committee adopts here, unquestioningly and without defence, an argument in common currency: that the only genuine representation is *sociological* representation, which mirrors the distribution of racial, ethnic, gender and sexual preferences in the population at large. Little concern is expressed for a curriculum representative of the wide range of philosophical options. Indeed, reading Aristotle or Rousseau is to be discouraged because they held some views unpalatable to the cultural left. What assumptions lie behind that argument?

From the onset, let us grant the CAUT one assumption—that by virtue of our limited reason, none of us could possibly imaginatively enact the whole range of human possibilities on our own. But more lies embedded within the argument for sociological representation. When the cultural left insists that all university boards, committees, departmental membership and curricula be "representative"—that women, visible-minority groups, gays and lesbians and disabled persons appear in at least the same ratio as they are distributed in the general population—they are simultaneously denying some cardinal principles of the scholarly culture. The possibility of holding principled grounds for action independent of one's biological make-up— trumped. The idea that reasoned discussions are something more than declarations of one's identity—trumped. The principle that historical accident is less significant than essential truths—trumped. The assumption that there is a hierarchy of meanings from sociological fact up to philosophical understanding—trumped. The idea that the university should not mirror, but transcend, the sectarian interests of society—trumped. When the cultural left speaks of "education equity," it does not mean a more intellectually balanced and comprehensive curriculum; it means curriculum reform on the basis of race, gender and ethnicity. The result, paradoxically, is the kind of modularized curriculum equally praised by the corporate right.

In fact, to drive the point home, the argument for sociological representation is actually an argument against representation: no one can adequately represent anyone else and nothing can effectively represent anything else. Therefore, to illustrate, men cannot articulate, and least of all endorse, the universal validity of women's claims for equality in the workplace, just as Westerners could make no claims regarding development or morality on behalf of non-Westerners. This utter breakdown of the idea of representation is what happened in the incident in 1993 at the University of Western Ontario, when an English professor was prevented, through angry protest by lesbian feminist students, from talking about a lesbian feminist poet because he was not a lesbian feminist, although he was gay.

One is tempted to offer a generous interpretation of where the arguments against representation lead—namely, to a form of populist democracy, which, while energetic, will also entail all of populist democracy's incumbent risks of mob and demagogic rule. But in fact it is hard to see how *any* democracy could really function on these assumptions. Since, arguably, no man can represent a woman, no older woman could represent a younger woman, no Caucasian woman could represent an Afro-American woman, no normally abled individual could represent a disabled person, and so on and so forth, what is this democracy where all that prevails is interest emanating from unassailable linguistic villages? The condition urged upon us by the cultural left takes us further back than the lesson contained in the story of the Tower of Babel. In that story, at least, while burdened with linguistic diversity, humankind was still left with the option of translation and an aptitude to learn a second or third language. In its postmodern form, if we follow out the logic of the argument, the cultural left would presumably have us return to a prelinguistic state where we could do little more than point at things, deprived of the powers of abstraction and of universals. This makes for lethal social policy and contributes decisively to the cynicism that is paralyzing this country.

Of course, the cultural left does not really want us to return to a state where nothing can represent anything. Compromises and brokering of interest would presumably continue; we just would never again be under the delusion that our public deliberations and rational insights were anything more than relative expressions of our position in society. This is why the cultural left so persistently indulges in the wink-wink of inverted commas—as in "academic freedom," "teaching," "reason"—by which is meant "so-called" academic freedom, teaching and reason. When the essence of literature, philosophy and history is politics, when teaching can only be advocacy, and when everything is about domination and subordination, there cannot really be any rational defence of academic freedom, teaching or freedom. Strictly speaking, there can also no longer be a distinction between teaching what is good and teaching what appears to be good, a distinction upon which, since the Platonic Academy, the university has rested.

What is occurring here is not dispassionate pursuit of vexing philosophical questions concerning truth and appearance or reality and illusion. When the cultural left says that everything is power, what else can it mean than that they want more power? They appear to have fully adopted Humpty Dumpty's answer to Alice's complaint that words can mean whatever a person wills them to mean: "When I use a word it means just what I choose it to mean…. The question is which is to be master—that's all."[31] Nowhere is this more evident than in the snippy dismissal of principled objections to political correctness, education equity and advocacy teaching as "backlash." This is turf war, not reasoned debate. Some have not held back from declaring themselves master.[32] As the CAUT "Status of Women Supplement" bluntly concludes: "When it comes to building an equity culture on your campus, are you in or out?"[33] But not everyone wants *in*. In 1994, Ruth Gruhn, professor of anthropology at the University of Alberta, took aim at "institutionalized feminism":

One must note that with the exception of schools of theology, no other single ideology or paradigm is securely codified in a separate university department. There are no departments of Marxist political science: political scientists of Marxist persuasion are individuals within open departments of political science in which their interpretations compete with other points of view. There are no departments of Freudian psychology; psychologists of Freudian persuasion are situated within open departments of psychology, in which their ideas compete freely with other approaches. But Women's Studies departments are solidly and uniformly feminist; and critique and competition of ideas within the Women's Studies department must remain within the framework of feminism.... Feminists have taken a stance of self-righteousness that views any critique of their fundamental tenets and political tactics as misguided if not immoral; and opponents will be castigated ad hominum if not vilified.[34]

Out has also become increasingly attractive to a new generation of women with the advent of an elegant riposte to postmodern feminism. After years of "victimization-feminism" promoted by such authors as Susan Faludi (*Backlash*) and Naomi Wolf (*The Beauty Myth*), young and successful feminists like Katie Roiphe (*The Morning After*), Daphne Patai (*Professing Feminism*) and Christina Hoff Sommers (*Who Stole Feminism?*) have opposed the feminism that abandons public obligations and the idea of equity based on legal and social equality.[35] They have questioned not only the assumptions behind campaigns against date-rape that depict women of pure virtue as victims of demon men, and the expansive meaning given to terms like "sexual assault" to include any remark of a hurting nature, but also a women's studies that focuses on therapy instead of instruction, where "feeling bad" is transmuted into "being oppressed." Though branded "*faux*-feminists" by Faludi and the editors of *Ms.* magazine, in a vindictiveness that only the cultural left has perfected, Roiphe, Patai and Sommers have a great following among young women who are sceptical of the hyperbole that has defined postmodern feminism.

Leah Bradshaw, a political scientist at Brock University, and Heather McIvor, a political scientist at University of Windsor, have been the voice of the same moderate feminism in this country, as has Supreme Court Judge Beverley McLachlin. Another moderate feminist, Ryerson history professor Margaret MacMillan, made this response to Stalker's complaints about universities being like harems: "[C]an Ms. Stalker really believe that we can learn only from people who are just like us? That we should study only subjects whose content mirrors our own lives? How dreary, how limiting, and how sad to assume women cannot learn from men and vice versa…. Ms. Stalker is welcome to enjoy her victimhood if she wants, but count me out."[36]

And those who remain *in* are flailing in confusion as the cardinal principles of a once-proud feminism fly in tatters. The battle raging in the National Action Committee on the Status of Women culminated in the committee's high-profile withdrawal from two significant investigations: the Royal Commission into New Reproductive Technologies and a panel on violence against women. This is a good example of what happens once the paralyzing logic of postmodernism is set loose. What has torn that committee apart is the catchword to which we just referred— "inclusion" or, more precisely, whether *some* women can speak for *all* women. Sunera Thobani, president since 1993, has made it clear that NAC had in the past been speaking only for white, middle-class women. NAC, she said, must "forge ahead under the leadership of the most marginalized women in society," for these "understand our society better than those who live in the four walls of relative privilege." The NAC has been torn by other forms of "identity politics," particularly by the lesbian caucus. As NAC's fundraising consultant, Gail Picco, complains, "Everyone's got a different piece of identity at NAC, and it's preventing them from coming together for collective action."[37] In the process of dividing the spoils, the cultural left is destroying the important gains made by a more moderate feminism.

Chapter 9

The Cultural Left: Political Correctness and Chilly Climates

So much of left-wing thought is a kind of playing with fire by people who don't even know that fire is hot.

George Orwell

The cultural left's politics have had the same damaging effects on another important issue in the university community: antiracist education. As we have seen, the aims of higher learning cannot be advanced if the university community is not a civil association. The intellectual life requires at its very core what the French philosopher Henri Bergson called *l'âme ouverte*—an openness of the soul towards the other. At the very minimum, such openness will be expressed as tolerance, and the university properly employs both legal and extralegal means to form and sustain tolerance among its members. But tolerance is a fickle virtue, easily derailing into indifference or diffidence, if it is not nourished by a moral will to see others as persons worthy of respect. The ladder of virtue which the scholarly culture invites its members to ascend is suspended from above rather than from below. If there is no possibility of friendships that transcend naked self-interest or elusive bonds of solidarity, then the moral substance upon which tolerance decisively relies degenerates into self-righteous moralism or sentimentality. It is only by aiming high—at the images of perfection and wholeness conveyed in books and sustaining conversations—that we will ever overcome the divisions in our society.

Lamentably, with the rapid growth in the proportion of people from the Carribean, Asians and Africans in Canada's population, and with the lively energy their cultures have brought to Canadian life, new forms of discrimination and hostility have erupted, even in university communities. Amidst the battery of instruments used to form the university into a civil association, antiracist education has as strong a presence on campus as programs promoting the recognition of the equality of women, and its intentions are noble. Unfortunately, it too has fallen under the spell of the cultural left's love affair with postmodernism, and the result is further discord and fragmentation.

"Different pieces of identity," to recall Gail Picco's summary of the goings-on at the NAC, were certainly apparent in the major spats in which the cultural left has been involved in the past six years. Few things have been so disgraceful as the hounding of June Callwood by the Writers' Union of Canada. After years of service to innumerable disadvantaged people, this great philanthropist was labelled a racist. The self-immolation of the cultural left, under siege by its own principles, is as riveting to watch as it is a bell-wether showing how social engineering has replaced education.

The cultural left's ambitions run to overturning the university as a whole based on its own inchoate sentiment that injustice pervades all aspects of Canadian society. Statistics Canada's *Canadian Social Trends* publication reports that 18 percent of Canada's 1.9 million visible-minority adults hold university degrees, while only 11 percent of other Canadians do.[1] Nonetheless, the cultural left believes that pervasive and systemic discrimination exists, so it seeks, not just to eliminate racism, but to make race one of the most potent ingredients of education. In an article in *Orbit*, Carole Ann Reed, an equity harassment prevention and antiracist officer, puts the point neatly: "Anti-racist education itself does not represent a single viewpoint but should be seen as an umbrella term that encompasses a variety of views and criticisms of the educational system."[2] "Anti-racist education," she says, "addresses racism as inherent in society's structure and institutions." Sensitivity towards race has come to mean hypercaution regarding all matters of religion, family heritage, social custom and sexual preferences.

Where have judgments like this led our university policy? Item One: When the Johnston Chair in Black Canadian Studies at Dalhousie University was advertised, nonblacks, even though they were acknowledged Black-Canadian studies scholars, were sharply told that eligibility was restricted to blacks only. Item Two: When the Greater Vancouver Sikh community discovered, after endowing a Sikh chair at UBC, that its incumbent, Professor Harjot Oberoi, was not using his position to promote Sikhism, and specifically not following the approved doctrine promulgated by the Akaltakhte in Amritsar, they demanded his immediate resignation. Item Three: At the University of Waterloo, Professor R.A. Harris argues that standard English (as in "John is late") is no more to be preferred than black English ("John be late"), for both are, after all, "dialects": "the only reason that the *New York Times* and the *Globe and Mail* celebrate one while denigrating the other is the difference in economic power and social prestige between the groups that speak them."[3] Item Four: A similar treatment of a religious issue occurred at University of Toronto's Hart House. At the annual tree ceremony each Christmas, the nativity story from St. Luke's Gospel is no longer read, so as not to offend non-Christians.

Does any of this justify and support the radical overthrow of traditional liberal education? Are there profound costs to employing a model that sees the university as a social welfare agency and change agent and views the salient terms of reference as "race, gender and ethnicity," empowerment and avoiding discomfort? There are surely better means of humanizing the members of the university community—such as focusing attention on intellectual and spiritual adventures. The cultural left has shifted away from books and conversations to hot-button politics.

The University of Alberta announced in a 1994 policy paper—"Opening Doors: A Plan for Employment Equity"— that it was adopting a quota system for admitting women and native applicants. The law school, it stipulated, would reach a numerical target of ninety-four women, and at least 5 percent of students accepted by each faculty in the university would have to be native. The University of Ottawa law school has adopted the same measures. One-sixth of its first-year students are enrolled there in a program to make the study of law more accessible for racial and cultural minorities, disabled, poor and mature students. Hiring quotas (though never so called) for aboriginal people, people with disabilities, members of racial minorities and women exist, in fact, at most of Canada's universities, signifying the attempt to redistribute faculty and administrative staff populations to promote greater equity.

Some find these practices abhorrent. One can understand the anxiety, particularly that of white males whose merit seems to them to be displaced by politics and who legitimately wonder why all the wrongs of history should be placed on their backs. But modest efforts to steer institutions in the light of approved public policy and constitutionally guaranteed principles are not unjustifiable. Political theory can show, and historical evidence can corroborate, that political leaders must exercise a guiding hand if they want their regimes to be something more than the result of a pragmatic brokering of interest. There can be no acknowledgment of duties and responsibilities, nor genuine civic friendship, unless there are publicly recognized laws and public policy, reflecting reasoned principles appropriate to the art of forming spiritual substance in a community. Those who oppose these policies appear to have an unfounded faith in the justice of the free market or in the natural goodness and beneficence of individuals left to their own devices. The art of political rule is a difficult one: too much law makes resentment flourish, but too little law gives rise to clannish conceit and vengeance-based power struggles. The current situation in Canada is one where both of these ills exist: extravagant idealism regarding the power of law to guarantee justice and cynical realism that nothing transcends, or should transcend, fierce jockeying for power.

The prospect of admission quotas, or special concessions to

minorities, in order to overcome historical injustices, has alarmed many individuals. Ezra Levant, an outspoken and eloquent critic of the University of Alberta's equity policy, expressed the views held by many ordinary Canadians, whether of old stock or recent vintage, when he questioned whether racial quotas, in the context of antiracism law, truly advanced mutual tolerance. Days after he published this opinion in the student newspaper of the university's law school, he was called by the assistant dean of the school and informed that his article was offensive and hurtful.

The University of Ottawa law school, not content with admission quotas, took yet another step in 1994. It announced that it would offer "any and all students who feel that traditional examination arrangements are prejudicial to their optimum performance the opportunity to apply for exam accommodation." Preferential treatment was particularly given to students facing "racial or cultural barriers."[4] Some, like single parents, according to the dean of the Common Law section, would be entitled to double time for an exam. The public denunciation was vociferous, questioning how these policies served political equality in any meaning of the term. "If these were medical students," asked Allan Kaufmann, "would you want...to graduate a student who was given double the time on an exam without good reason—and have these people operating on you?"[5]

The issue is not whether Levant or Kaufmann are right. I believe that extralegal mechanisms for the purpose of stimulating moral renewal and criticism of the status quo are legitimate expressions of political leadership in the university. They are legitimate, however, only when they are used in the service of genuine plurality and political equality. As Canadians, we have followed too strictly for too long a path set out for us by the intellectual patterns and traditions of Western civilization, in the evolution of mercantile markets, medical scientific knowledge and the puritanical and managerial ethos of the North American continent. While this has allowed for the development of many good things (political liberalism and technology), we could have adopted a very different path of development. We could have absorbed, for example, together with our own truly prodigious achievements, the rich cosmological visions of our aboriginal peoples and their respect for nature. Be that as it may, it is the immense fortune of our times that we now have an opportunity, through exposure to the worlds we have shunned, to proceed along a new path. But genuine plurality and political equality is not what the cultural left desires.

A conference designed to encourage "new liberationist strategies" for minority groups suffered from the same tendency to divert attention from the higher capacities that unite us to the biologically given attributes that divide us. Roy Miki's "Writing Thru' Race" conference, sponsored by the Writers' Union of Canada, denied access to whites because of the "urgency to construct public spaces" where nonwhites would feel unthreatened and "without the mediating screen of a binary 'white'/'coloured' dichotomy." Robert Fulford criticized the conference, justifiably arguing: "In his novel *1984*, Orwell described a society whose rulers taught their people that war is peace, ignorance is strength and freedom is slavery. Now the Writers' Union of Canada wants to tell us that closed is open, limited is free, exclusion is inclusion, and private is public." Roy Miki rebuked him for his "petulant paternalism."[6] "The kind of pluralism Mr. Fulford yearns for," Miki wrote, "is really the resurrected form of an earlier assimilationist ideology that was used historically to promote Anglo-European values and traditions as the Canadian norm."[7] The cultural left errs when it seeks to immure ethnic groups into solitudes, squeeze multiculturalism's potential for genuine plurality into the narrowest expression of uniform diversity, trivialize great civilizational achievements and reduce them to complaints of victimization and play the trump card of "offence" whenever Western customs or rites are celebrated. All these tactics smack of a humility that has degenerated into cravenness and intellectual charity that has become extravagance. Many of these projects also produce new forms of paternalism and cultural imperialism, a point made with much clarity and insight in Neil Bissoondath's book *Selling Illusions.*[8]

The cultural left does no one a favour. Politicizing language to celebrate the vernacular idiom of the oppressed, in hopes of expressing solidarity with them, leaves the "oppressed" in their solitudes. Politicizing language by euphemizing reality as if there were no evil or misfortune that could not be dispelled by language, emasculates the courage and patience required to accept those inevitable burdens and injustices of life that nothing, short of fantasy, can overcome. Safe-speak, in the end, simply immunizes so that no one undertakes the work that reality demands.

If the cultural left wanted real equity and diversity, it should not stop at *ethnic* diversity and gender balance, but also look at *intellectual* diversity and balance. Given the diverse intellectual breadth actually represented in the Western tradition (including widely divergent points of view—from the pre-Socratics to the gnostics, from the Brotherhood of the Free Spirit to the Albigensians, from D'Annunzio to Thomas Pynchon—many of whom are, in fact, "soulmates" of the cultural left), it is difficult to understand the cultural left's persistent rally cry that the West is blandly homogeneous. But true equity and diversity are not what the cultural left wants. The cultural left does not simply want more women and more non-Westerners; it wants more feminists and more cultural deconstructionists. This is evident in its argument that "diversity"—the code word for its own ideology of power—be evident in every book, course, program, and faculty, rather than, more reasonably, in the overall university curriculum.[9]

The cultural left is not even true to the cultures to which it wishes to give visibility. Consider, for example, the rich civilization of India and the remarkable elasticity that has given it the power to absorb centuries of invading cultures (including the Aryans and the Mongols) and make some of their most outstanding achievements its own. The cultural left's patronizing effort to represent India's civilization back to it, nostalgically willing India back into its own past, ignores how fluid and active "culture" is. The cultural left makes a patronizing presumption when it asserts that we will westernize civilizations like India's if we do not withdraw and hide our civilization's achievements. It is far more likely, given the vast depth of other civilizations, particularly of Eastern cultures, that vastly important hybrids will emerge out of the East's response to the West. (A nonacademic look at this non-Western creativity can be found in Pico Iyer's jaunty but suggestive book *Video Night in Kathmandu*.[10]) We could be seeing this age as an opportunity to renew our own tired doctrines and dogmas and to discover that there are important convergences of understanding between cultures on issues of spirituality, human excellence and dignity.

The fragmentation enjoined upon the universities by the cultural left buys deeply into the bias expressed by communitarians in their lively political-theory debates with liberalism. According to communitarians, there are no universal experiences that bind us beyond our evident differences. This kind of thinking also subscribes to the narrowest ideas of intellectual and spiritual achievement—that only aboriginals can teach aboriginal literature and that aboriginals should restrict themselves to that literature. David Bromwich has coined a neat expression for the balkanized state in which the cultural left leaves us—"a negotiated economy of ritual intolerances."[11] Should we decline to make moral judgments for fear of being Eurocentric when we confront bigotry, mutilation and ritual murder, as happens in "ethnic cleansing," female circumcision and the practice of *sati*—all known non-Western practices?

There are less dramatic, but similarly ironic, examples of the effects of the cultural left's "new liberationist strategies." Consider the following fiasco: Canadian universities have roughly twenty ethnic chairs. Conflict has arisen over many of these, but none has been as bitter as the controversy related to the UBC Sikh chair. The cultural clash of Professor Harjot Oberoi and the Greater Vancouver Sikh community, who paid $350,000 to endow the chair, began when Oberoi published his book *The Construction of Religious Boundaries*, a study sympathetic to Sikhism, but evidently not sufficiently so. The Sikh community took offence, particularly, to Oberoi's arguments that Sikhism was a fluid religious movement, synthesizing Hinduism and Islam, and that nineteenth-century Sikhs were involved in popular religion, including sorcery. This, the Sikh community alleged, was false and moreover compromised Oberoi's position to promote Sikhism. When they approached the UBC administration and proposed that the Sikh community be given tighter control over the Sikh chair, officials responded that the university retained all control over donations given to it. "To maintain credibility," UBC's community relations officer said, "UBC has to maintain autonomy. Academics don't always say popular things. If you don't question things, what's the point of having a university?"[12]

According to one interpretation, the officer is right. The university is now largely an Enlightenment institution and, for better or worse, knowledge must prevail over belief, and historical fact over mythology. Religious faith is decidedly pre-Enlightenment, and has no place, as religious faith, at the modern university. Nevertheless, the university is not merely a child of the Enlightenment. Its roots, as we have seen, extend to Socrates and Christ, conferring on it the great intellectual and spiritual purposes symbolized by those figures. According to another interpretation, then, the formation of moral solidarity is seen as one of the great tasks of the university. This view suggests that however much one may drive spirituality or morality out of the classroom with a pitchfork, they will still find their way back (even in the form of dangerous surrogates).

The UBC community relations officer, according to this argument, did not confront seriously the concerns of the Sikh community. Myths are powerful agents of community attachment, honour and justice, and to maintain such myths it is sometimes necessary to let the sleeping dogs of historical fact and ambiguity lie. The issue is not whether Oberoi is right, but whether knowledge, as the Enlightenment would have us believe, is the one thing needful in our lives. In an older time in the West, a balanced division of labour existed between the universities and society. Truth was the preserve of an elite who sought it at all cost, and society was left to live in myth, although the educated recognized that those myths needed occasional reform and correction. "Socratic irony" was used to prevent the indiscriminate dissemination of truths that could severely corrode society. (Socrates would adapt his speeches to the particular souls he addressed and would, when necessary, hold some truths in reserve.)

The cultural left recognizes the conflict between truth and important myths, but it does not hold up an intellectual and moral vision of the university that speaks of goods beyond bargaining and convenience. Everything, in short, is negotiable. As a consequence, Socratic prudence becomes, in the hands of the cultural left, Professor Vickers's unfortunate willingness to abandon the unalloyed commitment to truth in favour of "teaching parallel belief systems" that ultimately serve political interests. The consequence of such willingness is to reinforce and speed the breakdown of order. We are witnessing in this country overall a colossal breakdown of moral order in civil society. The university, with its openness to unconventionalism, is the primary site for this breakdown. And in the vacuum left by both the corporate right and the cultural left, there has arisen a culture that has taken to devising "zero-tolerance" behaviour policies to regulate the growing disorder.

In 1992 at the University of Calgary, a poster announcing a student party sported a bare-breasted woman. Two female students complained to the university administration that they were offended. The official response was to place a "censored" sticker over the woman's breasts.[13] This little story tells the whole tale of the breakdown of the moral society of the university: for failing to attend to the culture within which moral attitudes are formed, the university is brought finally to using technical regulations to impose social order, whose zealousness stamps out the opportunities for ambiguity and intellectual play that characterize a healthy scholarly culture. Conversations are opportunities for maturing and refining those powerful sexual desires that lead students to lust for bodily satisfaction. If desire is not sublimated and given a spiritualized outlet, then a student is left in a state of volatile internal conflict between enflamed desire and duty. And a desire, denied the opportunity of satisfaction, risks becoming perverted or monstrous.

In 1994 the Carleton University Students' Association sent out a memo to all faculty—a "no-party memo"—declaring that professor-student socializing beyond the classroom was "decidedly inappropriate." The memo read: "This type of social activity creates a haven for harassment and coercion." In the chilly climate descending on faculty-student relations, many faculty will now no longer meet a student behind closed doors, unless with a chaperon. Is this justifiable concern with the conditions needed to ensure civility and decency, or is it mere political correctness?

The "zero-tolerance policy" originated in a report produced by the Ontario Council of Regents for Colleges. Its opening words declared: "The government of Ontario has adopted a policy of zero tolerance of harassment and discrimination at Ontario universities." It set out prohibited behaviours and proposed a review of all courses or instructional materials for "sexist, racist, homophobic or Eurocentric content." It recommended that all students and employees be required to attend an orientation on antidiscrimination and antiharassment, that a module on harassment and discrimination be integrated into all courses and that there be a compulsory course on social relations which would include women's studies, race and ethnic relations, sexual orientation and the changing workplace. The real clincher came with the recommendation to "establish complaint procedures without legalistic constraints," meaning that complainants and respondents, ideally, should not be represented by lawyers at any stage of the process, and that the standard of proof should be that of the balance of probabilities—rather than the criminal law's demand for proof beyond a reasonable doubt and proof of intention.

The policy finally sent out to Ontario's colleges and universities defined harassment as "something known 'or might reasonably be known' to be offensive, hostile, and inappropriate" pertaining to race, ethnic origin, sexual orientation and disability. Central to the policy was the argument that harassment was not restricted to discrete incidents or specifiable actions, but could be "environmental" or "systemic":

> Negative environment: one of a series of comments or conduct that creates a negative environment for individuals or groups.... Examples include exposure to graffiti, signs, cartoons, remarks, exclusion, adverse treatment related to one or more of the prohibited grounds...gestures, remarks, jokes, taunting, innuendo, display of offensive materials.... A complainant does not have to be a direct target to be adversely affected by a negative environment.[14]

The zero-tolerance policy was to apply not only to what was said in the classroom but to books cited by professors, library reading materials, and art. It was to apply to visitors or guests with "no ongoing connection to the institution," to off-campus actions and even to telephone calls from another country to anyone in the university community. Ontario's NDP government pledged to make $1.5 million available to support the development and production of training packages, data-collection models, evaluation models and audit models if colleges and universities would make zero tolerance "the central goal" of their policy and assume a "proactive" role in a prevention campaign. The "framework," the government hastened to add, "reflects the Ministry's minimum expectation."

And what was the university response? Academic administrators and faculty unions were, characteristically, asleep at the switch. The Carleton Faculty Association simply denied that the directives existed, until *Ottawa Citizen* editor Peter Calamai took them to account: "The Ontario government has banned free thought and expression at the very institutions devoted to such freedoms—our universities—and there has been no public outcry."[15] Robert Fulford kept up a steady pressure, aptly describing the policy as "relentlessly grim priggishness" and asking, reasonably, whether the policy would apply to feminists who make men uncomfortable, economists urging welfare reform making those on social assistance uncomfortable, or law professors lecturing against shield laws in rape cases on the off-chance their views could be construed as sexist. "Being offended," he added, "is part of learning how to think." And Naomi Klein pointed out what should have been obvious—that "zero tolerance" began as low-cost grandstanding concerning workplace and classroom behaviour and ended as a proposal for high-budget judicial apparatus.[16]

At the University of Toronto there are eight equity officers, who command a per annum budget of $1.5 million. In 1991, when its only two investigated cases were thrown out, (one of which was Harry Klatt's) the University of Western Ontario's equity office spent between $400,000 and $600,000. Economy has now pared that budget down to $320,000 annually. Other universities continue to bring in consultants at $90,000 per annum (the average salary of a full professor) to professionally manage the education equity regulations they were compelled to institute.

Cost is not the only concern about the new regulations designed to monitor campus behaviour. Human rights jurisprudence is of recent vintage, and the administrative law developed to permit judicial review of its findings is still feeling its way tentatively. In criminal law, the awesome power of judicial authority is tempered by procedural hurdles that weight all proceedings in favour of the accused by putting the onus of proof on the plaintiff. Strict regulations govern every stage of the process. Offences are set out precisely in statute. Prosecutors must respect the presumption of innocence, are required to demonstrate their case beyond a reasonable doubt and must prove intention. Punishments are based on the application of a predetermined table of sanctions to the particular case. Tort law between private parties, by contrast, is not hampered by the complex onus of proof. Nonetheless, here too there is a concrete basis for judicial decisions—remedies, in the form of damages, are based on an objective measure of loss, namely, monetary costs incurred.

Human rights jurisprudence occupies a wholly new space. Like criminal law, its authority comes from statute and it enjoys criminal law's vigorous investigative powers. But its tribunals are not obliged to follow due process as defined in criminal law. They need not name the accuser, nor are they obliged to permit legal representation. Nor must complainants prove their case beyond a reasonable doubt or prove intention.[17] In this, human rights law is more like a public version of tort law, with one major difference: its remedies are damages based not on incurred losses but on punitive remedies. When "climate" or "environment" is the object of a tribunal's attention, these punitive remedies are no longer tied precisely to the alleged "offence"—particularly if the offence is "systemic" and thus has no discrete target—but can be anything deemed appropriate to the climate the tribunal wishes to create or foster.

The adjudication of "systemic" harassment, sexism, racism or homophobia by the new area of law is also slippery in one other way. In the law of negligence (nonintentional torts), the measure that is used to determine negligence is whether the "standard of care" held by a reasonable and prudent person under similar circumstances has been met. Particularly in allegations of "systemic" or "environment" forms of harassment, this last concrete standard also vanishes. The accused need never know, nor even be expected to know, what is required to prevent a "chilly climate." The particulars required to prove a "reasonable person" test are so diffused as to become meaningless. This new field of law, then, constitutes a fundamental shift in judicial procedure. Instead of being based on verifiable circumstances and weighted in favour of the accused, it is based on a dispersal of effects, which loads the deck in favour of the accuser.

The opportunity for politicizing the law under these conditions is endless. In formal human rights tribunals, accused persons have recourse to an apparatus of judicial review that can raise concerns about errors of fact and of law. The more informal tribunals operating at universities run roughshod over most of these options. Zero-tolerance policy is a dangerous political tool, especially when it has adopted an ideology intolerant of the dissenting views comprising the scholarly culture.[18] Moreover, zero-tolerance policy leaves open a huge window of opportunity for what University of Calgary political scientist Rainer Knopff has called "social technology"—using the judicial apparatus to socially remanufacture human relations.[19] But this is exactly what the cultural left is seeking in its persistent efforts to use the university for social engineering.

By vastly politicizing the terms of legal reference, zero-tolerance policy also increases the litigiousness of the university community. To be sure, the university community does need to be regulated by some quasilegal mechanisms. At King's College, University of Western Ontario, in a case that was profiled on Eric Malling's *W5* segment entitled "Harassment Police," Harry Klatt was accused of sexual harassment for, among other things, saying that the steps of a first child are "like a girl's first experience of menstruation" and for referring to women's breasts as "exuberant" or "Twiggy." In the video "Inequity in the Classroom," a student complains of a male professor who ends his course with a slide show that concludes with a bikini-clad woman on a beach and the statement "I like to end every course with a pretty sunset." In ordinary times, these kinds of statements would be seen as laughable or innocuous. In addition, the liberal argument that there is a distinction between unlimited freedom of speech and appropriately regulated freedom of action should apply in normal circumstances. But if there ever was a time when provocative thoughts could be judged separately from injurious actions, that time is not now. The distinction assumes a civil association of trust, even friendship. Justice Oliver Wendell Holmes, Jr., may have, like John Stuart Mill, defended the right to shout "Fire!" in general, but "the most stringent protection of free speech would not protect a man in falsely shouting fire in a theatre, and causing panic." Our times are like a crowded theatre, in which there is mutual suspicion and mutual provocation, and a highly volatile atmosphere of potent passions where speech too readily precipitates rash action.[20]

Our politics of rights as entitlements has greatly distorted sound social practice. Those who question the libertarian defence of an abstract freedom of expression are raising important questions as to whether the language of rights and the art of prudent statesmanship are always compatible with one another. Take the arguments of Somer Brodribb (the University of Victoria instructor who headed the Committee to Make the Department More Supportive to Women and whose "chilly climate" findings accused her department of "growing antifeminism"). If she is now excessively vehement in her actions of bringing down the University of Victoria political science department, part of the reason for her views seems legitimate in light of the inappropriate responses to earlier complaints she had made elsewhere. In 1986, Somer Brodribb gave a lecture in Montreal. During the event, a man carrying a rifle case seated himself in the front row. The moderator of the event called security. The man produced a licence, and so was merely asked to place the case under his seat! When the Montreal massacre occurred, Brodribb recognized Marc Lépine as the man with the rifle case. "I want the administrations," Brodribb later said, "to stop telling the men to put the guns under their seats."[21] A few years later, in the Counselling Psychology Department at UBC, where Brodribb was supporting a 1993 rally in support of women, women had been receiving antifeminist hate mail. Forensic experts brought in to review the letters concluded that they "were not written by a psychopath." Reasonably, Brodribb and the other UBC women replied, "We know there's a threat. We feel there's a threat and we don't need university officials buying time and hiring experts to tell us there's no threat."[22] I believe Brodribb is right. The narrowest interpretation of the letter of the law as rights—to bear firearms and of free expression—has, in these incidents, taken over the spirit of the law, which is to form a civil association. Rights without responsibilities and the web of civic friendships become dangerous instruments.

Yet it is precisely this absolute defence of freedom of speech that is put forward by the Society for Academic Freedom and Scholarship and the Trent University professors in their declaration of a "right to offend." The Society for Academic Freedom, like America's National Association of Scholars, performs an admirable watchdog task of monitoring bureaucratic zeal aimed at preventing the free exchange of ideas. But in these times, the society's passionate defence of unlimited speech and scholarship reinforces a political situation in the university that is highly vulnerable to the imposition of zero-tolerance policies. The society's warnings are often mired in polemical excess as, for example, when John Furedy, its president, equated all restrictions on freedom of speech to the Salem witch hunts and McCarthyism, and said that the indictment of UBC's political science department was equivalent to being charged as a "crypto capitalist" under Soviet totalitarianism or a Jewish sympathizer under Nazi totalitarianism. There is, of course, a respectable argument made in John Stuart Mill's *On Liberty*, suggesting that the value of airing even noxious opinions is that public debate will reveal them to be unfounded and indecent. Jack Granatstein echoes Mill's sentiments when he says, "Keegstra is talking crap, historical nonsense. But if he was in a university, I would defend his right to say what he said."[23] Joseph Fletcher, a political science professor at the University of Toronto, obviously agreed when he invited members of a nazi organization to his class on free speech. If, however, there is no public forum, and if genuine public conversation has deteriorated to a clamour of voices, then the liberal perspective advanced by Furedy, Granatstein and Fletcher risks degenerating into a defence of the "right to offend," as the Trent professors would have it.[24] The more entrenched libertarians become, the more the cultural left is able to advance successfully with its agenda of social revolution.

Behaviour codes at the university, initially designed to prevent sexual blackmail and explicit discrimination, now apply, thanks to the cultural left, to such an immense range of behaviour, that universities are utterly polarized and paralyzed. While some exercise what they believe is their right to provoke, others abandon all distinctions and criteria of preferment so as not to offend anyone. The true work of the scholarly culture is slipping between the cracks. I referred to our times as a "crowded theatre" where no one has the right to shout "Fire!" But where has this volatile and irascible environment sprung from? We need to entertain the possibility that the cultural left's postmodern identity politics, which deconstructs all the forms of human civility and perfectibility that once made up the moral core of a genuine liberal education, is the major culprit. One of the strange twists in Canadian academe is that the task of rebuking the cultural left's zero tolerance for dissenting viewpoints and of defending traditional conceptions of the scholarly culture has fallen to academics like Philip Resnick, Jack Granatstein, Reg Whitaker and Warren Magnussen—mainstay figures among the old left.

Once universities abandon the complex work of shaping moral attitudes, and then find it necessary to introduce hyperrationalist technical regulations to control the licence they have allowed to grow, we are hearing the death rattle of the university as an idea and institution. Codes and tribunals do not make for a civil association. We have permitted politicized moralism to replace the careful incubation of a moral attitude that transpires wherever good books are read and soul-leading conversations are pursued.

David Cooke, Ontario's minister of education, after considerable public pressure, on February 17, 1994, offered a disclaimer on the zero-tolerance policy by saying it was a framework and not proposed legislation. The retreat from policy to "framework" or "model" convinced very few. Moreover, the damage to the university community was already done.[25] The cultural left's turf wars continue unabated: zero tolerance for all programs it designates as "Eurocentric," despite the appeal to "inclusivity," for objectivity because it is deemed "phallocentric" (male perspective); for prescriptive core curricula, because they are "hegemonic"; and for university policy aimed at recruiting accomplished students, because it is "elitist." "Oppression," in the hands of the cultural left, has become infinitely elastic.

The mischief of zero-tolerance policies, and the potent passions that the cultural left's turf wars release, have manifested themselves in classic form in the upheaval in the University of British Columbia's political science department. The repercussions of the fiasco will probably be felt for over a decade. In June 1995 the story even made it to the pages of the *New York Times*.

The origin of the fiasco was a spring 1992 memo from graduate students to university officials, alleging inappropriate behaviour from faculty and bias arising from "environmental" irregularities arising from the prevailing faculty composition, curriculum and methods of instruction. A subsequent November 1993 exchange of memos between the students and deans did not accelerate the progress of departmental reform that the small cohort of nine students desired. The students' language became stronger, alleging "sexual terrorism" and "systemic racism." Finally, in 1994, before any allegations had been verified, the department acquiesced to an order to request an inquiry.

On the advice of the dean of the law school, who recommended a fellow feminist who had had experience in investigating charges of harassment at University College of the Cariboo, UBC's president David Strangway commissioned Joan McEwen to investigate the students' allegations. Strangway's fast action, given that no internal investigations had ever been conducted, may have had something to do with a desire to avoid a second ugly brush with political correctness. A few years earlier, as a consequence of unfortunate remarks he made in conjunction with a proposal that UBC host the international gay games, Strangway had been raked over the coals by the Vancouver press.

Be that as it may, the investigation brought some disturbing statements, actions, and behaviour to light. The most serious was the allegation that a white male visiting instructor, commenting on the tough grading of his black teaching assistant on his students' first assignments, said, "Yeah, now they probably think that you are just one big, bad, black bitch." Another allegation was that the department had taken insufficient action against a particularly virulent campaign of harassment against a female student, whose work in a feminist B.A. thesis attracted posters by an unknown perpetrator that read "Chopped her into little pieces, p.43" and "Silence is the mark of hysteria…choking… decapitation." Further allegations included: a member of faculty taking retaliatory action against a student; a male professor making sexual advances to a number of his female M.A. students; a professor posting crude cartoons on his office door; a professor interrupting conversations with looks at passing female students; and a professor failing to intervene when, after a black student gave her presentation, a white female student commented, "OK, now you can go to the back of the bus."

The McEwen Report repeated the students' allegations of sloppiness in admission procedures, uneven grading practices, poor dissemination of information, unequal treatment and favouritism, discrimination and inappropriate gossiping to students about other students. Past formal reviews of the department, while supportive, had raised procedural and curricular concerns. Many of the faculty acknowledged the difficulties nonetheless, and the department as a whole was correcting the faults—if at a snail's pace. This does not mean that a sensible person would not register surprise at what McEwen revealed. For a department whose primary scholarly employment is to study the relation between political fact and perceptions, not to say procedural rule of law, the lackadaisical attention to possible ambiguous and mixed messages is difficult to understand. One may also, with justice, question the style of an instructor who, believing himself to be expressing "solidarity" with the "oppressed," thinks, in peculiar sixties fashion, that he should use the idiom of the street. The instructor who called a woman student "one big, bad, black bitch" explained to McEwen that "She bantered with me, made jokes about her race and discussed personal matters…. How could I know?" Is this a mitigating factor upon which anyone would really wish to wage an all-out battle on behalf of academic freedom?

It is, however, a far cry from this apparent inefficiency and latitude of behaviour, to the charge McEwen makes of *systemic* racism, sexism and discrimination. Her logic is arresting. She cites a white male professor putting down a white female M.A. student by making comments such as "Even an undergraduate student would understand that!"; a white male professor silencing a mature white female Ph.D. student in the classroom while encouraging others to speak; professors discounting the Marxist perspective of their students; a white male graduate-advisor telling a white female Ph.D. student that she was "brave" to come to university when her child was just an infant; a white male professor, during an oral comprehensive exam, asking a female Ph.D. student of colour to distinguish between the words "discourse" and "intercourse"; a white male professor telling a Jewish female professor that feminism is a "Jewish-American princess conspiracy"; and professors demonstrating impatience when students who have difficulty with English talk in class. In a wholly unwarranted assumption, McEwen concludes that these are "manifestations of the reaction that the members of the socially dominant group, namely the white male group, has to persons who do not share their characteristics.... [The department's culture] is the product of a cohort of faculty who, for the most part, are older, white, male, heterosexual, middle-class and of Anglo-European heritage, proud (the students would say to the point of being arrogant) of their reputation as scholars, conservative in their ideological and methodological approaches [and] educated in the patriarchal and authoritarian traditions of Western society."[26]

Dissenting views by students and faculty who praised the department and denied the allegations were ignored and in some cases deemed inconsequential, because they came from "middle-class white women." The responses of faculty to the allegations were relegated to a four-page appendix. The finding that there was a basis for the allegations was therefore a foregone conclusion. Taking the students at their word, and evidently fond of "structural" analyses, McEwen found a climate where "perceptions" and forms of "social signalling" made the department systemically inhospitable to women and minority groups, which therefore formed a "basis" for the allegations.

In June 1995, on the recommendation of John Grace, the dean of graduate studies, Strangway announced that admissions to the department's graduate program were closed. Grace's recommendation did not endear him to many of the faculty, who saw this as an expression of his known sympathies for postmodern feminism. Strangway's action, in light of the intense criticism of McEwen's report that immediately arose, was also seen as precipitous. Concern that rashness had replaced good judgment was not allayed by his memo to the faculty that read "despite the limitations of the Report the University felt it had to act."

Apart from the allegations of bias, which McEwen did not verify, the burden of her conclusions rests on the two facts she appears to believe are most salient: (1) the poor representation of women in the department and (2) the apparent lack of encouragement for points of view like feminism, postmodernism and Marxism because, as one student put it, faculty were "still working with paradigms which are dated."[27] Both charges are, with some qualifications, factually correct.[28] It is another thing, however, to conclude that they add up to "systemic" sexism or other discrimination. Sociological representation, as I have argued, is an unwarranted demand that the cultural left has unabatedly pursued to further its own political agenda. Such representation says nothing about intellectual diversity or balance in points of view, far more important factors at a university.

While a 20 percent female membership is nothing to boast about, five women, arguably, do provide role models for UBC's political science women students. The charge that there is an absence of "alternative perspectives" is ideology parading under the banner of pluralism. It is hard to square the fact that the department contains internationally acclaimed specialists on Third World development and human rights—whose work is predicated on the affirmation of human dignity—and theorists who work exclusively on the philosophy of the Enlightenment, with the allegation that the curriculum is not receptive to women's and minority groups' desires for recognition of their worth. Once again, a narrow sociological model is being employed: women's equal worth can be affirmed only by reading women's writing, and people of colour must read writings by other people of colour. If the primary concern is to affirm the equal worth of women and non-Caucasians, must every department commit itself explicitly to gender studies, feminist political theory and "postcolonial" theorizing, to reach that end? If, on the other hand, the purpose is to do little more than advance the ideological concerns of the cultural left—as one suspects— why is this intellectual bias not made explicit? Since resources were already stretched very thinly in the department—one of the sources of the students' complaints—it is difficult to justify the request for the addition of advocacy education.

McEwen's report cost UBC $237,897.68. McEwen's logical fallacies and *non sequiturs*, her tarnishing of all by the actions of a few and her unwillingness to distinguish perception of offence from actual harm have endeared her to no one—either members of the department or dispassionate reviewers.[29] Two responses in particular contributed significantly to invalidating the report as a whole. The dean of arts, Pat Marchak, wrote: "...The report is deeply flawed. Among many weaknesses: it dismisses testimony and evidence contrary to the allegations and relegates faculty responses to a short appendix; evidence is lacking; allegations are repeated as if all were about sexism and racism even where there is no apparent or necessary linkage, and the context of alleged comments is not reported."[30] The *Globe and Mail* denounced UBC for its "most cringing conformity" and called the report "bone-chilling." Its editors suddenly remembered, after months of corporate-right musing on the need to pare the university's mandate down to market logic, that the university was "the protector and transmitter of the great intellectual traditions that underpin our society."[31]

Logic unfortunately rarely persuades, especially when ideology has intruded. Nothing political science faculty could say improved their bottomed-out status. When Don Blake, former head of the department, responded initially to the charges by proposing to implement "a more aggressive mentoring program for women" he was rebuked by the radical students for using the male-word "aggressive." His unsuccessful but diligent efforts to find the perpetrator of the poster campaign were castigated as a sign of his indifference. When faculty went back, allegation by allegation, to restore innocuous statements to their contexts and deny that they were racist, students wrote in a memo "The first symptom of racism is to deny that it exists."[32] The group of six students behind the allegations, who had most influenced McEwen's report, also made clear that they understood why the department's members appeared so intractable: white males, they claimed, could never understand the perspectives of women and Afro-Americans. This cohort also alienated other students when they refused to allow anyone but themselves to participate in the working groups on equity the department had established.

But the *coup de grâce* for the department was the blatantly ideological opposition of the dean of graduate studies, for whom the only salient terms of analysis of the whole affair were "race and gender" and a world inscribed with the indisputable fact of the "power elites...privileged positions."[33] In a memo he presented to Graduate Council, John Grace wrote: "Until relatively recently, universities have been dominated by senior white male faculty members. It is not surprising, but unacceptable, for this group to seek to perpetuate its domination of our university."[34] In the wake of his statements, allegations and innuendo have escalated. Faculty, the major protagonists announced, must sign a public apology acknowledging "racism, sexism, harassment, and the difference between these and 'academic freedom'" and take a mandatory twelve-week, twelve-step recovery program, in which they "vent their frustrations and explore their reluctance to lose the power and prestige which they have cultivated for so long as their natural 'right.'" "Early retirement," the students continued, "should be offered to those professors publicly identified as refusing to sign their names to [the apology] and/or refusing to be involved in the [re-education classes]."

"Unlimited numbers" of letters of reference should be made available to all graduate students. The demands go on and on, and the taunts of "coverup" and "evasiveness" continue—further evidence of how a small number of students have been permitted, under the aegis of the cultural left's adage "the personal is political," to vent their pathologies, insecurities and disappointments as intellectual perspectives. The radical minority of students have said they are "ashamed of Canada": "This should have been a moment of celebration, of victory for marginalized students." John Grace has continued to hold that the procedural questions raised by the political science department are an indication that its white males are in a "state of denial," though simultaneously, a larger contingent of thirty students petitioned to the president for the ban to be lifted.

Admissions to the political science department were reopened in November 1995, in the midst of the high-profile resignation of Tom Berger from the Board of Governors over the mishandling of the whole affair and a poster campaign opposing the president during his open-house week. The radical student group denounced the reopening as a "monumental betrayal." To this day, no allegations have been supported by evidence, but the university administration has not officially denounced the report. The more serious allegations of retaliatory action and conspiracy were exposed as fantasy, though the disgrace remains. The fear that a truck can be driven through the loose judicial procedure of harassment investigations was confirmed. Some of the faculty, though respected and distinguished political scientists, remain under a cloud of suspicion. Members of the department are now obliged to provide a squib of their careers, "confessing" their theoretical and methodological commitments to prospective students. The President's Council is divided and paralyzed. Some of the students have taken their complaints to the B.C. Council of Human Rights, where officials told one inquiring faculty member that 97 percent of complaints are upheld, often to the tune of tens of thousands of dollars in damages. Fairness, justice, reason and decency—all have fallen through the cracks in this quasijudicial process, where one person could be investigator, judge and jury, reinforcing deep concerns about the judicial procedure of the "zero-tolerance" war on discrimination. The UBC campus remains deeply divided: in a Faculty of Arts meeting faculty voted only 97–52 to lift the ban on admissions. Polarization of observers has further diminished any chance of addressing the problems of the department in a reasonable manner. At one extreme, Sima Godfrey, an associate professor of French, concluded: "[T]he only thing this report—and the president's hasty decision to act upon it—has clearly succeeded in doing is to allow too many (mostly male) members of the faculty of arts to utterly dismiss the issue of discrimination on campus and to portray themselves as the beleaguered victims of political correctness."[35] At the other extreme, the *Globe and Mail* editorial of September 12, 1995, compared the UBC affair to the contempt for academics in China's Cultural Revolution. The middle ground, the most minimal condition of civil society, has crumbled.

Other political science departments have experienced major disruptions and have become deeply divided over issues of sexism, racism or preferential hiring. Why the concentration of controversy in political science? Janice Newton, a University of Toronto political science professor who conducted one of the first harassment investigations early in the 1980s, offers one explanation: "Because we study power. Political science attracts people who are attracted to power, and it's also attracted people who want to critique power and the abuse of power."

Newton is only partly right. From Aristotle, who said that political science was the "queen of sciences," to David Easton, who distinguishes the political system from all others in its capacity to undertake the "authoritative allocation of values," is a tradition that sees politics as the source of the overarching authority that sets priorities to diverse human affairs. What is at stake in the agitations in Canada's political science departments is more than simply the discovery of how power is used and abused. Political science is a discipline that stands or falls on the distinctions between authority and force, between the public and the personal, and between universal and particular. It is also a discipline which believes that public life, and engagement in a civil society that transcends our personal and social lives, is the only means to preserve decency and common sense. In these commitments, political science resonates deeply with the core of the scholarly culture.

Yet all these assumptions are under siege from the cultural left. The UBC students, in a revealing use of words, complained about the "authoritative" atmosphere. They did not say "authoritarian," about which it might be appropriate to raise concerns. They didn't think there should be *any* authority—not the authority of reason, informed judgment, or repeatable experiment.[36] In the next few years, political science departments will continue to be an indicator of where the university as a whole is going. There are only two options: the further fragmentation of its civil society or an attempt to reunite men and women, Caucasians and non-Caucasions, heterosexuals and homosexuals, at a level that transcends their differences.

At this point, the signs that we will attempt the latter are not favourable. When Marlene Nourbese Philip accused Neil Bissoondath of "pimping the tawdry racist views of colonial powers," Bissoondath shot back with the only appropriate response: "It's the way public conversation is carried on in this country: lots of time to talk about everything except ideas."[37] Under the ceaseless politicking of the cultural left, all pretence at talking about ideas has been abandoned. The university's ultimate purpose is to reunite us at a higher level of our humanity—as reasoning and moral beings. But the reality is that the cultural left is doing little more than reinforcing the social fact, observed by Keith Spicer, that Canadians are 28 million "scorpions in a bottle." And, in the paradoxical twist that is so characteristic of today's university debate, the agitations of the cultural left—to create an environment where no group and no culture is dominant—reinforce the marketplace ideology of the corporate right. Michael Valpy reported recently in his *Globe and*

Mail column that when the decision was made to no longer read St. Luke's Gospel at University of Toronto's Hart House Christmas ceremony, it was also decided to replace the predominantly Anglo-Saxon food services at Hart House—in both cases so as not to offend other cultures. The cultural left's political agenda has played neatly into the hands of the corporate right: the new franchise operators are Taco Bell and Tim Horton Donuts. As Valpy wryly notes, something significant has been lost.[38] What has been lost is the humanizing force and the highest unifying purposes of the scholarly culture.

Chapter 10

New Directions

*Turn where we may, within, around, the voice of great events
is proclaiming to us, Reform, that you may preserve!*

Thomas Macaulay

"**N**ot since the Russians launched Sputnik and made for a
complete rethinking of higher education, have people
looked so hard at what the university is doing and what it is
not," reads a recent *Globe and Mail* column.[1] With good reason.
This country has mortgaged its economic growth and social
development to the university. The cracks that have now
appeared, and which together form what pundits have identified
as the universities' "perception problem," call into question the
future contribution of the university to Canada. While I have
suggested that this "perception problem" is a consequence of the
persistent politics of the corporate right and the cultural left, it
would be naïve to say: everything is fine on the home front, just
send money.

Only six parameters are currently defining Canada's university
debate. Outside observers call for "accessibility, accountability
and efficiency." The university responds with "equity, academic
freedom and autonomy." All of these are important procedural
matters that pertain to the conditions necessary for a genuine
scholarly culture. But in paying attention to these questions
alone, we neglect the substantive questions: what are the university's purposes; in what way does the scholarly culture sustain

and nurture these purposes and what good is the university serving? Many aspects of the current debate remain at the level of *means*, disregarding the fact that today it is the *ends* that are at stake.

The essence of the university is the important and complex interaction of the scholarly culture and the needs of students. This process is stimulated, and its respective parts are refined, through conversations and books. The forms of understanding and friendship that comprise the university's highest accomplishment emerge in the leisurely dialogues and meditative withdrawal that the university affords its members. While this leisure is time lost from the explicit productive purposes of society, it is time invested in future gains to society, in which understanding is matured and the tendencies of overcertainty and rashness are corrected.

But this essence has been corrupted, as the university has overstretched itself and developed into a multiheaded beast that believes it can offer everything to everyone. The university stands on the verge of financial, spiritual and political collapse. It is now discovering that it is incapable of satisfying all desires and wants. In the place of coherent curricula and principled priorities, the university is becoming a hybrid of pragmatic compromises arising from the turf wars of sectarians and from the invented crises thrust upon it by government, business and interest groups, each of whom has declared it to have a "perception problem." From the cultural left's mantra of "race, gender and ethnicity" to the corporate right's imperative of efficiency and free-market principles, politicized agendas are being entrenched. But this is a zero-sum game, where one protagonist's gains are another's losses. If sanity and decency are to be restored to the university, we need to revive the historical tensions that characterized the formation of the university (*civitas* and *universitas*) and remember the distinctive virtues that sustain the idea of higher learning.

The university both as an idea and as an institution is at a crossroads. It is not difficult for one to conceive the alternatives that might lie in store for Canada's universities. The institution as we presently know it may be divided up, one fragment comprised of scattered monastic enclaves, another consisting in a network of training and research centres, operating perhaps as that strange new hybrid of "virtual university" and community college. If this should happen, part of the university will have become utterly irrelevant to future society, its scholars ensconced in an Epicurean garden and engaged in arcane diversions. Its other part will have been seamlessly joined with the technological dynamo of modern society, for having lost its critical detachment and independence, it will concern itself with little more than adjusting students to the ever-changing norms of society. This scenario is not particularly far-fetched. For centuries, the university has been at the forefront of how we interpret our potential as human beings. The current signs that the university can weather the historical changes occurring worldwide and that the university will continue to be central to our lives in the future are not optimistic.

Many hot buttons are being pressed in today's debate. I have described the politics of these issues in light of an ideal of the university—a polyphony of voices, an odyssey of the soul, a ship afloat on a boundless sea. The hot buttons nearly always reflect zero tolerance of the ambiguities and inefficiencies of the practices these metaphors support. The effect of pressing the hot buttons is that Canada's universities are overreacting and attempting to meet every expectation and combat every perception. The result is rash action, perplexity, waste and a politics where nearly every party has its back up. The university cannot simultaneously be an engine of economic growth, a social welfare agency, a laboratory for a new consciousness, a training centre and a home for the scholarly culture. Something has to give.

However, while I think these hot buttons are playing havoc with the essence of the university, I also believe that they serve a purpose. Their value lies in stimulating us to think of the real changes the universities must undertake. A few modest suggestions follow. Desperate times call for desperate measures, even measures which in ordinary times would appear quite mad. Perhaps now is the time to turn a few things on their heads.

Hot Button One: Abolish tenure.

Recommendation One:
The university cannot continue to operate as it traditionally has. Under the power of faculty associations, tenure has become job security for a portion of the faculty who neither engage in scholarship nor teach responsibly. But the argument for abolition of tenure is rash and short-sighted. It ignores the real risks to independent scholarship represented by overzealous governments and their granting agencies, especially when teaching and research are expected to mirror the opinions and prejudices of the day, when "relevance" or "use" is defined narrowly, or when an artificial time frame is imposed on the progress of research.

While the scheme of replacing tenure with renewable contracts appears to ensure greater accountability, it raises questions for which there seem to be only disquieting answers. Who would control the process? And who would determine the criteria of what research productivity or teaching effectiveness might be? Government? The market, as manifested in student's choice of popular courses? The various constituency groups that have elbowed their way onto boards of governors? Faculty themselves? By any way the options are parsed, the jockeying of power and the corruption of good judgment that would follow the introduction of this scheme would be worse than current practice.

But it remains that current practice must change. Every three years, faculty in every rank should be subjected to a substantive review of their work, and signs of significant potential in scholarly accomplishment should be evident. Tenure should be granted at arm's length from the institution in which it is given, by an independent commission of scholars. It should be granted only after the publication of a major study or finding, and its recognition as an important accomplishment by the wider scholarly community. It should also be subject to periodic review—a time frame of ten years is generous but reasonable—and if the finding is that no further major work of scholarship has been produced, recourse should be taken in revoking tenure. In the case of those who, despite a want of scholarship, have maintained excellence in teaching, the alternative of renewable contracts should be implemented. If reform of this magnitude is undertaken, it must come swiftly and decisively. Grandfathering the present generation of academics would only compromise the renewal that universities have no option but to undertake, and it would increase intergenerational conflict.

The likely effect of these changes is that far fewer faculty will be tenured (as few as one-third), institutions will have the flexibility to undertake serious renewal, and it may be that, as a general rule of thumb, the awarding of tenure will be delayed until the rank of full professor is achieved. The fallout of these changes will not be attractive for those who have taken tenure as a privilege that would never be assailed, or the faculty associations who have protected their weakest members by acting on the belief that equity means sameness. Academic administrators must learn to defend their colleagues' unseasonable or apparently irrelevant work, if it displays creative potential, with far greater aptitude and conviction—and this will be a boon to the university's public relations. Administrators will also have to learn to act resolutely when dismissal is appropriate. The reforms would be a breath of fresh air to the growing surplus army of highly accomplished but unemployed scholars, and to students who want their education to resonate with passion and rigour—characteristics evident only in academics who actively participate in the scholarly culture.

Hot Button Two: Back to teaching.

Recommendation Two:
While in principle, teaching and research are correlates of one another, in practice, especially in the humanities, and arguably

also in the social sciences, some research is worth little and some diverts faculty from the responsibility of teaching. There *is* a publish-or-perish mentality in the universities, and few institutional efforts are made to invest deeply in instruction. The public is evidently not amused. While 83 percent of Canadians think universities are doing a good job, only 7 percent think the research role of the university is important.[2] The report of Stuart Smith's Commission of Inquiry on Canadian University Education, while flawed, struck a powerful respondent chord in the public at large. Many faculty do not want to teach undergraduate classes, since the very structure of the university is set up to reward graduate training and research. Like slum landlords, absentee professors leave the teaching of undergraduates to unripened sessional instructors whose work often amounts to little more than rent collection. Being released from undergraduate teaching is considered to be the great university plum.

Like the University of Toronto, every university should sponsor forums on teaching—especially for pretenured faculty—and institute ongoing efforts to improve aptitude. Universities should have a mentorship program for new faculty and make stronger efforts to monitor and correct teaching practices, even when such efforts at improvement are interpreted as an incursion on academic freedom. There is, without question, a plurality of acceptable teaching practices, and initiatives to reduce that richness to one alone must be shunned, but when what passes as teaching is little more than reading of unrevised lecture notes or political advocacy, intervention is essential. Since the soul of the university is at stake if the needs of students are not genuinely met, all initiatives to foster greater emphasis on teaching must be applauded: the preparation of how-to teaching manuals, across-the-board peer reviews of teaching, designing teaching evaluations with teeth (unlike the soft evaluations in current usage at most universities) and the awarding of grants based on demonstrated correlation between teaching and scholarship.[3]

Nonetheless, it is a far cry from these necessary cosmetic changes to schemes that would see "learning" as the primary mission of the university or which would even have the university system evolve into a two-tiered set of institutions, one devoted to teaching and the other to research. The purpose of the university is to sustain and enrich the scholarly culture in particular, and the wider culture in general, by stimulating the pursuit of "inconsequent adventures" and by extending myriad invitations to look, to listen and to reflect. The studies that show no correlation between teaching and research are counterintuitive to the experience and common sense of the real scholar. They demand a causal relationship in the learning process—as if the components were not inextricably bound up with one another in a culture of scholarship. Teachers do not put on different hats for teaching and research. Moreover, a student, as Frye says, is not "'taking' a subject" but is being taken up by the culture of scholarship. To abstract either element distorts severely the culture and the benefits its members can derive from it.

A different two-tiered system might be vastly preferable—one grounded on the approximate distinction between theoretical reason and practical reason. What if all professional schools—medicine, engineering, journalism, business, nursing and education—were shifted out of the university and together with the existing colleges, brought into partnership as a new institution—the polytechnic? The solution would have a variety of benefits. Universities would remain places where the culture of scholarship could proceed undisturbed and where primary attention would be paid to frontier research, to cultivating critical reason and imagination and to fostering political citizenship and public service. It would, of necessity, contain the humanities, the social sciences and most of the sciences. The polytechnics would house the research facilities associated with our "engines of economic growth" and "engines of social change," and with research in the fields of the applied sciences, thus serving the primary task of preparing students for vocations and fostering the pragmatic aspects of social reform. To be successful, such polytechnics would have to be given the level of financial support and recognition that went into building up a superlative school like the

Massachusetts Institute of Technology. The refurbished and more lustrous polytechnics could then serve students who are seeking assured know-how and whose expectations are not currently met by a university environment that must, of necessity, never cease asking "But why?" and perennially respond "Yes, but...." Cost savings, effectiveness in meeting the concerns of employers and taxpayers, clarity in the implementation of mandates, and improved public relations would result, taking us out of the current state of confusion and disappointment, where all the status has been given to the universities and the burden of multiple conflicting social agendas has equally been placed in their laps.

Hot Button Three: Rankings and performance indicators.

Recommendation Three:
In a time when "comparative advantage" is everything, sticking one's head in the sand and refusing to be ranked is not an option. Living on inheritance, or exaggerating the complexity of sector comparisons, only reinforces the judgment that universities are irrelevant and have something to hide. The *Maclean's* ranking project will continue to be with us for many years, as will the demand from the universities' observers, who insist on performance indicators as the means of accountability. The available measuring sticks are deficient, however, and need to be revised.

The *Maclean's* ranking suffers, above all, from its incapacity to assess quality, other than through the ambiguities and distortions to be seen in its quantitative indicators. A report on quality can emerge only if the evaluation of institutions begins to consider individual schools, departments and faculty, and looks to the many nonquantifiable factors that signal scholarly excellence. Distinctions need to be made: What contribution has the Queen's School of Policy Studies made to Canadian public policy? What breakthroughs has University of Toronto's School of

Medicine made in its field? What do John Polanyi's students gain from his stellar scholarly achievements? How has Women's Studies at the University of British Columbia advanced the recognition of equal worth of women? How does the University of Northern British Columbia's Department of First Nations bring the perspective of aboriginal peoples to public debate? Universities will resent this type of assessment, but it must be made.

There are only two ways in which such quality could be entered into the rankings equation. One would be to extend to universities the opportunity to supply a narrative that highlights their distinctive excellences and achievements. The second would be to compose a body of "reasonable and prudent persons" from within the scholarly culture (for starters, one could look at some of the members of the Royal Society of Canada), funded equally by the sponsoring magazine and the Association of Universities and Colleges of Canada. This group would examine the data currently collected and make an informed judgment as to the strengths and weaknesses of each university. These are only the most minimal means of improving the current scoring system.

The same kind of improvement is necessary in the discussions on student performance indicators. We need to institute Canada-wide scholastic achievement tests for graduates of high schools and follow this up with entrance and graduation examinations at universities, akin to the foreign service exams written for application to Foreign Affairs, which evaluate judgment and understanding. Our current practice of compiling numerical data based on graduation and attrition rates, operating costs per student or library acquisitions, is just whistling against the wind. What the public wants to know is whether students are acquiring theoretical literacy (sound judgment, a moral attitude of detachment and impartiality, an understanding of competing perspectives), the very "value-added" that input-output analysis avoids analyzing. Exit exams will not offer results with the precision expected by the corporate right. But if designed by a commission of "reasonable and prudent persons" and if aimed at testing more than just an accumulation of factual knowledge (like Hirsch's dictionary of cultural literacy) or abstract skills, the exams would supply some measure of what occurs in the "black box" that the university is really about.

Hot Button Four: Value-for-money and value-added auditing.

Recommendation Four:
Nothing riles the public more than leaked news about waste and unaccountable expenditures. The current drive to have universities reveal the salaries and perquisites enjoyed by their senior administrators is fuelled, among other things, by stories of one-dollar memberships in swanky private clubs and lavish residences. "Opening the books" has become not only the rallying cry of the corporate right, but also the rallying cry of faculty and staff within the university. Universities have difficulty accounting for their expenditures in neat "investment for profit" formulae quite simply because, in its very nature, the scholarly culture is speculative, inefficient and ambiguous. If universities have avoided bringing in professional managers, it is because academics alone are sufficiently acquainted with the nuance of that culture, especially the understanding that no single vector will bring the ship to port. "Value-added" or "value-for-money" auditing, especially when it demands a precision inappropriate to the subject matter, risks severely narrowing and flattening the scholarly culture.

But notwithstanding this, a large component of the university is still a business. The university culture has come to include parts that are not essential and that its academic administrators manage poorly. Value-added auditing, when applied to the management of investments, capital expenditures, brick-and-mortar disbursements and pension funds and to the services universities provide (health, instructional technology, maintenance, public relations, recruitment, bookstores, computer facilities, library), can only be beneficial—especially when such audits reveal the greater cost effectiveness of opening the competition for such management and services to the private sector. Tradition and stubbornness ("the way it has always been done") can impede the sound efficiencies that technology and superior management techniques provide.

Libraries are a case in point. Academics and librarians often romanticize the experience of roaming through library stacks and the serendipitous discoveries resulting from such wanderings, but the cost of books and journals is skyrocketing and library acquisition budgets cripple the flexibility needed to make other necessary allocations. With information technology, there is no sound option but to transform libraries from collection-based facilities to access-based services, just as librarians will have to become information managers.

Noses will be put out of joint, and unions will agitate noisily when large sectors of the university are privatized, but there is no alternative to taking a scalpel to the university and subjecting its budget to the strictest financial scrutiny. The universities must have the resoluteness, even ruthlessness, to distinguish the essential from the accidental, to cut their losses and strengthen their successes, and to declare redundant what is failing. They cannot go on continuing to believe that every one of their programs has a leading role. Across-the-board cuts and whittling away at the periphery, which is current practice, produces only mediocrity overall. The practice also fails to recognize that the scholarly culture is a compound of diverse elements, and that treating all of them in the same way exhibits extravagance towards one and parsimony towards another.

Hot Button Five: Tuition as user fee.

Recommendation Five:
The seriousness of our national debt and the necessary limits that must be imposed on cash flow to universities require us to abandon the idea that the public trough is the only pool of

resources. Just as universities have to learn to shake off the unessential, so students must learn the value of what is necessary. Increased tuition fees are a form of moral education and should be taken on the chin in the same way that the demanding challenges of university education must be shouldered.

There are, however, additional ways to correct the serious cash flow that need to be considered—ones that would avoid depositing the responsibility for the national debt on students alone. It is an injustice that one generation can enjoy public largesse without limit, while the next pays for that generation's sins. Justice demands an intergenerational pact. Just as today's taxpayer absorbs the penalty for yesterday's abuse of the environment, so the baby-boomer generation, who have enjoyed the benefits of the system, should bear some financial responsibility for the crippling deficits with which universities are encumbered. Now is the time, in other words, for alumni to pay up, either by a "tithing tax" (such as one-half percent of income tax) or by outright gifts to their alma mater. The former may be preferable, since, without a sufficient tax incentive, few have been inclined to undertake the latter.[4]

Enforced philanthropy may be distasteful, but this country has a poor track record of any other form of giving. In 1993, the last year for which there are data, individual donors and corporations in Canada gave to teaching institutions a total of $56 million in receipted donations (further differentiation to determine the university component is not available), as compared to government expenditures of $16 *billion*. Funding to universities from private sources hovers between 3 percent and 7 percent of the university's operating budget. That funding is also quirky, such as the immensely generous but idiosyncratic gift of $12 million to Queen's University to buy a fifteenth-century English moated castle and convert it into an international study centre.[5] What Robert Reich and Christopher Lasch identify as the "secession of the successful"—wealthy families who have only a marginal concern about public goods—is as evident in Canada as in the America they describe. But unless the universities give them something to be proud of, it is not surprising that their gifts have been modest.

A more radical solution is called for. Whether or not we adopt the recommendation of shifting professional programs to the colleges, all professional programs should operate on a cost-recovery basis. Professional training, while it gives our society as a whole an enviable expertise and technical advantage, primarily lines the pockets of individuals. Since the first-employment salaries and the lifetime earnings of professionals are vastly greater than that of other graduates, the cost of their training should be borne by them. While it is true that their future taxes will also be higher, contributing more to the public coffers than other graduates, professionals are benefitting from historical investments that far exceed the immediate costs of the education they are provided. Future taxes pay past sacrifices, while full-cost tuitions would square present costs.

The public savings derived from operating professional programs on a cost-recovery basis should not be recouped by governments seeking to meet their deficit-reduction goals but should be invested in nonprofessional university degree programs. Such investment would be a recognition that liberal education is a good enjoyed by Canadians as a whole in the shape of a more informed political citizenry, responsible leaders, a productive workforce and, generally, a segment of society that enjoys a firmer sense of moral and intellectual purpose. Bachelor program tuitions should remain at their current ratio to operating budgets—approximately 20 percent—while graduate program tuitions should rise gradually to approximately 50 percent.

Hot Button Six: Distance-learning technology.

Recommendation Six:
If the emerging technologies are pushing us towards the "virtual university" of electronic classrooms and pay-per-service instruction, then we should not shop only in our local market.

Distance television and videoconferencing should bring together talents from every continent—in science, literature or politics—into "virtual seminars" and world-class lectures. Stephen Hawking and John Polanyi, V.S. Naipaul and Milan Kundera, Vaclav Havel and Benazir Bhutto should be available if we take seriously the potential of the electronic medium. Instead, what commonly transpires is more of the same tired shuffling of lecture notes from instructors who, while well intentioned, lose much in the translation to television or, worse, use the opportunity to pursue thwarted theatrical careers. The technology is in its infancy, but some of its cast are in their dotage.

However, even if we could marry Matthew Arnold's "the best which has been thought and said in the world" with an electronic medium, would this be "education"? The clarity required to make such an assessment is clouded by pointing to examples from medical surgery "virtual" classes and business-management seminars, where the transmission of factual information, and even guidance in honing of skills, is apparently highly effective. But at the heart of university education are also talents developed from practice and habit: understanding, discerning judgment and cultivated imagination. While not even a classroom can offer any guarantee that during a four-year incubation such abilities will be formed, the evidence that electronic technology can even approximate the classroom is immensely weak. Dissemination of information and demonstrations of skills are only minimal conditions for learning. "Learner-centred" models of education are predicated on the idea that students can develop these additional talents unassisted (taking unrealistically the example of self-educated scholars), but it is the ordinary, middle-ability student who loses in these structures. It is hard enough to practice Socrates' effective teaching style in a real classroom. He "adapted speeches to souls" and thus prudently individualized what he taught by assessing the characters of his students. It is virtually impossible to do this in a disembodied classroom. The keen desire to re-engineer teaching to make it more "effective" constitutes not a praise of teaching, but its denigration. Classes of four to nine hundred students connected by projection screens is not education but entertainment. In entertainment, one is not teaching a plurality of minds, but prodding mass response.

Technology must be applied assymetrically. Electronic technology—interactive CD-ROM language acquisition, "virtual libraries" and mail or chat-lines—are all powerful and useful tools. Much of the factual and skill-based information they are capable of handling effectively is better done electronically than by traditional teaching methods. But while such technology is most appropriate in professional training, it can convey none of the passion of discovery or the surprise of comprehending meaning that are evident in even the most ordinary embodied conversations and that are the lifeblood of the scholarly culture.

Hot Button Seven: A modularized curriculum.

Recommendation Seven:
No academic, not even an entire faculty or university, can do justice to the breadth and richness of the intellectual understanding in any society. This is one fact that favours "outsourcing"—the use of extrauniversity scholarly achievement in a curriculum composed of the hues of many experts. The scholarly culture is, moreover, a strangely amorphous being, bringing forth achievement only through a slow and incremental collective activity and, as a form of collective behaviour, is often stiflingly conformist. Renewal is critical if the scholarly culture is to survive—whether that renewal comes in terms of discrete units in a curriculum that shake up the complacency of accepted opinion, or as provisional troops brought in from the network of approximately thirty-thousand-plus private scholars, who work in government ministries and private corporations waiting against all hope for tenured faculty to retire. Modularizing, in short, has its attractions.

But curricula are more than a set of course offerings. They are organic phenomena that have evolved gradually and whose components have been refined in their interaction with one another. Opening them up and restacking components, as if a curriculum was a piece of Ikea furniture, overlooks the complexity that informs them, especially in its purpose of meeting the diversity of student needs. Moreover, as with all human creations, curricula are a fragile balance of political artifices, made all the more so with recent government insistence that all the university's affairs be ground through the mill of "stakeholders." Modularizing curricula will open the process of coordination to even further politicization, culminating in a set of course offerings that are an incoherent hodge-podge of interests and agendas.

A far superior prospect for making universities relevant, cost-effective and infused with fresh ideas is one that fills an old bottle with new wine—the core curriculum. In these days of irascible empowerment and the subsequent loss of commonalities that reunite us above our differences, the last thing we need is a curriculum that fragments the experience of students further. The thousands of courses the university offers with little prescription as to how they should be sampled already reinforces the absence of common experiences and the loss of virtues that come only from being a member of a community. A core curriculum is a countermeasure to the prevailing social forces, and when it is designed sensitively and with discerning connoisseurship, it can be an oasis nourishing the general social barrenness.

Hot Button Eight: The inclusive university.

Recommendation Eight:
One of the university's wild cards, which it will play after all the trumps are down, is its claim to universality. In opposition to parochialism and provincialism, the university as an idea and institution stands or falls on its proficiency to deliver on this claim. It must say, as Terence, the Roman dramatist, did: "I am human and let nothing human be alien to me." Thus, all efforts

to recognize and engage the plurality of voices comprising the human chorus are to be encouraged. It is unconscionable that any university worthy of its name could ever have proceeded otherwise.

The efforts that confer unqualified equal status and dignity on women and members of minority groups, as much as the separate initiatives that accelerate the progress of those conferrals, are an unmitigated blessing. One praiseworthy initiative undertaken in recent years at the University of Calgary is a mentoring program set up by the Academic Women's Association for incoming women faculty. Paired with a more senior faculty member, new women faculty receive advice on the range of opportunities and pitfalls they will encounter as university instructors. "Inclusivity," however, ought not to be restricted to gender and race alone. It could also include age, which is precisely the category targeted recently by Wilfrid Laurier University with its Laurier Fellows program. Through an aggressive fund-raising campaign, the university raised $2.5 million for twenty-five new gifted scholars to work as "bridging appointments" until faculty retire. The initiative is an important commitment to renewal brought by the young in particular.

But if the university is to live up to its mandate fully, and to enjoy real inclusivity, then it must also continue to sponsor true intellectual diversity. It is the strange fate of our times that the political agenda for "inclusivity" constitutes a relentless campaign against curricular breadth and depth. When the Western inheritance is seen as nothing but the preserve of "dead, white males," it is a short step to closing off entirely any serious attention to the rich diversity of forms of human perfectibility and transcendence that its thinkers invited us to entertain. The result is a narrowing of our perspective, as the whole university curriculum comes to reflect one perspective alone—the project of empowerment. This project increases the litigiousness of the university community, focusing an individual's attention on rights and entitlements, rather than on responsibilities and forms of friendship. Postmodernism has now had its day in court and has served a useful role as a sceptical corrective to the terrible presumptions of our age. A new generation of young scholars is far more cautious of the arrogant rationalism which, in our past, reinforced unwarranted prejudice and discrimination. It is time now to retire postmodernism as the only theory to be entertained, and lay aside its corrosiveness, especially where it gives us social policy and jurisprudence in which material facts, logical argument and demonstrable truth have no standing.

True inclusivity is more than mere sociological representation of gender, racial, ethnic and "lifestyle" differences—it is openness to the range of intellectual options that compete for our attention as thinking and acting beings. Detached contemplation, filial piety, spiritual charity, moral action, material acquisitiveness, political glory, communal solidarity, Romantic rebellion, scientific mastery and pragmatic common sense—these are only a sampling of the competing paradigms of human opportunity with which students should be acquainted if the array of their intellectual and spiritual needs are to be truly met. These options are articulated in one way in our own Western inheritance and in another way in the texts and works of other cultures. The challenge is to move beyond the dogma and doctrine that have encrusted these differing ways and to encounter the essential experiences that bind us across cultures and historical accident. Until we overcome the radical idea that all of these alternatives are nothing but expressions of unjustifiable privilege, we will never enjoy the intellectual invitation to become acquainted with genuine universality, which the scholarly culture extends to everyone courageous enough to ask questions.

Hot Button Nine: Academic freedom.

Recommendation Nine:
The university's second wild card is academic freedom. As the cornerstone of the university, academic freedom is the sole basis

for the university's claim of uniqueness among other postsecondary institutions. Practices such as tenure and paid sabbatical make no sense unless academic freedom is seen as the primary purpose of the university. Academic freedom is a privilege given to the few to pursue in leisure "inconsequential adventures" that will appear from the outside as frivolous and irrelevant. It is also the privilege to cultivate understanding and critical judgment without fear of reprisal, the means and results of which will be seen from the outside as controversial and uncomfortable. Yet, from the apparently useless and irrelevant exercise of academic freedom are generated by-products that society will find useful—from gene therapy to CD players—and from the controversial and uncomfortable will stem, among other goods, progressive political and legal reform. Without academic freedom, and an institution that enshrines its privileges, our society would lack direction and purpose.

But academic freedom is also a responsibility. It is not the same as freedom of speech and action, for these the law and constitution extend to everyone. Academics are asked for more. Academic freedom is the opportunity to speak and act with a refinement and maturity higher than the conduct permitted by law. When academics are forgiven their inappropriate and indecent remarks with the excuse that their conduct is no worse than that of the rest of society, we are hearing the death rattle of academic freedom. Once academic freedom violates the canons of good taste, it is a violation of the trust that civilization invests in the privileges it has given to the few.

The horizon of good taste is, of course, elastic and open to interpretation, but there is conduct that legitimately pushes the envelope and that should be tolerated, and there is conduct that falls outside the pale. In the abstract, freedom of speech and action is a great good which should never be assailed because, from the public airing of opinion it encourages, private prejudice and fantasy are exposed and driven out. But such freedom must also be exercised in a manner appropriate to the times. Ours is not a time when jaunty jocularity and dubious teaching techniques based on provocation are acceptable. The university, appropriate to its origins in the tension between *universitas* and *civitas*, is an institution which tolerates difference but does so within a common recognition of the dictates of decency and civility. Its price may be freedom and reason, but its worth comes from its ability to compose those moral attitudes, within the intellectual and spiritual adventures upon which it invites its members, that transcend the letter of the law and subscribe to its spirit. Anything less deprives the university of its distinct status in our society.

The great travesty of our times is that while accommodation and compromise between the diverse parties of our civil association were still possible, the wildcard of academic freedom was played precipitously and without good judgment. Now we are polarized and the middle ground has been vacated, while "ignorant armies clash by night," one favouring "zero-tolerance policy" and the other the "right to offend."

Hot Button Ten: Accountability.

Recommendation Ten:
Every "stakeholder" is now demanding that the university be accountable to it—the corporate right, the cultural left, government, media, policy wonks, education pundits, the taxpaying public that voted for reductions in public expenditures. Their concerns are not without merit, since the disbursement of public funds, especially in our times, must constitute a sound and responsible investment. The demands for transparency are reasonable, especially when reality matches the opinion that universities suffer from swollen university administrations, gutted bachelor programs, unproductive faculty, irrelevant research and overall inefficiency. "Accountability," while a catch-word for elusive perceptions and crisis mongering, is nonetheless also an entreaty whose time has come. Nowhere could accountability be more sufficiently tested than in examining the services faculty

members extend to the community in which they live. Until the universities abandon the idea that service is met through involvement in the internal administration of the institution and recognize the responsibilities academics have to society, academic privilege will be scorned by outsiders.

There is, however, one constituency to which the universities have not thus far been obliged to be accountable: the students. A 1992 survey by Statistics Canada of thirty-six thousand graduates reported that the major reason students attended university was for general self-improvement. The acquisition of job skills ranked at the bottom of the list of reasons. The voice of students should tell us something.

In the current jockeying for power, the university and the curriculum are becoming nothing more than the sum total of the agendas of interest groups. One powerful group sees education as agitation propaganda, with students and professors equipping themselves to be revolutionaries. Another sees education as a set of services with students and professors as consumers and providers. Students—with their complex needs and longings— are falling through the cracks. The philosopher Hannah Arendt once wrote that education is "where we decide whether we love our children enough not to expel them from our world and leave them to their own devices, nor to strike from their hands their chance of undertaking something new, something unforeseen by us, but to prepare them in advance for the task of renewing a common world."[6]

The cultural left and the corporate right have nearly succeeded in bringing about the two dangers Arendt feared. Only a return to the scholarly culture that truly looks to the range of student needs will restore the preparation that Arendt saw as essential. The university is the gatekeeper to the self-understanding and refinement of society, and without tolerance for its ambiguous ways, that self-understanding and the projects for improvement are in danger of becoming superficial or dogmatic. To centre once again on the needs of students, as these are swept up and given form within the scholarly culture, is to restore the university to its rightful place.

What the university needs above all is a robust public relations campaign. Though a new expense, such a campaign would serve the important task of public education by stimulating tolerance of the university's practices and extending anew an invitation to young women and men currently disappointed in their expectations of what the university offers. It is unbelievable that the Association of Universities and Colleges in Canada or the Canadian Association of University Teachers have not undertaken the initiative. The university's mysterious processes are poorly understood and its cultivation of human longings appears remote. The discriminating graces it confers on society as a whole are elusive and even shunned. To date, the universities have disdained advertising themselves. Collectively, the universities must now unite, or divided they will fall under the opprobrium of misunderstanding and false expectations. The campaign must profile what universities do best: form individuals who exhibit thoughtful reflection, cultivated imagination and informed criticism; produce citizens who look upon politics as a noble enterprise on behalf of the public good, not simply interest; and stimulate intellectual and spiritual journeys that offer meaning and purpose.

The campaign must make a pitch to restore the past practice where government ministries of universities were separate from college and manpower training ministries. It must communicate a picture of the university's proficiency in forming the character and discerning talents of students, so that the private and public sector will set up internships for university students (even unpaid ones), that would express concrete endorsement of the "value-added" that universities supply. The campaign could aim at creating a partnership of the private and public sector in founding an Institute of Advanced Research, akin to the Woodrow Wilson Centre in Washington or the Social Affairs Unit in London, where academics are invited to participate in the formation of public policy.

The campaign must also initiate a process to enhance our

public intellectual life. It is incredible that a country with such superlative talent does not have newspapers and journals like the *New York Times* and the *Washington Post*, or *Harper's* and *The Atlantic Monthly*, which offer opportunities for direct engagement between the scholarly culture and the public. It is even more astounding that the professional associations representing the university's interests have made no effort in this direction, but instead have pursued more pedestrian agendas that keep the scholarly culture in an ivory tower.

Perhaps the public relations campaign would find it useful to employ one final metaphor of the university that I can offer. In many ways, the university is a gothic mansion, filled with secret rooms and hidden staircases. It is filled with surprises, some horrors and many unanticipated discoveries. Its labyrinthine hallways contain a comfortable clutter, almost a studied dishevelment, that despite the muddle may afford the opportunity for serendipitous finds, rediscoveries and even acts of greatness. This mansion is not at home in the suburbs, where the public safety authorities would not tolerate its disorder. It is only at home in the centre of the city, where corruption, decay and some rot prevail, but also where the hopes of renovation and renewal are dreamt. Though it rises up above the common and everyday, it confers distinction and grace on everything around it. If it were razed to the ground, to make way for a more hygienic and efficient structure, in its very consonance with the surrounding social world, it would have become drab and uniform, and its wayfarers would have no landmark by which to gauge their movements.

The particular recommendations for change I have made reflect only one perspective on the scholarly culture. There are many others. More important is the fact that we must abandon the expectation that the university can be all things to all people and that by re-engineering it we will find a shortcut to the millennium. The university cannot be an engine of economic growth, a social welfare agency, a laboratory for a new consciousness, a training centre and also a home for the scholarly culture. When we expect the university to be all these things, and seek to prepare it for the twenty-first century with this view in mind, we simply manufacture the "perception problems" that invite even more extravagant dreams. The jewel in the crown of the university is the scholarly culture. From time to time that jewel must be examined, held up to harsh lights and polished so that the encrustations of age are removed. The hot-button politics of the last six years have chipped away at the university but have done little to polish it. For the sake of our society and generations to come, now is the time for the academic world and others who know and love the university well to unite in order to revive and nurture its soul.

Endnotes

Chapter 1: Wilting Ivy?

1. Statistics are drawn from the following sources: "Federal Transfers for Higher Education," *CAUT Special Bulletin*, November 1995, p. 11; Miles Wisenthal, "Education and Research in Canada," *Policy Options* 14 (4) (May 1993); Council of Ontario Universities, "The Financial Position of Universities in Ontario: 1995" (May 1995); and Statistics Canada, *Education Quarterly Review* (Spring 1994), cat. no. 81–003, vol. 1, no. 1.

2. "The Universities: A Measure of Excellence," *Maclean's*, 2 November 1992.

3. "Change or Be Changed: A Lesson in History," *CAUT Bulletin*, December 1991, p. 3.

4. H.W. Arthurs, Roger Blais and Jon Thompson, "Integrity in Scholarship: A Report to Concordia University," 1994 (private circulation).

5. John Cowan, "Lessons from the Fabrikant File: A Report to the Board of Governors of Concordia University," 1994 (private circulation).

6. As cited in Barry Gross, "The Case of Philippe Rushton," *Academic Questions* 3(4) (Fall 1990): 36. Cf. Philippe Rushton, *Race, Evolution, and Behavior: A Life History Perspective* (New Brunswick, NJ: Transaction, 1994).

7. *Surface*, 23 September 1993, p. 3.

8. Gordon Freeman, "Kinetics of Non-homogenous Processes in Human Society: Unethical Behaviour and Societal Chaos," *Canadian Journal of Physics* 68 (September 1990): 794–98.

9. As cited in "Students Ban Whites from Minorities-only Lounge," *Montreal Gazette*, 24 June 1995, p. B1.

10. As quoted in "Political correctness attacked," *The Calgary Herald*, 10 June 1994, p. B1.

11. As cited in "Granting Agencies Tie Funds to Ethics," *Winnipeg Free Press*, 1 December 1994, p. C16.

12 "Who You Gonna Call? Prof Busters!" *Halifax Chronicle Herald*, 9 February 1993, p. B1.

13. *Maclean's*, 23 May 1995, pp. 51–52.

14. "Survey of the Perception of Universities among Provincial Government Officials," Research Report no. 5, in *Report on the Commission of Inquiry on Canadian University Education* (Ottawa: Association of Universities and Colleges in Canada, 1991), p. 15.

15. Uwe Poerksen, *Plastic Words: The Tyranny of a Modular Language* (Pennsylvania State Park: Pennsylvania State University Press, 1995).

16. "Whatever Happened to the University?" reprinted in *The Globe and Mail*, 28 December 1993, p. A15.

17. The wording is not always as clear as this. Manitoba's Education Minister Clayton Manness veiled his threat to have government "restructure" the universities after universities balked at his "Manness Challenge" document, saying "I hope those challenges don't produce a non-product, but if they do, ultimately we're going nowhere but continuing to dilute the product because of funding that doesn't increase at a level everyone's expected. Then I would think that ultimately these discussions will be taken to a so-called different level." ("A Challenge to Change," *Winnipeg Free Press*, 7 January 1995, p. A15.)

18. Christine Tausig Ford, "A Solid Showing," *University Affairs*, April 1993, p. 40.

19. Zero tolerance appears to have been one of David Cooke's favourite terms. More recently, he has announced "zero-tolerance" of violence in schools.

20. "Universities Mull Demand to Rationalize," *Winnipeg Free Press*, 12 January 1995, p. B2.

Chapter 2: The Needs of Students and the Scholarly Culture

1. As cited in "Students Want Just the Facts, Shun Thinking, Academics Say," *The Globe and Mail*, 19 June 1993, p. A6.

2. As cited in "Universities: Measuring Excellence," *Maclean's*, 14 November 1994, p. 17.

3. Northrop Frye, "A Revolution Betrayed," in *On Education* (Markham: Fitzhenry and Whiteside, 1988), p. 92.

4. Two good introductions to this complex cultural interaction are Philip Sherrard, *The Greek East and the Latin West* (London: Oxford University Press, 1959) and Hans Jonas, *The Gnostic Religion* (New York: Beacon Press, 1958).

5. See Michael Oakeshott, "On the Character of a Modern European State," in *On Human Conduct* (Oxford: Clarendon Press, 1975).

6. Ibid., pp. 324–25 (emphasis added).

7. Matthew Arnold, *Culture and Anarchy and Other Writings*, ed. Stefan Collini (Cambridge: Cambridge University Press, 1993), p. 190.

8. The major protagonists in today's curriculum battles are: Allan Bloom, *The Closing of the American Mind* (New York: Simon and Schuster, 1987), Dinesh D'Souza, *Illiberal Education: The Politics of Race and Sex on Campus* (New York: Free Press, 1991), E.D. Hirsch, Jr., *Cultural Literacy: What Every American Needs to Know* (Boston: Houghton Mifflin, 1987), Russell Jacoby, *Dogmatic Wisdom: How the Culture Wars Divert Education and Distract America* (New York: Doubleday, 1994), Stanley Fish and Gertrude Himmelfarb, *Looking into the Abyss: Untimely Thoughts on Culture and Society* (New York: Alfred A. Knopf, 1994). For a good summary of the issues, see W.B. Carnochan, *The Battleground of the Curriculum: Liberal Education and American Experience* (Stanford: Stanford University Press, 1993).

9. Virginia Woolf, "How Should One Read a Book," in *The Common Reader*, 2nd series (New York: Harcourt, 1948), p. 142.

10. Michael Oakeshott, "Education: The Engagement and Its Frustration," reprinted in Timothy Fuller, *The Voice of Liberal Learning: Michael Oakeshott on Education* (New Haven: Yale University Press, 1989), p. 71.

11. John Henry Newman, "General Knowledge Viewed as One Philosophy," in *The Idea of a University Defined* (Oxford: Clarendon, 1976).

12. "What's Hot… What's Not," *Maclean's*, 1994, p. 54.

13. See here the discussion in Chapter 9.

14. William Thorsell, "Rising above Philistinism," *Globe and Mail,* 10 June 1995, p. D3. One might only wish that the *Globe and Mail* generally would take its bearings from the vision expressed in this convocation address. In fairness, Thorsell acknowledges that the media is "a giant skepticism-manufacturing industry." Cynicism, would be more like it.

15. As quoted in Michael Valpy, "The Day the Professor Defended the Monarchy," *The Globe and Mail,* 6 April 1995. The anachronism is particularly acute in light of the sensible opinions being expressed by the successor to the throne. Prince Charles has made it clear, in light of the contemporary social world, that he will not be "defender of *the* faith" (that of the Church of England), but rather the defender of faith, be it Catholic, Islamic, Hindu or Zoroastrian, just as he is opposed to the duty of the sovereign to be an "agent of national unity." An inevitable, and fresh, push towards republicanism.

16. Michael Oakeshott, "The Voice of Poetry in the Conversation of Mankind," in *Rationalism in Politics* (London: Methuen, 1962), p. 199.

17. F.R. Leavis, "Literature and the University: The Wrong Question," in *English Literature in Our Time and the University* (London: Chatto and Windus, 1969), p. 47.

18. Michael Oakeshott, "The Universities," (in *The Voice of Liberal Learning,* ed. Fuller,) p. 124.

19. Michael Oakeshott, "A Place of Learning," in Fuller, *The Voice of Liberal Learning,* p. 29.

20. Matthew Arnold, quoted in Fuller, *The Voice of Liberal Learning,* p. 142.

21. Northrop Frye, "The Critical Discipline," in *On Education,* p. 34.

22. Statistics from Statistics Canada, *Education Quarterly Review* (Spring 1994), cat. no. 81–003, vol. 1, no.1.

23. Horace, *Epistles,* I.xi.27.

24. F. Scott Fitzgerald, reprinted in *Afternoon of an Author,* ed. Arthur Mizener (New York: Scribner's, 1957).

Chapter 3: Academic Privileges in the Spotlight

1. The rebellion of faculty against academic administrators was nowhere as vitriolically fought as at Carleton University (with the exception

perhaps of Memorial, Manitoba and Mount Allison). Political science professors Glen Williams and Sharon Sutherland took on Carleton University's admission policy, which had resulted in a change of its moniker from "Second Chance U" to "Last Chance U." Carleton, they argued, was accepting seven out of every ten Ontario high school students with less than 65 percent averages. It had the lowest share of Ontario Scholars: those with averages greater than 80 percent. "The administration's chosen course of action is a ruined path," Sutherland said, having led, as Williams charged, to a "dedication of an entire institution to the province's weakest students," particularly in the B.A. program. The university had become, in short, an "admissions treadmill." Sutherland and Williams' report spurred other departments to complain widely about the "negative halo" that had fallen on them by the poor image of the B.A. program. In 1995, university management capitulated to the faculty boards, and the Senate raised admission standards. Concerns of fiscal mismanagement still poison relations between faculty and administration.

2. One such growing cleavage is between the thirty-five thousand regular university faculty and twenty-five thousand term appointments. The Canadian Association of University Teachers fears that the presence of so many term appointments weakens their negotiation power, while term appointees are principally using their union power to lobby solely for higher pay. CAUT fears a group that has acted as a whistle blower on tenured faculty's alleged abuse of privileges, while the various CUPE unions representing sessional appointees have been clear that they have little concern about benefits that may contribute to institutional continuity or curricular coherence. The special pleading by each side ensures only that the university itself will be the loser.

3. As reported in *The Ottawa Citizen*, 13 September 1995, p. A1.

4. See Robin S. Harris, *A History of Higher Education in Canada, 1663–1960* (Toronto: University of Toronto Press, 1976); Paul Axelrod, *Scholars and Dollars: Politics, Economics, and the Universities of Ontario, 1945–1980* (Toronto: University of Toronto Press, 1982); Paul Axelrod, *Making a Middle Class: Student Life in English Canada during the Thirties* (Kingston and Montreal: McGill-Queen's University Press, 1990); David M. Cameron, *More Than an Academic Question: Universities, Government, and Public Policy in Canada* (Ottawa: IRPP, 1991); Davis J. Bercuson, Robert Bothwell

Endnotes

and J.L. Granatstein, *The Great Brain Robbery: Canada's Universities on the Road to Ruin* (Toronto: McClelland and Stewart, 1984); A.B. McKillop, *Matters of Mind: The University in Ontario, 1791–1951* (Toronto: University of Toronto Press, 1994); J.A. Corry, *Farewell the Ivory Tower: Universities in Transition* (Kingston and Montreal: McGill-Queen's University Press, 1971).

5. Jo Anne Sommers, "Not... Tenure!" *University Manager*, Winter 1995, p. 15.

6. "Letter to the Editor," *The Globe and Mail*, 10 May 1995, p. A12.

7. For an excellent review of academic freedom, see Michael Horn, "The Mildew of Discretion: Academic Freedom and Self-Censorship," *Dalhousie Review* (Winter 1992/93): 439–66.

8. John Cowan, "Lessons from the Fabrikant File: A Report to the Board of Governors of Concordia University" (1994), p. 7 (private circulation).

9. As quoted in "Tenure Pumps Up the Pace," *The Calgary Herald*, 1 May 1994, p. B2.

10. Robert Moody, "Tenure and Research," *CAUT Bulletin*, 11 February 1995.

11. Charles Sykes, *Profscam: Professors and the Demise of Higher Education* (Washington, DC: Regnery, Gateway, 1988), p. 103.

12. *McKinney* v. *University of Guelph* [1990] 3 S.C.R. 229.

13. Walter Burgess, "Letter to the Editor," *The Globe and Mail*, 13 October 1993, p. A23.

14. As quoted in Vivian Smith, "When Academe Draws the Line," *The Globe and Mail*, 1 October 1995, p. A8.

15. Ibid.

16. Freeman's essay is filled with unfounded, contradictory, overly speculative, and on occasion silly statements. Abjuring survey work, he claimed that such social science techniques were "distorted by the artificiality of the gathering situation" and that what was needed was "wisdom." He went on to define wisdom as the "knowledge of [the] body of empirical correlations." Using a pseudoscientific jargon of "kinetics," an approach that tries to extrapolate from discrete events to long-term trends, Freeman offers his own version of this dubious approach by moving from a set of nonverifiable statements made in his office about cheating to "analogous events in society at large."

It leads him to say that the "largest single root" of the drug problem is "the decay of stable families as the basic unit of society" and that "about half of the children of two-career families suffer serious psychological damage." Freeman offers a chain of causes that is literally incredible: the pill has led to more infidelity because there is a direct link between the pill and more casual sex and then "the rest follows: decreased mutual respect, decreased self-respect, decreased ethical behaviour, and societal decline." As Dancik, editor-in-chief of thirteen scientific journals, wrote: "The article does not comprise science and has no place in a scientific journal."

17. One recent example of the clash between knowledge (or what is taken as knowledge) and political myth is the ruckus that broke out in 1994 at McGill University, when it was calculated that a new pension plan paid smaller monthly benefits to women than to men, because women's average life expectancy is 7.4 years longer than men's, based on actuarial tables.

18. See "The Academic Profession in Canada," produced at the Institute for Social Research, York University, under the direction of J. Lennards. For further discussion of the survey, see "The Structure of Academic Work," Task Force on Resource Allocation, Ontario Council on University Affairs (August 1994).

19. John Sewell, "Letter to the Editor," *The Globe and Mail*, 5 June 1995, A16.

20. "Back to School for the University," editorial, *The Globe and Mail*, 3 January 1994, p. A10.

21. Paul Axelrod, *Making a Middle Class* (Kingston and Montreal: McGill-Queen's University Press, 1991).

22. From a survey by the Canadian Research Management Association, 1991, private circulation.

23. Angus Reid/AUCC Survey, 1993, as reported in "A Solid Showing," *University Affairs*, April 1993, p. 40.

24. Harry Arthurs, "Resolved: Canadian Universities Undervalue Teaching," *CAUT Bulletin*, 15 January 1994, p. 15.

25. Ibid.

26. Gilbert's conclusion is also flatly contradicted by the more detailed and extensive studies on small group teaching undertaken by Richard Light at Harvard University.

27. As cited in "Undergraduate Teaching, Research, and Consulting/Community Service," Task Force on Resource Allocation (Toronto: Ontario Council on University Affairs, August 1994), p. 2.

28. Ibid.

29. D.H. Lawrence, 4 May 1908, *Letters of D.H. Lawrence,* vol. 1, ed. James T. Boulton (Cambridge: Cambridge University Press, 1979).

30. Robert Burton, "Democritus to the Reader," *Anatomy of Melancholy* (Oxford: Clarendon Press, 1989), p. 215.

31. Press release, Office of Randy White, Reform MP, Fraser Valley West, 1995.

32. The money for the paintings came, in fact, from an endowment fund committed to sustaining the traditions of the university, and not university sources, as CUPE officials alleged.

33. Virginia Woolf in *The Sickle Side of the Moon: Letters of Virginia Woolf,* vol. 5, ed. Nigel Nicolson (London: Hogarth Press, 1979), p. 211.

34. "Aging Professors Target of Study," *The Globe and Mail,* 20 September 1995, pp. A1, A7.

35. "University Officials Wrestle with Age Bulge," *The Globe and Mail,* 20 September 1995, p. A11.

36. "Aging Professors Target of Study," *The Globe and Mail,* 20 September 1995, p. A11.

37. Roger Kimball, *Tenured Radicals: How Politics Has Corrupted Our Higher Education* (New York: Harper and Row, 1990), p. xvii.

38. Arthurs, Blais and Thompson, "Integrity in Scholarship," p. 4.

39. Ibid.

40. An audit by an independent accounting firm confirmed that some portion of research funds had been used for purposes other than those intended; that account balances had been manipulated, thus mixing research grants with contract funds and diverting funds to discretionary research accounts; that there were examples of duplicate expense claims, camouflaging of personal expenses, and conflicting expenses. Following the Fabrikant murders, the Natural Sciences and Engineering Research Council (NSERC) asked the RCMP to investigate and (with Fonds FCAR, the Quebec granting council) withheld research funds from the university and gave the university an ultimatum of sixty days to improve its procedures.

41. Arthurs, Blais and Thompson, "Integrity in Scholarship," p. 7.

42. Calculation based on listings in the *Universities Telephone Directory,* Association of Universities and Colleges of Canada, 1994/95, and on discussions with policy analysts in the AUCC.

Chapter 4: Growing Discord on Canada's Campuses

1. Plato, *Republic*, 539b. Translation and notes by Allan Bloom (New York: Basic Books, 1968).

2. "When Rules Overtake Common Sense," *The Globe and Mail*, 1 July 1994, p. A11.

3. See here the discussion in Chapter 9, note 17.

4. As quoted in "Revolting," *Montreal Gazette*, 10 February 1993, p. B3.

5. One of the ironies that intellectual historians are enjoying is that the more immediate source of postmodernism is the work of Friedrich Nietzsche and Martin Heidegger. The leftist postmodernism of de Man, Foucault and Derrida is therefore ironical in view of Nietzsche and Heidegger's connections with Nazism and in view of the fact that works like *The Geneology of Morals* and the *Letter on Humanism* were, as one American commentator has wryly noted, at one time the reserve of "gentlemen on the right." See Werner Dannhauser, "The Trivialization of Friedrich Nietzsche," *The American Spectator* 15 (5) (May 1982): 7–13.

6. Stanley Rosen, *Hermeneutics as Politics* (New York: Oxford University Press, 1987).

7. Allan Bloom, *The Closing of the American Mind* (New York: Simon and Schuster, 1987), Dinesh D'Souza, *Illiberal Education: The Politics of Race and Sex on Campus* (New York: Free Press, 1991), E.D. Hirsch, Jr., *Cultural Literacy: What Every American Needs to Know* (Boston: Houghton-Mifflin, 1987), Russell Jacoby, *Dogmatic Wisdom: How the Culture Wars Divert Education and Distract America* (New York: Doubleday, 1994), Stanley Fish and Gertrude Himmelfarb, *Looking into the Abyss: Untimely Thoughts on Culture and Society* (New York: Alfred A. Knopf, 1994).

8. Jean Bethke Elshtain, *Democracy on Trial* (Toronto: Anansi, 1993), p. 120.

9. Gerald Graff, "Teach the Conflicts," in *The Politics of Liberal Education*, ed. D.J. Gless and B. Hernnstein Smith (Durham, NC: Duke University Press, 1991).

10. Northrop Frye, "Language as the Home to Human Life," in *Salute to Scholarship: Essays Presented at the Official Opening of Athabasca University*, ed. Michael Owen (Athabasca: Athabasca University, 1986).

11. Amy Gutman, "Introduction," in *Multiculturalism and the "Politics*

of Recognition," Charles Taylor and Amy Gutman (Princeton: Princeton University Press, 1992), pp. 20–21.

12. Robertson Davies, "Shakespeare over the Port," Stratford papers on Shakespeare, 1960, reprinted in *The Enthusiasms of Robertson Davies,* ed. Judith Skelton Grant (Toronto: McClelland and Stewart, 1979).

13. As reported in "University Rankings," *Montreal Gazette,* 9 November 1994, p. A6.

14. "Making the Grade," *The Globe and Mail,* 23 June 1994, p. C3.

15. Universities in Ontario currently submit financial statements, enrolment reports, ancillary fees reports, reports on capital spending, audit reports, annual reports on institutional revenues and expenditures, annual reports on applications and admissions, faculty renewal grant reports, reports to pay equity commissions, employment standards branch, federal granting councils, Revenue Canada, Statistics Canada, the Public Trustee in compliance with Ontario Charities legislation, plus submissions to the Ontario Council of University Affairs and the Ontario Council on Graduate Studies. They undergo accreditation of their professional programs. They also generate internal university documents from the annual report, to mission statement, academic plan, financial plan, enrolment forecast, academic program reviews, reports on research centres, fund raising, status of women, equity, safety, outreach education and student financial aid.

16. I am indebted to Imelda Mulvihill, whose paper "A Measure of Excellence: A Critique of the 1993 *Maclean's* Survey of Canadian Universities" is a sustained critique of the survey's methodology (private circulation).

17. As cited in "Taking the Campus Pulse," *Maclean's,* 14 November 1994, p. 44.

18. Ibid.

19. One has to wonder though why *Maclean's*, with its enthusiasm for rankings, has not turned its eye to hospitals, charitable organizations, courts or other publicly funded institutions.

20. "If It's OK to Rank Cars, Why Not Universities," *The Globe and Mail,* 29 June 1994, p. A23.

Chapter 5: Skirmishes over the University's "Perception Problem"

1. *University Accountability: A Strengthened Framework,* Report of the Task Force on University Accountability, May 1993. The Task Force

was composed of representatives from the Ontario Confederation of University Faculty Associations, the Council of Ontario Universities, the Ontario Federation of Students, and the Ontario Council on Graduate Studies, among others. It reported to Ontario's Ministry of Education and Training.

2. Association of Universities and Colleges of Canada, "A Primer on Performance Indicators," *Research File* 1(2) (June 1995).

3. See *Measuring Up: Using Indicators to Manage Change,* Proceedings of the AUCC Symposium, 14–16 November 1993 (Ottawa: AUCC, 1994); *Accountability in Education in Canada,* Special Issue of the *Canadian Journal of Education* 20(1) (March 1995); Alberta Education, *Educational Quality Indicators: Annotated Bibliography* (Edmonton: Alberta Education, Corporate and Fiscal Planning Branch, 1990); James Cutt and Rodney Dobell, eds., *Public Purse, Public Purpose: Autonomy and Accountability in the Groves of Academe* (Halifax: Institute for Research on Public Policy, 1992).

4. *University Accountability,* p. 140.

5. Ibid, p. 5.

6. Ibid, p. 57.

7. Even the celebrated Scholastic Aptitude Test is a questionable mea-sure of accomplishment and potential, since recent studies show that the correlation between high SAT scores and university success is less than that between height and weight and university success.

8. "A Private Life," editorial, *The Globe and Mail,* 28 November 1995, p. A22.

9. As reported in "Suspended Prostitute Prof Back in Class," *The Ottawa Citizen,* 21 December 1995, p. A3.

10. One of the few sensible commentaries on the Hannon case was Martin Levin's "Fifth Column" essay entitled "Gerald and Jane," *The Globe and Mail,* 21 December 1995, p. A20.

11. "A Primer on Performance Indicators," p. 2.

12. Ibid, p. 1.

13. Ibid, p. 2.

14. René Hurtubise and Donald C. Rowat, *The University, Society, and Government: The Report of the Commission on the Relations between Universities and Governments* (Ottawa: The University of Ottawa Press, 1970), p. 88. The commissioners, however, took a naïve view of the benevolence of governments vis-à-vis the universities, writing "Universities, like all other human organizations, are selfish, and

without sanctions will not co-operate in any but a trivial sense. Since the only agency of society that can supply the necessary sanctions is the government, it must provide the framework within which this co-operation can take place" (88). History may have proven them wrong.

15. As cited in *The Transition Years: A Report for Schools in the Carleton Board of Education* (Ottawa: Carleton Board of Education, 1992).

16. "Executive Summary," *Research Report No. 5: Survey of Perceptions of Universities among Provincial Government Officials* (Toronto: Public Affairs Management, Inc., 1991).

17. See Paul Axelrod, *Scholars and Dollars: Politics, Economics and the Universities of Ontario, 1945–1980* (Toronto: University of Toronto Press, 1982) and David M. Cameron, *More Than an Academic Question: Universities, Government and Public Policy in Canada* (Ottawa: IRPP, 1991).

18. For an analysis of the Lewis Report, see David Warrick, "The Lewis Report and New Anti-Racist Education in Canada," in Peter C. Emberley and Waller R. Newell, eds., *Politicizing the Classroom: How Liberal Education Is Being Bankrupted and How Its Virtues Can Be Restored* (Toronto: University of Toronto Press) (forthcoming).

19. In August 1992 Allen sent a letter to the universities alerting them to the changes to come. In September 1993 the universities received the document "Guidelines for the Appointment of Members of University Bodies" from the Ontario Ministry of Education and Training.

20. "Colleges Upgrade Downgrading," *The Vancouver Sun*, 4 December 1994, p. B1. See also Norma Vale, "The Thaw Begins," *University Affairs*, June-July 1994, pp. 6–8.

21. As cited in Jennifer Lewington, "Academic, Lobbyist Appointed Ryerson University President," *The Globe and Mail*, 19 January 1995, p. A7.

22. As quoted in "Class Distinctions Beginning to Blur," *The Globe and Mail*, 14 July 1993, p. A3.

23. As quoted in "The Thaw Begins," *University Affairs*, June-July 1994, p. 7.

24. As quoted in "Re-Inventing our Schools," *University Affairs*, June-July 1993, p. 8.

25. There is currently a joint Council of Ministers of Education and Statistics Canada project to devise Pan-Canadian Education

Indicators and considerable work proceeds on distance education and open learning, but removing barriers to credit transfer has been the most evident achievement.

26. This was already preordained in Ontario's 1990 Premier's Council Report, *People and Skills in the New Global Economy*, which read "Although universities and colleges serve often distinct functions, they are now facing some very similar demands. Like colleges, universities are increasingly being pressured to provide a more sophisticated general foundation in communications and interpersonal relations, science and technology, teamwork and problem-solving for all students, whatever their discipline" (68). By 1993, the Pitman Task Force on Advanced Training could recommend in its report *No Dead Ends* that "the equal value of vocational and academic education be recognized by all the partners engaged in Ontario's post-secondary system" and that credit be given for work experience.

27. Benjamin R. Barber, *Jihad vs. McWorld: How the Planet Is Both Falling Apart and Coming Together and What This Means for Democracy* (New York: Times Books, 1995).

28. Jean Bethke Elshtain, *Democracy on Trial* (Toronto: Anansi, 1993), p. 3.

29. Robert Hughes, *The Culture of Complaint: The Fraying of America* (New York: Oxford University Press, 1993).

30. George Grant, *Technology and Empire: Perspectives on North America* (Toronto: Anansi, 1969) and *Technology and Justice* (Toronto: Anansi, 1986).

Chapter 6: The Corporate Right: Ending "Business as Usual"

1. As quoted in "Axworthy Not Saying of Students, Let Them Eat Kraft Dinners," *The Vancouver Sun*, 25 October 1994.

2. Lloyd Axworthy, "Federal Support to Post Secondary Education," Human Resources Development Canada (Ottawa: Department of Supply and Services, 1995).

3. "Can Our Universities Manage Change?" *The Globe and Mail*, 24 October 1995, p. A20.

4. See, especially, Organization for Economic Co-operation and Development, Centre for Educational Research and Innovation, *Education at a Glance: OECD Indicators*, 2nd ed. (Paris: OECD, 1993).

Endnotes

5. Magna International Inc., for example, undertook the highly praise-worthy initiative of establishing a "Magna for Canada Scholarship Fund" setting aside $1 million for winners of an essay contest "If *You* Were the Prime Minister of Canada, What Would You Do to Improve Living Standards and Unify the Country?" The National Winner, a Carleton University engineering student, was also offered a one-year paid internship with the CEO of Magna.

6. "Just Who's Out of Touch Here?" *Winnipeg Free Press*, 7 January 1995, p. A15.

7. Monique Jérôme-Forget, "Foreword," in *Ending the Squeeze on Universities*, ed. Stephen T. Easton (Ottawa: IRPP, 1993), p. 3.

8. Ken MacQueen, "Education Is a Commodity," *The Ottawa Citizen*, 30 June 1995, p. A8.

9. John Cowan, "Herding Sacred Cows," *University Manager*, Fall 1992, p. 11.

10. Peter J. George, "The Expanding Role of the State in Canadian Universities: Can University Autonomy and Accountability Be Reconciled?" in *Higher Education Management*, vol. 7, no.3, November 1995, p. 318.

11. Alberta Advanced Education and Career Development, Government of Alberta, "An Agenda for Change," March 1994, p. 5.

12. "Universities Mull Demand to Rationalize," *Winnipeg Free Press*, 12 January 1995, p. B2.

13. *University Accountability*, p. 33.

14. As cited in "Storming the Ivory Towers: Schools across Canada Navel-gazing," *Winnipeg Free Press*, 12 January 1995, p. B1.

15. Suspicion that faculty salaries are wildly inflated can be allayed. While 10 percent rollbacks would hurt few faculty, the following data might justify the disbelief of academics when school teachers, civil servants and hospital administrators cite fat university salaries as a factor in the public debt.

Salary Analysis for Canadian Universities and Colleges for 1993–94

| University | Average Salary Level | | | | 1993 | 1992 |
	Lect.	Asst.	Assoc.	Full	Combined	Combined
Alberta		52 297	63 246	85 442	72 927	74 095
Calgary		48 916	63 735	85 402	69 788	70 935
Carleton	58 493	58 127	79 102	90 798	79 217	75 728
McGill	43 310	44 367	65 482	86 889	66 842	68 101

McMaster	49 872	56 342	72 926	92 619	79 013	79 122
Queen's	43 375	56 201	71 365	88 190	74 183	74 963
Regina	41 113	51 128	67 557	84 185	67 750	69 566
Simon Fraser	51 736	56 210	72 282	91 432	75 933	73 687
Toronto	60 504	56 944	80 535	99 363	83 519	82 599
Waterloo	55 931	56 394	77 157	93 415	78 117	79 375
York	48 826	56 995	71 624	92 821	73 900	74 750
Average	49 632	53 570	70 730	89 060	73 627	73 467

Statscan average for *Major Canadian Universities to Date* (41/65).

16. Cameron, *More Than an Academic Question*, ch. 2 and 3.

17. As cited in "Universities, provinces fear loss of money," *The Globe and Mail*, 4 October 1994, p. A4.

18. "Social Reform Price Tag: $7 Billion," *The Toronto Star*, 5 October 1994, p. A1.

19. "Federal Support to Post-Secondary Education: A Supplementary Paper," Minister of Human Resources Development, 1994.

20. Ibid.

21. As cited in "Elites Should Pay, Axworthy Says," *The Globe and Mail*, 16 November 1994, p. A9.

22. Ibid.

23. "Cost Cuts Go Too Deep, U of T Head Says," *The Globe and Mail*, 30 November 1994, A3.

24. Local student federations, however, refused to participate, and Mike Burns, the executive director of the Ontario Undergraduate Students' Alliance, commented, "Protests are passé." See "The Times, They Are A-changing," *The Ottawa Citizen*, 22 February 1995, p. C3.

25. As quoted in "Proposal Fuels Student Ire," *The Calgary Herald*, 26 January 1995, p. B1.

26. As quoted in "Students Rally against Tuition Hikes," *The Toronto Star*, 26 January 1995, p. A14.

27. AUCC's counterproposal was to cut in half the current federal cash support of $2.6 billion; fund a $1 billion student loan program with $250 million start-up; and spend $500 million on research infrastructure and $500 million in transfer payments to redress regional disparities. In contrast to the government's starving of basic research in Canada, AUCC also pointed to a Clinton administration that had affirmed its commitment to university research.

28. This has to be placed in historical context, though. Sponsored and contract research funding from the three federal granting agencies and the centres of excellence in Ontario, for example, rose 68.2 percent in the period 1981–1991. In 1992/93, $858 million was provided to university researchers in Canada by federal research granting councils.

29. See "The Financial Position of Universities in Ontario: 1995," External Relations Division, Council of Ontario Universities.

30. Honourable Richard Allen, Minister of Colleges and Universities, "Memorandum to Executive Heads, Colleges and Universities and Members of the College and University Round Tables," 21 January 1992.

31. See Spruce Riordon, "Comments on OCUA Paper, Sustaining Quality in Changing Times" (August 1994) (private circulation).

32. As cited in "Taking the Campus Pulse," *Maclean's*, 14 November 1994, p. 44.

33. As quoted in *CAUT Bulletin* (December 1994).

34. Christopher Lasch, *The Revolt of the Elites and the Betrayal of Democracy* (New York: Norton, 1995). See also Conor Cruise O'Brien, *On the Eve of the Millennium* (Toronto: Anansi, 1994).

Chapter 7: The Corporate Right: Taking Care of Business

1. "Culture and Education," *Salute to Scholarship: Essays Presented at the Official Opening of Athabasca University* (Athabasca, AB: Athabasca University, 1986), p. 11.

2. Another plan that was in the air was a contingent-repayment bursary program in which the federal government would issue a bursary certificate to students upon their offer of admission from a university. When students registered, they would present the certificate as payment for tuition and the university would submit the certificate to the government for reimbursement.

3. As quoted in *The Globe and Mail*, 2 August 1995, p. A5.

4. By one calculation, a $20,000 loan not repaid after fifteen years of being below the threshold costs, at 8.2 percent, $68,139!

5. Robert Sheppard, *The Globe and Mail*, 31 October 1994.

6. While the data show that where women make 72 percent of what men make, for university graduates, the gap between women and men in 1990 was nearly closed.

7. As quoted in *The Globe and Mail*, 2 August 1995, p. A5.

8. Mariem Martinson, "University Enrolment and Tuition Fees," *Education Quarterly Review* (Winter 1994), Statistics Canada, cat. no. 81–003, vol. 1, no. 4.

9. "Higher Tuition Could Mean Better Access," *The Globe and Mail*, 22 September 1995, p. A20.

10. "Fee Increases Will Not End Problems," "Letters to the Editor," *The Globe and Mail*, 7 October 1995, p. D7.

11. "Letters to the Editor," *The Globe and Mail*, 11 November 1994.

12. As cited in "Students Protest Federal Cuts That Imply Rise in Tuition Fees," *The Globe and Mail*, 10 October 1995, p. A2.

13. As cited in "Universities: Measuring Excellence," *Maclean's*, 14 November 1994, p. 17.

14. As quoted in "The Electronic Classroom," *The Globe and Mail*, 9 December 1994.

15. Ibid.

16. Alberta, Alberta Advanced Education and Career Development, *New Directions for Adult Learning in Alberta*, 1994, p. 6.

17. Ibid.

18. "The Technology of the Future Is Already Here," *CAUT Bulletin*, November 1993, pp. 14–15.

19. "The Electronic Classroom: A New Reality," *University Affairs*, March 1992, p. 4.

20. As cited in "Universities Mull Demand to Rationalize," *Winnipeg Free Press*, 12 January 1995, p. B2.

21. Neil Postman, *Amusing Ourselves to Death: Public Discourse in the Age of Show Business* (New York: Viking, 1985).

22. See George Grant's essay "The Computer Does Not Impose on Us the Ways It Should Be Used," in *Beyond Industrial Growth*, ed. A. Rotstein (Toronto: University of Toronto Press, 1976), pp. 117–31, a sizzling rebuttal of those who believe that computers are simply tools to be used as we wish, and also Hubert Dreyfuss, *What Computers Can't Do* (New York: Harper and Row, 1972).

23. Jack Ady, *New Directions for Adult Learning in Alberta* (Edmonton: Government of Alberta, 1994), p. 6.

24. Andrew Coyne, "A Citizen Is a Consumer Who Knows His Place," *The Globe and Mail*, 27 November 1995, p. A20.

25. Ibid.

Endnotes

26. Arthurs, Blais and Thompson, "Integrity in Scholarship."

27. "N.S. Plans to Offer Warranties on Grads," *Winnipeg Free Press*, 6 August 1994, p. A13.

28. "Corporate Involvement in Education a Sign of the Times," *The Vancouver Sun*, 12 September 1994, p. 41.

29. As referred to in "Chequebook Paleontology Raises Problems for Universities and Taxpayers," *The Globe and Mail*, 1 October 1994, p. D8.

30. George Grant, "A Platitude," in *Technology and Empire* (Toronto: Anansi, 1969), p. 143. Interestingly, the Roblin Report, which goes far in advancing the corporate right's agenda, also recognizes the potential conflict between technology and the human good: "Technology may be the mantra of the day, but the wider uses of education have not lost their importance. In teaching the values, the ethics and the principles of culture, the contributions of the liberal arts and sciences continue to be at the centre of good education. These disciplines encourage the capacity to learn and appreciate, to reason and understand, to adjust and apply, and to acquire added knowledge. Without these capacities, technology and the economy lose their way. The well-rounded mind will help to manage the complexities, the speed, and the implications of the extraordinary changes modern technology imposes." Regrettably, in the hands of Clayton Manness, this advice has been quietly forgotten.

Chapter 8: The Cultural Left: Gender Politics

1. Paula Rothenberg, "The Inclusive University," CAUT Conference 1994 (private circulation).

2. "A few are influencing a lot at UBC," *The Globe and Mail*, 6 October 1995.

3. Aaron Wolfgang, "Needed: Intercultural Training of Teachers and Counsellors for the Year 2000," Symposium on Educational Issues in a Pluralistic Society, *Orbit* 22(3) (1991).

4. Reg Whitaker, "The Cutting Edge of Ontario's Bad Law, *The Globe and Mail*, 6 January 1994.

5. Stephen Richer and Lorna Weir, eds., *Beyond Political Correctness: Toward the Inclusive University* (Toronto: University of Toronto Press, 1995).

6. Stanley Aronowitz and Henry A. Giroux, *Postmodern Education: Politics, Culture, and Social Criticism* (Minneapolis: University of

Minnesota Press, 1991), p. 91.

7. Misao Dean, *The Canadian Forum* (July/August 1995): 17.

8. Paula Prime, "Speaking of Sex/Parting our Lips," in *Women Changing Academe*, ed. Sandra L. Kirby (Winnipeg: Sororal Publishing, 1991).

9. The petition "On Free Inquiry and Expression," signed by one-third of the Trent academic community read: "We defend, therefore, the right to certain types of speech and academic expression which, in fact, we do not condone, and in some cases deplore. This includes the right to offend one another. It includes the right to express— and the right of access to intellectual materials which express— racially, ethnically, or sexually discriminatory ideas, opinions, or feelings, just as it includes the right to expressions that favour inequality of incomes or benefits. It also includes the right to make others uncomfortable, to injure, by expression, anyone's self-esteem, and to create, by expression, atmospheres in which some may not feel welcome or accepted" (private circulation).

10. Robert Fulford, "Defending the Right to Be Offensive," *The Globe and Mail*, 25 July 1995, p. C1.

11. Oakeshott, "A Place of Learning," in Fuller, *The Voice of Liberal Learning*, p. 23.

12. As Professor Roxana Ng, who teaches sociology at OISE, said at a conference on the "inclusive university," "We need proactive strategies that recognize that we are all gendered and racialized subjects."

13. Elsa Schieder, "Integrating Lesbian Content," in ed. Debra Martens, *Weaving Alliances: Selected Papers Presented for the Canadian Women's Studies Association at the 1991 and 1992 Learned Societies Conferences* (Ottawa: Canadian Women's Studies Association, 1993), p. 56.

14. Jackie Stalker, "The Chill Women Feel at Canada's Universities," *The Globe and Mail*, 25 July 1995, p. D6.

15. Cf. "The Progress of Women," *The Globe and Mail*, 11 August 1995, p. A18.

16. As quoted in Leo Groarke, "The Tyranny of Group Talk," *The Literary Review of Canada* (April 1995): 9; M. Grenier and L. Hachey, "The Attribution of Causality in Lépine Murder News," in *Critical Studies of Canadian Mass Culture*, ed. M. Grenier (Toronto: Butterworths, 1992), p. 231.

17. As cited in Patty Fuller, "Fear-mongering 101: Feminists Wildly

Overstate the Hazards of Campus Life," *Alberta Report,* 6 December 1993, p. 28.

18. "Killer's Letter Blames Feminists," *The Globe and Mail,* 8 December 1989, p. A1.

19. Susan Mann-Trodinmenkoff, ed., *Women in Scholarship: One Step Forward, Two Steps Back* (Ottawa: Royal Society of Canada, 1990), p. 3.

20. An able historian of intellectual ideas Sheinin is not. She might try reading Stephen C. Ferruolo's excellent study *The Origins of the University* for a more historically accurate account. Her comments about the University of Paris are contradicted by the fact that Abelard's theological writings and later Aristotle's logical treatises— both condemned as heretical by the Church—were actually the mainstay of the mediaeval University of Paris. The widespread use of Abelard's art of disputation and the general prominence enjoyed by late twelfth-century figures like Siger de Brabant and John of Salisbury also significantly decentred the metaphysics Sheinin believes sustained mediaeval misogyny.

21. Kai Nielsen, "Harming Women: The Backlash to Feminism," in Trofimenkoff, *Women in Scholarship,* p. 18.

22. University of Western Ontario's Caucus on Women's Issues and President's Standing Committee for Employment Equity, *The Chilly Climate for Women in Colleges and Universities,* University of Western Ontario, 1991.

23. Anne Vézina, "Letter to the Editor," *The Globe and Mail,* 7 July 1995, p. A12.

24. Paula J. Caplan, *Lifting a Ton of Feathers: A Woman's Guide to Surviving in the Academic World,* Project of the Council of Ontario Universities Committee on the Status of Women (Toronto: University of Toronto Press, 1993).

25. Caplan, *Lifting a Ton of Feathers,* p. 45.

26. Kirby, "Introduction," in *Women Changing Academe,* p. i.

27. *The Ottawa Citizen,* 26 May 1995, p. A3.

28. I have explored some of the dangers of these exercises in my book *Values Education and Technology: The Ideology of Dispossession* (Toronto: University of Toronto Press, 1995).

29. Jill Vickers, "Are Efforts to Renovate the Concept of Academic Freedom Useful?" "Status of Women Supplement," *CAUT Bulletin,* 1994, p. 7.

30. Ibid.

31. Lewis Carroll, *Alice's Adventures in Wonderland and Through the Looking-Glass* (Oxford: Oxford University Press, 1982), p. 190.

32. Battle lines, rather than reasoned debate, also characterize the discussion of preferential hiring. To illustrate, Linda Williams, chair of the Canadian Federation of University Women, Status of Women and Human Rights Committee, justifying reverse discrimination, writes, "Whenever a decision comes between hiring a woman and a man with the same qualifications, the woman should get the job. At least until we get rid of the old boys' network."

33. Karen Grant and Hilda Taylor, "Insert," *CAUT Bulletin* (April 1995).

34. *Fraser Forum, Critical Issues Bulletin III*, (Toronto: The Fraser Institute, 1993), pp. 12-13.

35. Susan Faludi, *Backlash: The Undeclared War against American Women* (New York: Crown, 1991); Naomi Wolf, *The Beauty Myth* (Toronto: Vintage, 1991); Katie Roiphe, *The Morning After: Sex, Fear, and Feminism on Campus* (Boston: Little Brown, 1993); and Daphne Patai, *Professing Feminism: Cautionary Tales from the Strange World of Women's Studies* (New York: Basic Books, 1994).

36. "Letter to the Editor," *The Globe and Mail*, 29 July 1995.

37. "Feminist Group at Critical Crossroad," *The Ottawa Citizen*, 6 March 1995, p. A3. In early 1995, as a sign of the new resolve, NAC voted against a deal with Random House of Canada, which would have provided its members with major discounts on books by female authors and would have seen NAC's imprimatur on these books. Whether the major reason was financial or a matter of control, the decisive blow fell when two members of the executive declared the first book, Judy Steed's book on child sexual abuse, *Our Little Secret*, as "homophobic." Gail Picco, who had arranged the deal with Random House, explained: "What happened here was the lesbian caucus saying, "We're the lesbians, and if we say it's homophobic, it is. My oppression is worse than yours."

Chapter 9: The Cultural Left: Political Correctness and Chilly Climates

1. Alanna Mitchell, "Members of Minorities Hold More Degrees," *The Globe and Mail*, 14 June 1995, A1.

300

Endnotes

2. Carole Ann Reed, "The Anti-Racist Dimensions of Holocaust Education," *Orbit*, Vol. 25, no. 2, 1994, p. 15.

3. As cited in Dr. R.A. Harris, "Letter to the Editor," *The Globe and Mail*, 24 January 1995, p. A21.

4. As cited in "Examination by Disadvantage?" *The Globe and Mail*, 19 February 1994, p. A19.

5. As cited in "Extra Time for Law Exams Challenged by Professor," *The Toronto Star*, 18 February 1994, p. A18.

6. Robert Fulford, "George Orwell, Call Your Office," *The Globe and Mail*, 30 March 1994, p. A10.

7. "Commentary," *The Globe and Mail*, 7 April 1994, p. A17.

8. Neil Bissoondath, *Selling Illusions: The Cult of Multiculturalism in Canada* (Toronto: Penguin, 1994).

9. The York University Anti-Racist Policy has a statement on curricular inclusivity that reads: "Included in these efforts is a critical analysis of the narrowness, or exclusivity, of curriculum, which, in turn, is often a result of disciplinary and cultural assumptions, or viewpoint…. The purpose of these reconsiderations is to encourage faculty, over time, to challenge their disciplinary and cultural assumptions, extend their knowledge, and construct courses that, as appropriate, include a diversity of racial ethnocultural contributions and experience…and to promote pedagogical change."

10. Pico Iyer, *Video Night in Kathmandu: And Other Reports from the Not-So-Far East* (New York: Vintage Departures, 1989).

11. David Bromwich, *Politics by Other Means: Higher Education and Group Thinking* (New Haven: Yale University Press, 1992).

12. As quoted in "UBC Stands by Sikh Professor's Right to Publish, *The Vancouver Sun*, 20 June 1994, p. B2.

13. Jeff Adams, "Few Universities Address Sexual Harassment Problem," *Calgary Herald*, 17 November 1994, p. B12.

14. *Framework Regarding Harassment and Discrimination in Ontario Universities and Colleges* (Toronto: Ministry of Education and Training, 1993), p. 3.

15. Peter Calamai, "Universities Kowtow to Big Brother," *The Ottawa Citizen*, 23 January 1994, p. A8, and "Universities Really Have Lost Nerve," *The Ottawa Citizen*, 29 January 1994, p. B11.

16. Naomi Klein, "Why Universities Feel Harassed by Zero Tolerance," *The Globe and Mail*, 6 January 1994.

17. See the very useful and sensible article by W. Anita Braha, "Sexual Harassment at the University: *Torfason* v. *Hummel*, A Test Case," in Debra Martens, ed., *Weaving Alliances*.

18. In 1993 the British Columbia Supreme Court said that universities were subject to the provincial human rights codes prohibiting various forms of discrimination. The case it had heard was a grievance by a student with a history of depression who had been refused an evaluation she required for a dietetic internship and a key to gain access to labs after hours. The court ruled she had suffered "humiliation and embarrassment." David Mossop, the lawyer arguing the case, said that the following types of complaints could now be taken legitimately to the B.C. Human Rights Commission: a blind student arguing that the university must provide braille textbooks or a female student complaining if she thought she had received a lower mark than that given males.

19. Rainer Knopff, *Human Rights and Social Technology: The New War on Discrimination* (Ottawa: Carleton University Press, 1989). See also Knopff's *Charter Politics* (Scarborough: Nelson, 1992).

20. The University of Victoria affair is an obvious example. Somer Brodribb's committee charged that members of the department were subject to pervasive sexist and racist harassment. Male faculty responded: "If you have any credible evidence to support these assertions we insist that you immediately provide such evidence to the proper university authorities.... If you are not in a position to provide [that], then we demand an unqualified apology and retraction." The response was interpreted by the complainants as a threat, and they demanded retraction of the letter. Warren Magnussen, one of the male faculty, responded in a paper entitled "Sexism, McCarthyism and Feminist Fundamentalism," suggesting that the banner of sexual harassment was being used to further a radical feminist agenda. "What is expected of men," he wrote, "is a recognition of their complicity with Marc Lépine. The only good man is a dead one. Or, as Somer Brodribb put it, 'I wish they'd all kill themselves.'" Among other things alleged in the original report was that departmental secretaries had been subjected to abuse. Doris Lam, a departmental secretary for fifteen years, wrote to David Strong, the university's president, saying there was no evidence of a chilly climate for women and that she had never even been consulted by the committee. Many female students and graduates of the department also wrote letters defending the department's reputation. An impartial

inquiry set up by the President found no basis for the serious allegations. The student society and the graduate students' Women's Caucus demanded president David Strong's resignation. A subsequent report written by Tom Berger, a former Supreme Court justice, criticized the inadequate procedure of the committee's investigation, but also denounced Magnussen's essay for its "intemperate tone" and "highly personal nature," denying that it was an academic analysis. Stab, riposte, counter-riposte, and meanwhile the scholarly culture burns.

21. "Brush with Killer Related as Women Demand Safer Campus," *The Vancouver Sun*, 12 November 1993, p. C3.

22. Ibid.

23. As cited in Lisa Dempster, "Political Correctness Attacked," *The Calgary Herald*, 10 June 1994, p. B1.

24. Underlying Fekete's provocative book *Moral Panic: Biopolitics Rising* is the same libertarianism: "Freedoms DO NOT entail responsibilities. This is exactly what makes them freedoms rather than contractual goods. They are entitlements of 'natural rights'.... Freedoms are exactly those things that permit us NOT to have to be good or obedient or agreeable or conforming in return for the right to exercise them; indeed that permit us to commit ourselves to unpopular things, including the pursuit of knowledge and the dialectic of conflicting ideas (on which, at least since Socrates, knowledge was considered to rest)" as quoted in "Political Correctness Attacked," *The Calgary Herald*, 10 June 1994, p. B1). A far more sensible discussion of academic freedom, and its incumbent responsibilities, can be found in "Some Perspectives on Academic Freedom and Accountability," Task Force on Resource Allocation, Ontario Council on University Affairs, March 1995.

25. The cultural left's rhetoric, of course, continues. A year after the brouhaha over a policy that was probably the NDP government's most ideological tract ever, Bob Rae, in a classic case of the pot calling the kettle black, observed the politics of the government that had thrown him out of office and commented: "I don't like the government. I find it meanspirited. In many, many cases it is doing things just for ideological reasons. Ideological governments and governments that run on theory are bad governments and I had a continuing argument with some people in my party about that very issue and I refused to run an ideological government." "Bob Rae Readjusts to Life on Opposition Side," *The Ottawa Citizen*, 24

September 1995, p. A2.

26. Joan McEwen, *Report in Respect of the Political Science Department of the University of British Columbia* (Vancouver: University of British Columbia, 1995), pp. 21–22.

27. As cited in McEwen, ibid., p. 159.

28. Between 1976 and 1987, there were no full-time hirings in the department. Since 1990, there were five hirings of which four were women.

29. See the first-rate analysis of the report in Graham Good, "Facecrimes," *The Literary Review of Canada*, October 1995, pp. 17–19.

30. *The Vancouver Sun*, 15 July 1995.

31. *The Globe and Mail*, 23 June 1995, p. A20. See also 12 September 1995, p. A19.

32. For example, one instructor made the comment "A pretty girl is like a melody," but in the context of explaining heuristic devices and how perceptions are formed. On another occasion, he said, "Blacks are at the bottom of the racial order," in the context of a discussion and critique of apartheid.

33. Memo to various faculty, 27 October 1995 (private circulation).

34. John R. Grace, Memorandum to the Graduate Council, October 10, 1995 (private circulation).

35. "UBC Has Shown It Is Indifferent to Its Crisis," In "Letters to the Editor," *The Globe and Mail*, 7 October 1995, p. D7.

36. The point is made very elegantly by Vilma Dubé, a teacher evidently astonished by the students' complaint, in a letter to *The Globe and Mail*, 11 September 1995.

37. As quoted in Ray Conlogue, "Hoping to Heal Canada's 'Intellectual Sickness,'" *The Globe and Mail*, 10 October 1994, p. A10.

38. "A Buffet at the U of T," *The Globe and Mail*, 20 October 1995, p. A23.

Chapter 10: New Directions

1. As quoted in "The Gloom Factor in University Rankings," *The Globe and Mail*, 9 November 1993, p. C1.

2. Angus Reid/AUCC Survey, 1993, as reported in "A Solid Showing," *University Affairs*, April 1993, p. 40.

3. A reorientation to teaching in the universities will not be effective, however, without serious school reform. The universities exhibit far too much reluctance, possibly for fear of stepping on toes, in expressing their opposition to the persistent whittling away at the high school curriculum, despite the fact that decades of experimentation in the schools have severely handicapped university teaching. While the schools cannot address only the needs of the 25 percent of Canadian students who go on to postsecondary education, it is also the case that school reformers have exhibited an immensely patronizing attitude towards those who do not go on to university when they urge that high schools underemphasize academics in favour of vocationalism. Such an attitude is predicated on the assumption that these students should not be challenged intellectually.

4. In Alberta alone, donors can write off 100 percent of their gift.

5. There have been other lavish gifts: $25 million to McMaster University, $6 million to University of Victoria, $15 million to Queen's University, $10 million to UBC for a performing-arts centre and another $15 million in the early 1990s.

6. Hannah Arendt, "The Crisis in Education," in *Between Past and Future: Eight Exercises in Political Thought* (Harmondsworth: Penguin Books, 1977), p. 196.

Copyright Acknowledgments

For Further Reading

Berman, P. *Debating PC: The Controversy over Political Correctness on College Campuses.* New York: Laurel, 1992.

Bérubé, Michael, and Nelson, Cary, eds. *Higher Education under Fire: Politics, Economics, and the Crisis of the Humanities.* New York: Routledge, 1995.

Bloom, Allan. *The Closing of the American Mind: How Higher Education Has Failed Democracy and Impoverished the Souls of Today's Students.* New York: Simon and Schuster, 1987.

Bloom, Harold. *The Western Canon: The Books and School of the Ages.* New York: RiverHead Books, 1995.

Bromwich, David. *Politics by Other Means: Higher Education and Group Thinking.* New Haven: Yale University Press, 1992.

Cameron, David M. *More Than an Academic Question: Universities, Government and Public Policy in Canada.* Ottawa: The Institute for Research in Public Policy, 1991.

D'Souza, Dinesh. *Illiberal Education: The Politics of Race and Sex on Campus.* New York: Free Press, 1991.

Elshtain, Jean. *Democracy on Trial.* Toronto: Anansi, 1993.

Emberley, Peter C., and Newell, Waller R. *Bankrupt Education: The Decline of Liberal Education in Canada.* Toronto: University of Toronto Press, 1993.

Ferruolo, Stephen C. *The Origins of the University.* Stanford: Stanford University Press, 1985.

Gates, Henry Louis, Jr. *Loose Canons: Notes on the Culture Wars.* New York: Oxford University Press, 1993.

Graff, Gerald. *Beyond the Culture Wars: How Teaching the Conflicts Can Revitalize Education.* New York: Norton, 1992.

Himmelfarb, Gertrude. *Looking into the Abyss: Untimely Thoughts on Culture and Society.* New York: Knopf, 1994.

Jacoby, Russell. *Dogmatic Wisdom: How the Culture Wars Divert Education and Distract America.* New York: Doubleday Books, 1994.

Kibre, Pearl. *Scholarly Privileges in the Middle Ages.* Cambridge, MA: Medieval Academy of America, 1962.

Kimball, Roger. *Tenured Radicals: How Politics Has Corrupted Our Higher Education.* New York: Harper and Row, 1990.

Lodge, David. *Small World.* New York: Macmillan, 1984.

Montgomery, Marion. *Liberal Arts and Community: The Feeding of the Larger Body.* Baton Rouge: Louisiana State University Press, 1990.

Ontario Institute for Studies in Education, Higher Education Group. *The Professoriate: Occupation in Crisis.* Toronto: OISE, 1985.

Pelikan, Jaroslav. *The Idea of the University: A Re-examination.* New Haven: Yale University Press, 1992.

Rashdall, Hastings. *Universities of Europe in the Middle Ages.* 3 Vols. Oxford: Oxford University Press, 1895.

Ridder-Symoens, Hilde de. *A History of the University in Europe.* Cambridge: Cambridge University Press, 1992.

Sykes, Charles. *Profscam: Professors and the Demise of Higher Education.* Washington, DC: Regnery, Gateway, 1988.

Index

Index

Symbol - 18, 26, 30, 32-33, 39, 41

Systemic Discrimination - 141, 210, 213-214, 229, 241, 243n.20, 246, 248-249

Technology - 2, 18, 95, 101, 140, 149-150, 152, 155, 160, 169, 187, 190-193, 199n.30, 201, 233, 242, 258, 266, 268-270

Tenure - 5, 8, 10, 12, 17, 59, 61-73, 99, 212, 259-260, 274

Therapy - 23, 56-57

Tolerance - 34, 36, 45, 54, 93, 149, 192, 207, 222, 228, 232, 277

Tradition - 14, 48, 51, 60, 108-110, 228, 231, 254, 266

Transcendance - 17, 33, 36, 42, 75, 78, 83

Trent University - 15, 44, 90, 197, 208, 208n.9

Understanding - 13, 19, 24-25, 28-29, 44, 190, 222, 257, 269

Unions - 160

Universitas - 27-29, 98, 207, 257, 275

University
1) administrators - 21, 62-63, 93-96
2) industry partnerships - 154, 194-196
3) litigiousness - 61, 97- 99, 101-103, 114, 125, 242
4) relation to colleges - 143-148
5) salaries - 95, 139, 184n.15
6) service - 78

University of Alberta - 47, 77, 100, 215, 230, 232

University of British Columbia - 4, 6-7, 9, 87, 101, 138, 218, 230, 235-326, 246-254

University of Calgary - 66, 158, 183, 237, 242

University of Guelph - 7, 82, 197

University of Manitoba - 7, 8, 60, 100, 101, 120, 139, 195, 211

University of Toronto - 3, 5, 7, 10, 60, 70, 119, 159, 166, 180, 191, 253, 261

University of Victoria - 7, 89, 121, 206, 242, 242n.20

University of Waterloo - 52, 60, 121, 145, 163, 189, 194, 230

University of Western Ontario - 48, 185, 213, 217, 224, 240, 242

Value-for-money Auditing - 12, 67, 197, 265

Virtual University - 13, 183-184, 186, 189, 193-194, 258, 268-269

Virtue - 24, 31, 36, 103, 133, 172, 182-183, 189, 192, 228, 257, 271

Vocationalism - 40, 140, 143-144, 147n.26, 148, 179, 193

Vouchers - 162, 175, 221

White, Randy - 79, 86-87

Yaqzan, Matin - 6, 75-76, 134

York University - 7, 79, 138, 167, 203, 218, 234n.9

Zero-Tolerance Policy - 15-17, 68, 138, 199, 209, 237-242, 244-246, 253, 275

313